OXFORD MODERN LANGUAGES
AND LITERATURE MONOGRAPHS

Editorial Committee
C. DUTTLINGER   N. GARDINI   A. KAHN
I. MACLACHLAN   C. SETH
J. THACKER   W. WILLIAMS

Dante's Masterplot and Alternative Narratives in the *Commedia*

NICOLÒ CRISAFI

Great Clarendon Street, Oxford, OX2 6DP,
United Kingdom

Oxford University Press is a department of the University of Oxford.
It furthers the University's objective of excellence in research, scholarship,
and education by publishing worldwide. Oxford is a registered trade mark of
Oxford University Press in the UK and in certain other countries

© Nicolò Crisafi 2022

The moral rights of the author have been asserted

First Edition published in 2022

Impression: 1

All rights reserved. No part of this publication may be reproduced, stored in
a retrieval system, or transmitted, in any form or by any means, without the
prior permission in writing of Oxford University Press, or as expressly permitted
by law, by licence or under terms agreed with the appropriate reprographics
rights organization. Enquiries concerning reproduction outside the scope of the
above should be sent to the Rights Department, Oxford University Press, at the
address above

You must not circulate this work in any other form
and you must impose this same condition on any acquirer

Published in the United States of America by Oxford University Press
198 Madison Avenue, New York, NY 10016, United States of America

British Library Cataloguing in Publication Data

Data available

Library of Congress Control Number: 2021948621

ISBN 978-0-19-285767-5

DOI: 10.1093/oso/9780192857675.001.0001

Printed and bound in Great Britain by
Clays Ltd, Elcograf S.p.A.

Links to third party websites are provided by Oxford in good faith and
for information only. Oxford disclaims any responsibility for the materials
contained in any third party website referenced in this work.

A Vittoria

splendifera e magnificente

Acknowledgements

A story can be told of the many encounters that led to the present book.

My supervisors Elena Lombardi and Manuele Gragnolati chose this project in its doctoral form and secured the support of Lady Margaret Hall and the Clarendon Fund at Oxford. They encouraged and inspired this monograph and its author through beginnings, middles, ends, and beyond—it could not have been without them. The environment of ICI Berlin provided further material support and new scholarly challenges as I prepared the manuscript for publication.

I was lucky to find in Martin McLaughlin and Nicola Gardini ideal assessors and in Francesca Southerden and Heather Webb ideal examiners, who recommended the thesis to OUP. Their feedback made the doctoral milestones both a pleasure and an opportunity for progress. I am similarly grateful to the anonymous readers at OUP, who demonstrated that kindness is not incompatible with intelligent critique.

Jenny Rushworth and David Bowe offered tips, friendship, and a model to follow, making it enviable to be a Dante scholar at Oxford in the mid-2010s.

Not least, Xavier Buxton, Matt Phillips, and Vittoria Fallanca read these pages with sensitivity and wit. Someday people will find it hard to believe that there was a time when these three concerned themselves with proofreading.

To all the above, my gratitude.

This book is dedicated to Vittoria, *parce que c'est elle*.

Contents

Editions, Translations, and Abbreviations xi
Figure xiii

Introduction: Dante's Masterplot 1
I.1 Keywords of the Masterplot 1
I.2 Masterplots and the Masterplot 10
I.3 The Cases of *Vita nova* and *Commedia* 17
I.4 Exemplariness, Credibility, Reproducibility 27
I.5 Reading Hermeneutic Writing 33
I.6 'The good' and 'the other things' 37

1. Paradox in the Poem 43
   1.1 Paradox in the Middle Ages: Scholastic Theology and Mystical Writings 44
   1.2 Oxymoron as 'compact verbal paradox' 53
   1.3 Long-range Paradox in the *Commedia* 62
   1.4 Coexistence of Narrative Models of Teleology and Paradox 66
      1.4.1 Teleological Plot and Paradoxical Content 67
      1.4.2 The 'Time' of Antanaclasis 70
      1.4.3 The Ineffability Topos 74
   1.5 The Role of the Reader 80

2. Alternative Endings and Parallel Lives 83
   2.1 The Affective Space: *Paradiso* VIII 89
   2.2 The 'Disnarrated' and Free Will in the *Commedia*: a Comparison with Two Twentieth-century Poems and the *Convivio* 96
   2.3 'La tecnica dell'episodio parallelo': Parallel Lives as Narrative Correlative of Alternative Endings 102
   2.4 Interpreting Alternative Endings and Parallel Lives: *Paradiso* XIII 107
   2.5 Secret as Narrative Freedom 113

3. The Future In/Out of the *Commedia* 116
   3.1 *Poeta* Writing into the Future 119
   3.2 The Proems of the Poem 123
   3.3 Unfinished Writing 135

    3.4 Vulnerable Narrator, Vulnerable Text   139
    3.5 Future's Messes in the *Inferno*   147
    3.6 The Ageing Author   158
    3.7 Between Vulnerability and Performance: *Paradiso* XXV   163

    Epilogue: Dante's Narrative Pluralism   168

Bibliography   173
Index of Passages   189
Index of Names   191
Index of Concepts   193

Editions, Translations, and Abbreviations

Works by Dante

Unless otherwise stated, editions and translations of Dante's works are as follows.

Conv.   *Convivio*, ed. Franco Brambilla Ageno, 3 vols (Florence: Le Lettere, 1995).

Dante's Convivio (The Banquet), trans. Richard H. Lansing (New York: Garland, 1990).

DVE   *De vulgari eloquentia*, ed. Pier Vincenzo Mengaldo, in Dante Alighieri, *Opere minori*, ed. Domenico De Robertis et al., 2 vols (Milan and Naples: Ricciardi, 1979–88), II, pp. 1–237.

De vulgari eloquentia, trans. Steven Botterill (Cambridge: Cambridge University Press, 1996).

Ep.   *Dante Alagherii epistolae = The Letters of Dante*, trans. Paget Toynbee, 2nd edn (Oxford: Clarendon Press, 1966).

Epistole, ed. Claudia Villa, in *Opere*, ed. Marco Santagata, 3 vols (Milan: Mondadori, 2011–14) III, pp. 1417–592.

Inf., *Purg.*, and *Par.*   *Inferno*, trans. Jean and Robert Hollander (New York: Anchor, 2000).

La Commedia secondo l'antica vulgata, ed. Giorgio Petrocchi, 2nd edn, 4 vols (Florence: Le Lettere, 1994).

Paradiso, trans. Jean and Robert Hollander (New York: Doubleday, 2007).

Purgatorio, trans. Jean and Robert Hollander (New York: Anchor, 2003).

Mon.   *Monarchia*, ed. Prue Shaw (Florence: Le Lettere, 2009).

Monarchia, trans. Prue Shaw (Cambridge: Cambridge University Press, 1996).

Rime   *Dante's Lyric Poetry*, trans. Kenelm Foster and Patrick Boyde, 2 vols (Oxford: Clarendon Press, 1967).

Rime, ed. Gianfranco Contini, 4th edn (Turin: Einaudi, 1980).

VN La Vita Nuova di Dante Alighieri: Edizione critica, ed. Michele Barbi (Florence: Bemporad & Figlio, 1932).
Vita Nova, trans. Andrew Frisardi (Evanston: Northwestern University Press, 2012).

Works of reference

DDP Dartmouth Dante Project, https://dante.dartmouth.edu/. All commentaries to the *Commedia* are taken from the DDP.

ED *Enciclopedia dantesca*, ed. Umberto Bosco, 6 vols (Rome: Istituto della Enciclopedia Italiana, 1970–8).

Figure

3.1 Domenico di Michelino, *Dante and his Poem* (1465). Fresco. Cathedral of Santa Maria del Fiore, Florence. 166

Introduction
Dante's Masterplot

I.1 Keywords of the Masterplot

There is a handful of words that most Dante scholars use and all encounter while studying the poet. These include (in English): *conversion, palinode, synthesis, reconciling, resolving, abandoning, purifying, surpassing, sublimating, overcoming*—the list goes on. Each comes with its own history, nuances, and intentions, but together they suggest a general narrative arc that the seasoned Dantist will recognize and the first-time reader can probably imagine. This narrative arc is what I call *Dante's masterplot*: the trajectory of progress through which the poet, at various stages in his path, understands in retrospect the most significant events of his autobiography, his writing career, and his protagonist's progress in the *Commedia*. This model, embedded in Dante's texts, promotes the hermeneutic practice of reading them teleologically, by subordinating earlier works or earlier parts of the poem to the revisionist gaze of its endpoint, towards which everything is said to have always aimed. The keywords have helped scholars elucidate this teleological pattern in a variety of ways. Scholars will argue for different degrees of continuity and discontinuity between old and new experiences; they will propose different periodizations and establish different turning points and endpoints in Dante's path; they will chart its course by tracking a wide array of themes and interests; and they will attribute varying significance and moral value to the overall trajectory of his path. Some of the keywords used to articulate these divergences have generated articles and entire monographs; others keep a low profile in the language employed by scholars and attract less critical attention. Among the most popular keywords, *conversion* indicates a radical break with past existential or religious stances;[1] whereas the more technical term *palinode* describes a *recantation*

---

[1] Two seminal works on the theme of conversion are Charles S. Singleton's *Dante studies: Vol. 2. Journey to Beatrice* (Cambridge, MA: Harvard University Press, 1958), and the collection of essays by John Freccero, *Dante: The Poetics of Conversion*, ed. Rachel Jacoff (Cambridge, MA: Harvard University Press, 1986). More recently, Christine O'Connell Baur, *Dante's Hermeneutics of Salvation* (Toronto: University of Toronto Press, 2006), esp. pp. 98–131;

of previous works or poetics, which might be explicit or implicit.[2] *Synthesis* often appears as the third stage of a dialectic between disparate elements (as in the case of Dante's *reconciliation* of pagan culture and Christian beliefs), implying the *resolution* of its conflicting aspects which are *sublimated* into a higher, and often less troubling, formulation;[3] while describing Dante's work as *syncretic* or *encyclopaedic* (for example, in the context of Dante's intertextual relations with medieval culture) may allow for the edges of its disparate elements to remain a little rougher.[4] All keywords come with their specific

---

Monica Bisi, *Poetica della metamorfosi e poetica della conversione: Scelte formali e modelli del divenire nella letteratura* (Bern: Peter Lang, 2012); Heather Webb, 'Deceit, Desire, and Conversion in Girard and Dante', *Religion & Literature*, 43.3 (2011), 200–8; Pierluigi Lia, *Poetica dell'amore e conversione: Considerazioni teologiche sulla lingua della 'Commedia' di Dante* (Florence: Olschki, 2015). For a critical review of the term see also Jennifer Petrie, 'Conversion', in *The Dante Encyclopedia*, ed. Richard Lansing (New York: Routledge, 2000), pp. 222–4, and Jennifer Rushworth, 'Conversion, Palinode, Traces', in *The Oxford Handbook of Dante*, ed. Manuele Gragnolati, Elena Lombardi, and Francesca Southerden (Oxford: Oxford University Press, 2021), pp. 529–45. For conversion (and its alternatives) in the medieval lyric context, see David Bowe, *Poetry in Dialogue in the Duecento and Dante* (Oxford: Oxford University Press, 2021).

[2] The most comprehensive reflection on the palinode is in Albert Russell Ascoli, *Dante and the Making of a Modern Author* (Cambridge: Cambridge University Press, 2008), pp. 274–300, based on his previous 'Palinode and History in the Oeuvre of Dante', in *Dante Now: Current Trends in Dante Studies*, ed. Theodore J. Cachey Jr (Notre Dame, IN: University of Notre Dame Press, 1995); see also Rachel Jacoff, 'The Post-Palinodic Smile', *Dante Studies*, 98 (1980), 111–22; Teodolinda Barolini, *Dante's Poets: Textuality and Truth in the 'Comedy'* (Princeton, NJ: Princeton University Press, 1984); Roberto Antonelli, 'Bifrontismo, pentimento e forma-canzoniere', in *La palinodia: Atti del XIX Convegno interuniversitario, Bressanone, 1991*, ed. Gianfelice Peron and Gianfranco Folena (Padua: Esedra, 1998), pp. 35–49; and, again, Rushworth, 'Conversion, Palinode, Traces'.

[3] See, for instance, Olivia Holmes writing that 'Dante is not a binary thinker, in any case, but a Trinitarian one, and when he proposes a thesis and an antithesis he generally looks for a synthesis' (*Dante's Two Beloveds: Ethics and Erotics in the 'Divine Comedy'* (New Haven, CT: Yale University Press, 2008), p. 3); Guy P. Raffa reviews dialectical understandings of Dante (including De Sanctis, Croce, and even Auerbach) in his *Divine Dialectic: Dante's Incarnational Poetry* (Toronto: University of Toronto Press, 2000), pp. 8–9, before proposing his own. For examples of the term *synthesis* in relation to Dante's intertextuality, see Michelangelo Picone's 'Dante and the Classics', in *Dante: Contemporary Perspectives*, ed. Amilcare A. Iannucci (Toronto: University of Toronto Press, 1996), pp. 51–73; and Reto R. Bezzola, 'L'opera di Dante: Sintesi poetica dell'antichità e del Medioevo cristiano', in *Studi danteschi*, ed. Martina Albertini and Johannes Bartuschat (Locarno: Pro Grigioni Italiano, Armando Dadò, 2015), pp. 133–51. Gianfranco Contini famously defined the *Commedia* as a 'sintesi ed enciclopedia degli stili' in his influential 'Dante come personaggio-poeta della *Commedia*', repr. in *Un'idea di Dante: Studi danteschi* (Turin: Einaudi, 1970), pp. 33–62 (p. 57).

[4] Contini's notion of the 'enciclopedia degli stili' is developed by the contributors to *L'enciclopedismo medievale: Atti del Convegno, San Gimignano, 8-10 ottobre 1992*, ed. Michelangelo Picone (Ravenna: Longo, 1994). Zygmunt G. Barański has written extensively on the *Commedia* as a '*summa* di sincretismo polisemico' ('Dante *poeta e lector*: "poesia" e "riflessione tecnica" (con divagazioni sulla *Vita nova*)', *Critica del testo*, 14.1 (2011), 81–110 (p. 89)); see also Simon A. Gilson, 'Sincretismo e scolastica in Dante', in *Studi e Problemi di Critica Testuale*, 90.1 (2015), 317–39.

value judgements, which are implicit in their use and often fly under the radar. Writing that earthly attachments and passions are *purified* and *purgated*, for instance, is not the same as saying that they are *abandoned*: the former reflects the assumption that the product of the purification process is preferable to its original unrefined form, whereas the latter arguably allows more neutral uses, even though it is by no means used only neutrally. If previous beliefs or poetics are *surpassed*, this implies the obsolescence of the past and an advantage to be had in the new position, much like *overcoming* agonistically evokes the idea of an obstacle, a struggle, and a victory over previous stances, whereas *transcendence* suggests instead a more ascetic detachment.

Naturally, these keywords have served, and continue to serve, a vast range of arguments, relating Dante's work to a dazzling array of historical insights, scientific ideas, theological conceptions, artistic productions, literary influences, theoretical frameworks, and cultural contexts. Nevertheless, at their baseline the keywords used to phrase these different approaches arguably have in common four assumptions about Dante's life, writing career, and/or his path in the *Commedia*. First, they portray the relationship between past and present, as expressed in the poet's life and works, in linear terms: the past flows into the present, through momentous upheavals or more fluidly, but nevertheless in one continuous and mostly one-way stream. Second, even when authorial decisions and revisions are taken into account, the keywords suggest that the author always seeks ultimate coherence within his writings, not least between his past and his present; in this view, contradictions are typically revealed to be only the appearance of contradiction, and what is paradoxical tends to be resolved in the name of consistency. Third, in cases where such contradictions and aporias arise, specifically, in the relationship between Dante's past and his new experiences, these keywords suggest a kind of solution that is modelled after Dante's masterplot, the poet's pattern of retrospection and self-understanding. Authorized by this dominant narrative, such keywords teleologically subjugate previous experiences to the newest point of view. In this regard, they work in a generally predictable direction: *ubi maior*, new experiences are given the last word over previous ones and coherence is ultimately restored. One final characteristic of these keywords is that the subordination of the past that they manifest is typically conceived in positive and productive terms, with an emphasis on what Dante and/or his readers will have gained from this sacrifice: moral improvement, greater understanding, experience, meaning, truth, peace, purity, beatitude, consolation, consistency—different readers will claim different benefits depending on their focus and the target of their argument. Here, too, we find a common denominator: in order to produce this added value, an earlier experience must be recontextualized, its intrinsic meaning and purpose replaced with the purpose and meaning of a new experience.

These basic assumptions are variously reflected in the teleological language that pervades critical discourse on Dante. Thus, when it comes to the complex question of erotic love in *Paradiso*, a popular view, championed here by Lino Pertile, is that 'true love must ultimately *surpass* the object of its desire. *To achieve the ultimate purpose of the journey*, the pilgrim must learn to direct all his love toward God, thus *leaving behind* not only Virgil but even Beatrice. *The aim* of true love is *to reach beyond* human love.'[5] Or, with respect to Dante's fraught relationship with his lyric past, John Freccero writes that '[his] poetic career was a continual *askesis* in preparation for his last work. In such a *linear evolution*, a glance backward to a previous poetic achievement is more likely to be a sign of *transcendence* rather than of return.'[6] Or, apropos the problem of subjectivity and earthly attachments, Christian Moevs argues that 'Dante's *Comedy* is built on the principle that…the individual subject of experience' reaches 'the point through which Bonaventure said one is "totally *transferred* and *transformed* into God"' and thus 'begins to *dissolve* its exclusive self-identification with a particular finite identity and its attachments'.[7] Similar examples are countless. Their lines of

---

[5] Lino Pertile, 'Does the *Stilnovo* Go to Heaven', in *Dante for the New Millennium*, ed. Teodolinda Barolini and H. Wayne Storey (New York: Fordham, 2003), pp. 104–14 (p. 110), italics mine. The phrase 'true love' ('vero amore' in the Italian version of the article) also appears in the title of Donato Pirovano's discussion of Dante's *caritas*, *Dante e il vero amore: Tre letture dantesche* (Pisa: Fabrizio Serra, 2009), which shares Pertile's outlook on Dante's progressive detachment from earthly love. Pertile's article was placed by the editors of the collection in dialogue with that of F. Regina Psaki, 'Love for Beatrice: Transcending Contradiction in the *Paradiso*', pp. 115–30. On the *querelle* and Beatrice's historicity and corporeality, see Elena Lombardi, *The Wings of the Doves: Love and Desire in Dante and Medieval Culture* (Montreal: McGill-Queen's University Press, 2012), esp. p. 14 and n. 25 therein; Tristan Kay, *Dante's Lyric Redemption: Eros, Salvation, Vernacular Tradition* (Oxford: Oxford University Press, 2016), pp. 80–90; and Heather Webb, *Dante's Persons: An Ethics of the Transhuman* (Oxford: Oxford University Press, 2016), pp. 126–8.

[6] John Freccero, 'Casella's Song: *Purgatorio* II, 112', in *Poetics of Conversion*, pp. 186–94 (p. 186), italics mine, except for *askesis*. For different critiques of this view, see Gianfranco Contini, 'Introduzione alle *Rime* di Dante', repr. in *Un'idea di Dante*, pp. 3–20; Barolini, *Dante's Poets*; and Kay, *Dante's Lyric Redemption*.

[7] Christian Moevs, *The Metaphysics of Dante's 'Comedy'* (Oxford and New York: Oxford University Press, 2005), pp. 169 and 185, italics mine. Bonaventure's phrase 'totally transferred and transformed into God', appropriated by Moevs, is taken from a passage in Bonaventure, *Itinerarium mentis in Deum* (Turnhout: Brepols, 2010), VII, 4, which stresses the role of affect in the soul's journey to God: 'In hoc autem transitu, si sit perfectus, oportet quod relinquantur omnes intellectuales operationes, et apex affectus totus transferatur et transformetur in Deum'. For a critique of this specific position, see Manuele Gragnolati, *Amor che move: Linguaggio del*

argument, as expressed through teleological vocabulary, will be familiar to most Dantists. After all, they are inspired and sustained more or less directly by metaphorical discourses that are arguably endogenous to the *Commedia*: Aristotelian teleology, the conversion narrative, spiritual pilgrimage, seafaring voyage, penitential progress, mystical *excessus*, *itinerarium mentis in Deum*, the genre of comedy, and conceivably more.

It might come as a surprise, then, that the language in which these arguments are couched is not as native to Dante's text as one might evince judging solely by the scholarship. If one investigates the language of the critics just quoted, *superare*, used by Pertile, and its synonym *sorpassare* never appear in the poem; similarly absent are *evoluzione* and its cognates, used by Freccero, and *trasferire*, used by Moevs. Moreover, *trasformare*, in Dante's hands, has quite a different tone than in Moevs's, considering that it is reserved for the monstrous metamorphosis of the pageant of *Purgatorio* into the beast of the apocalypse, traditionally identified with the Antichrist (*Purg.* XXXII, 142). *Trascendere* occurs once in the etymological sense of (pseudo-)physically 'ascending through' the heavens ('ammiro | com'io trascenda questi corpi levi' ['I am amazed | that I can *glide through* these light bodies'], *Par.* I, 98–9), and is otherwise reserved to God's transcendence, not to a human path toward it.[8] The one time the verb *dissolvere* does occur in the *Commedia* it describes the physical effects of death on the mortal body:

> Con quella fascia
> che la morte *dissolve* men vo suso,
> e venni qui per l'infernale ambascia.
>
> [With the very swaddling clothes
> that death *unwinds* I make my way above,
> and I have come through agony of Hell.]
>
> (*Purg.* XVI, 37–9)

---

corpo e forma del desiderio in Dante, Pasolini e Morante (Milan: Il Saggiatore, 2013), esp. pp. 155–61. For the continuing presence of the embodied individual in *Paradiso*, see also Manuele Gragnolati, *Experiencing the Afterlife: Soul and Body in Dante and Medieval Culture* (Notre Dame, IN: University of Notre Dame Press, 2005); Vittorio Montemaggi, 'In Unknowability as Love: The Theology of Dante's *Commedia*', in *Dante's 'Commedia': Theology as Poetry*, ed. Vittorio Montemaggi and Matthew Treherne (Notre Dame, IN: Notre Dame University Press, 2010), pp. 60–94; Webb, *Dante's Persons*, esp. pp. 164–205, as well as Kay, *Dante's Lyric Redemption*.

[8] In 'colui lo cui saver tutto trascende' (*Inf.* VII, 73), 'letizia che trascende ogni dolzore' (*Par.* XXX, 42); see 'trascendere' in *ED*. A similar pattern is found in *soblimare*: physically expressed by Dante in his posture (*Par.* XXVI, 87) and referring to the gospels as 'la verità che tanto ci soblima' (*Par.* XXII, 42); see 'soblimare' in *ED*.

The verb's use, in this case, is rhetorical: first, it helps sharpen the contrast with the protagonist's embodied condition of living among the dead, who are 'unwound' from their own flesh; and second, this state of *dissolution* is only temporary, lasting until the resurrection of the body, the gratuitous gift that will rewind it.[9] In the *Commedia*'s eschatological framework, announced repeatedly throughout the poem, Dante's verb *dissolvere* connotes a process that is not as teleological as Moevs's 'irreversible dissolution of the ego'.[10] The same can be said about many teleological keywords that do not feature in the three quotations above. *Sviluppare, sintetizzare, palinodiare*, and the related nouns are never used by Dante, and the same applies to *purificare*.[11] Its synonym *purgare*, on the other hand, occurs nine times, as a technical term specific to, unsurprisingly, the purging souls of the second cantica.[12]

The keywords Dante does use are employed with nuance and often unpredictably. It is true, for instance, that he describes his journey in terms of what the protagonist (and the narrator) *leaves behind*. Dante's *lasciare* has as its objects, variously, 'lo passo | che non *lasciò* già mai persona viva' ['the pass | no mortal being ever left alive'] (*Inf.* I, 26–7); '[l]o fele' ['bitterness'] of Hell's torments (*Inf.* XVI, 61); 'Lucifero' ['Lucifer'] (*Inf.* XXXIV, 89); the metaphorical 'mar sì crudele' ['that cruel sea'] of the first cantica (*Purg.* I, 3); but also, more tragically, 'ogne cosa diletta più caramente' ['all you most dearly love'] (*Par.* XVII, 56). Contrary to what Lino Pertile seems to suggest in the quote above, Dante never leaves Virgil but is, rather more poignantly, left by him in *Purgatorio* XXX, 49–50 ('Ma Virgilio n'*avea lasciati* scemi | di sé' ['Virgil had departed, *leaving us bereft*']), an event which had been announced by the pagan poet as early as *Inferno* I, 123 ('con lei ti *lascerò* nel mio partire' ['I'll *leave* you in her care when I depart']). It is perhaps with this announcement in mind that Dante expresses his fear of being *abandoned* by his guide on two occasions (*Inf.* VIII, 109 and *Purg.* III, 20). These two instances of *abbandonare* are emblematic of its use more generally: in the *Commedia* the verb has stronger pathetic connotations than *lasciare*, and the stories it tells are hardly ever uplifting. Many occurrences, scattered throughout the poem, trace a rather more negative trajectory from a

---

[9] In Statius's brief history of the human body from conception to the afterlife, told in *Purgatorio* XXV, the verb *solversi* is used about the soul releasing itself from the body upon death: 'Quando Lachesìs non ha più del lino, | *solvesi* da la carne' (*Purg.* XXV, 79–81).
[10] Moevs, *Metaphysics of Dante's 'Commedia'*, p. 11.
[11] Dante is, of course, '*puro* e disposto a salire alle stelle' at the end of *Purgatorio* (XXXIII, 145).
[12] As such it is absent from *Inferno* and appears once in *Paradiso* XXVIII, where it is paired with *risolvere* and employed figuratively, in a comparison between a sky cleared by the wind ('per che *si purga* e *risolve* la roffia | che pria turbava', 82–3) and Dante's mind cleared of doubts.

desirable situation to its wilful or accidental loss, as when Dante abandoned 'la verace via' ['the one true way'] (*Inf.* I, 12) and Fetonte '*abbandonò* li freni' ['*released* the reins'] of his father's chariot (*Inf.* XVII, 107), or in the case of Emperor Albert I of Habsburg leaving Italy in a state of anarchy (*Purg.* VI, 97), and of Ganymede forsaking his comrades as a result of his kidnapping at the hand of Zeus (*Purg.* IX, 23). There are other instances where teleological readings of *abbandonare* can and will be proposed. For instance, when Dante compares his hesitancy to ask a question to that of a storkling who 'non s'attenta | d'*abbandonar* lo nido' ['does not dare | to *leave* its nest'] (*Purg.* XXV, 11–12), he is promptly encouraged by Virgil to overcome his shyness and ask on, in the spirit of his journey of increased knowledge. Further, when the pagan poet explains the structure of Purgatory, the last three circles of avarice, gluttony, and lust come under the normative heading of 'L'amor che...troppo s'*abbandona*' ['The excessive love which *gives itself*'] to earthly attachments (*Purg.* XVII, 136), although it is worth noting that the adverb *troppo* tempers and contextualizes the negativity of s'*abbandona*, suggesting that more moderate abandonment would perhaps not be censured as severely (these sins of incontinence can, after all, be expiated).[13] As scholars point out, Virgil's definition of incontinence in *Purgatorio* harkens back to Francesca's famous speech in *Inferno* V, where the lady draws her listeners' attention to the continuing presence of, depending on interpretations, either her love or her lover, 'che, come vedi, ancor *non m'abbandona*' ['as you see, it *has not left me* yet'] (*Inf.* V, 105).[14] Traditional readings of the passage reproach the lady for fixating on the past, but the text makes multiple interpretations possible when it comes to the specific quality of this fixation. Do Francesca's words portray the continuing presence of her love/lover as positive or negative, welcome or imposed? Is her unabandoned state 'a source of...consolation or desolation'?[15]

---

[13] As indeed has been argued, specifically in the case of sodomy, by some readers of the terrace of the lustful (*Purg.* XXV–XXVII). See Joseph Pequigney, 'Sodomy in Dante's *Inferno* and *Purgatorio*', *Representations*, 36 (1991), 22–42; John E. Boswell, 'Dante and the sodomites', *Dante Studies*, 112 (1992), 63–76; Claudio Giunta, '*Purgatorio* XXVI: àmbito e modelli della poesia volgare', in *La poesia italiana nell'età di Dante: La linea Bonagiunta-Guinizzelli* (Bologna: Il Mulino, 1998), pp. 58–68; Teodolinda Barolini, 'Dante and Cavalcanti (On Making Distinctions in Matters of Love): *Inferno* V in its Lyric Context', *Dante Studies*, 116 (1998), 31–63, and 'Dante's Sympathy for the Other', *Critica del Testo*, 14.1 (2011), I, 177–204; Heather Webb, 'Power Differentials, Unreliable Models, and Homoerotic Desire in the *Comedy*', *Italian Studies*, 68.1 (2013), 17–35.

[14] Lombardi, *Wings of the Doves*, pp. 139–40. On the issue of the speech's capacity to 'produce multiple interpretations' (p. 139), see esp. pp. 132–74.

[15] Lombardi, *Wings of the Doves*, p. 140.

The poem tells us that she is not abandoned, not what not being abandoned must be like. And yet, elsewhere, the poem ascribes some merit to *not* letting go: *abbandonarsi* can only make exile hit Dante harder ('colpo... | tal ch'è più grave a chi più *s'abbandona*' ['a blow... as falls most heavily on one *proceeding heedless*'], *Par.* XVII, 107–8), and perhaps expose him to accusations of pride for his decision to undertake the otherworldly journey ('se del venire io *m'abbandono*, | temo che la venuta non sia folle' ['If I [*let myself*] come | I fear it may be madness'], *Inf.* II, 34).[16] The verbs *lasciare* and *abbandonare* thus paint a morally and affectively rich picture of what moving forward entails: progress, of course, but also uncertainty, regret, pain, danger, and even hubris. This is also the case with the important keyword *convertire* and its cognates, which in Dante's usage are capable of cutting both ways: they can describe the pious 'anime *converse*' of Purgatory (*Purg.* XIX, 116) just as well as deride the wicked '*conversi*' of Malebolge (*Inf.* XXIX, 41).[17] Indeed, conversion is perfectly capable of a negative trajectory: it leads from joy to tears, as 'la letizia *si convertia* in amarissimo pianto' ['his happiness *gave way* to bitterest weeping'] in the *Vita nova* (III, 7), and from good will, through greed, to sin, as 'la pioggia continüa' metaphorically '*converte* | in bozzacchioni le sosine vere' ['*reduces* | the ripening plums to blighted rot'] (*Par.* XXVII, 125–6). In the three appearances it makes as a noun, one per cantica, *conversion* is associated with an element of tragic untimeliness: Pope Adrian's conversion comes too late ('La mia *conversion*, omè!, fu tarda' ['My *conversion*, alas, came late'], *Purg.* XIX, 106), and Francis's conversion of the people in the Holy Land comes too early ('per trovare a *conversione* acerba | troppo la gente' ['finding the people unripe for *conversion*'], *Par.* XI, 103–4), while Constantine's own conversion is the accidental cause of much evil and greed, through his misjudged donation of land to the pope (*Inf.* XIX, 116). The poetics of conversion, therefore, are far from univocal in the *Commedia*, but deterioration, grief, and untimeliness remain available as possibilities in its poetic universe, as indeed they are in life. For some reason, however, these possibilities are not as popular with Dante scholars. What makes positive teleological connotations so dominant in the critical discourse on Dante? And what picture of the *Commedia* would arise if we were to follow its alternatives instead?

---

[16] The remaining instances of *abbandonare* are in *Par.* V, 117 (the pilgrim not having abandoned the mortal condition yet, i.e., being still alive) and XVIII, 9 (the narrator giving up on his attempt to express Beatrice).

[17] *Converso* is a technical term for a lay friar, etymologically derived from *convertire*. See 'convertire' in *ED*.

This study aims to answer these questions. Its core purpose is twofold. First, this extensive Introduction interrogates the critical expectations and practices that accompany teleological readings of Dante with a view to investigating their basis in the poet's writings. Second, the body of the monograph identifies, over the course of three chapters, three possible alternative paths carried out in the poetic practice of the *Commedia* with the aim to explore their hermeneutic implications. The starting point of this Introduction, then, is the observation that, embedded within the text and conditioning these readings, lies Dante's masterplot: a 'constant in Dante's personality' which, as Gianfranco Contini put it, consists in 'downgrading an earlier experience, removing from it its intrinsic aim, and repurposing it as part of the new experience'.[18] The teleological pattern in Dante's works has been detected by a handful of scholars with whom I enter in frequent dialogue in the following pages, starting with Erich Auerbach in his pioneering essay on medieval hermeneutics, 'Figura', and Gianfranco Contini in his edition of the *Rime*, the source of the above quotation. Most importantly, Teodolinda Barolini's own edition of the *Rime* builds on her work on narrative theory (first and foremost, *The Undivine 'Comedy'*), which I can credit as the main methodological interlocutor of this monograph, alongside Albert Russell Ascoli's critique of the palinode in his essential *Dante and the Making of the Modern Author*. Building on this scholarship, this Introduction shows how the teleological masterplot is so pervasive in the author's oeuvre, and its narrative of past mistakes and new beginnings has proved so suggestive, engaging, and inspiring to generations of readers that it often takes on a life of its own in their imagination. Influenced, with varying degrees of awareness, by the textual mechanisms of the masterplot, scholars of Dante continue to reproduce teleological dynamics in their readings of the poem, leaving evidence of its workings in the vocabulary, arguments, and structures of their writings. It is, for instance, common practice in articles and monographs to explore Dante's oeuvre through a variety of approaches and methodologies, yet largely in the order in which he himself has articulated them, from youthly lyric poetry to the seriousness of the *Commedia*, from the dark wood to the Empyrean, from Francesca's love to that of Mary. By reproducing the master narrative of linear development

---

[18] 'una costante della personalità dantesca .... [Q]uel suo degradare un'esperienza precedente, toglierle la sua finalità intrinseca, usufruirla come elemento dell'esperienza nuova' (Contini, 'Introduzione alle *Rime* di Dante', pp. 4–5, trans. mine). Contini's magisterial essay offers one of the earliest and most perceptive explorations into what is called here *Dante's masterplot*.

first suggested to them by the author, his readers thus become more Dantean than Dante. Indeed, this kind of reproducibility is a defining trait of any masterplot. Let us then identify what makes a masterplot.

I.2 Masterplots and the Masterplot

The term *masterplot*, as used throughout this monograph, is defined as a basic narrative pattern that is prevalent within a text and, in various ways, directs its interpretation. The prefix *master-* is employed in its richness but with three main connotations: first, *master* as 'main', indicating (as neutrally as possible) the higher frequency of this pattern relative to other patterns within the text; second (less neutrally), *master* as 'dominant', a gendered term signalling the hegemonic tendency to prevaricate over other patterns and other interpretations of the text; and lastly, *master* as 'original' or 'matrix' (as in 'master recording'), suggesting the masterplot's capacity to be reproduced over and over, and not exclusively by its author.

Although T. K. Seung's 1961 monograph *The Fragile Leaves of the Sibyl: Dante's Master Plan* promotes at length the thesis of a 'master plan' in Dante's *Commedia* (also featuring it in the title),[19] the term *masterplot* used here has a different technical origin in Peter Brooks's work of narrative theory *Reading for the Plot: Design and Intention in Narrative*.[20] Brooks's focus is on modern novels that are very different from the *Commedia*. Nonetheless, he is interested in many of the questions that are explored in the present monograph and that have attracted theorists of narrative ever since Aristotle: beginnings, middles and ends, delays and digressions, the relation between time and narrative, between writing and meaning, between reading and pleasure. In chapter 4 of his book, 'Freud's Masterplot: A Model for Narrative', Brooks rearranges these elements to create an original model for narrative based on Sigmund Freud's *Beyond the Pleasure Principle*. Freud's paper, published in 1920 and traditionally regarded as a watershed in his conception of the human psyche, is not specifically concerned with narrative, but Brooks derives from it a dynamic narrative model for 'the movement of the plot and its motor force in human desire, its peculiar relation to

---

[19] T. K. Seung, *The Fragile Leaves of the Sibyl: Dante's Master Plan* (Westminster, MD: Newman Press, 1961). On the gendered, hermeneutically violent connotations of a masterplot see the Epilogue.
[20] Peter Brooks, *Reading for the Plot: Design and Intention in Narrative* (Cambridge, MA: Harvard University Press, 1984); ch. 4 'Freud's Masterplot' is at pp. 90–112.

beginnings and ends, its apparent claim to rescue meaning from temporal flux'.[21] Brooks calls this particular model 'Freud's own masterplot'.[22]

The focus of Brooks's analysis oscillates from describing the dynamics internal to texts to the experience of reading them, an ambiguity that he believes can never fully be resolved when thinking about narrative—an intuition which bears on this study's understanding of Dante's masterplot.[23] Thus, on the one hand, Brooks treats the text as a living organism pulled and pushed by contrasting forces that are inherent in it; on the other, he shifts seamlessly to the experience of reading, with the pleasure and terror of suspense, recognitions, closure, and so forth. In the model of Freud's masterplot, narrative is shaped by the tension between two basic and contrasting principles: desire for more narration (mapped onto Freud's 'pleasure principle') and wish for closure (mapped on Freud's 'death drive'). If left unchecked, the 'pleasure principle' of narration would stimulate endless storytelling without aim or reason, while the 'death wish' for closure, if left similarly unchecked, would drive the story to a premature end, interrupting the narrative before it has had a chance to make closure meaningful.[24] The distinctive path of narrative is shaped by the interplay between these conflicting forces and their respective risks. Thus, readers find supreme pleasure in following the twists and turns of plots that are delayed by obstacles and thrown off course by detours but eventually reach the desired end.[25]

Arguably, Freud's masterplot provides a useful model for thinking of Dante's *Commedia* as it stands. Olivia Holmes has already noted their affinities. 'The story of Dante-the-pilgrim's journey to blessedness', with its deviation from the straight path and descent before ascent, 'is always also a metatextual story': 'the drive of narrative is ultimately the desire for the end and quiescence, but...always on the verge of premature death or short-circuit'.[26] The protagonist's meandering yet teleological path in the *Commedia*— Holmes thinks of it specifically in terms of Dante's tentative and progressive

---

[21] Ibid., p. 90.   [22] Ibid., p. 96.
[23] 'Ricoeur's emphasis on the constructive role of plot, its active, shaping function, offers a useful corrective to the structural narratologists' neglect of the dynamics of narrative and points us toward the reader's vital role in the understanding of the plot' (Brooks, *Reading for the Plot*, p. 14).
[24] Ibid., pp. 108–9.
[25] In contrast to Peter Brooks, another reader of Freud, Leo Bersani, offers a critique of 'teleologically narrativized' readings of *Beyond the Pleasure Principle* (*The Freudian Body* (New York: Columbia University Press, 1986), p. 66). Bersani is interested, instead, in showing the ways in which Freud's line of argument in *Beyond the Pleasure Principle* fails to proceed linearly as it incessantly returns to the pleasure principle it purports to move beyond (see also pp. 54–67).
[26] Holmes, *Dante's Two Beloveds*, p. 31.

detachment from a 'mistaken erotic choice'[27]—thus emblematizes the kind of narrative described as Freud's masterplot, where the possibility of errancy 'can be represented by "all manner of threats to the protagonist or to... completion: it most commonly takes the form of temptation to the mistaken erotic object choice".[28] This model, however, is not specific to the dialectics between *eros* and *caritas* in Dante but can be said to apply to desire and textuality more generally. Take the following passage from *Convivio*, for instance, which depicts 'the wanderings of the soul's desire toward God as the drive that pushes the pilgrim forward on the road' in terms that seem to anticipate the *Commedia* and its journey:[29]

> E sì come peregrino che va per una via per la quale mai non fue, che ogni casa che da lungi vede crede che sia l'albergo, e non trovando ciò essere, dirizza la credenza a l'altra, e così di casa in casa, tanto che a l'albergo viene; così l'anima nostra, incontanente che nel nuovo e mai non fatto cammino di questa vita entra, dirizza li occhi al termine del suo sommo bene, e però, qualunque cosa vede che paia in sé avere alcuno bene, crede che sia esso.
>
> [And just as the pilgrim who walks along a road on which he has never traveled before believes that every house which he sees from afar is an inn, and finding it not so fixes his expectations on the next one, and so moves from house to house until he comes to the inn, so our soul, as soon as it enters upon this new and never travelled road of life, fixes its eyes on the goal of its supreme good, and therefore believes that everything it sees which seems to possess some good in it is that supreme good.]   (*Conv.* IV, xii, 15)

The passage mixes images of pilgrimage with the Aristotelian teleological drive alluded in the incipit of the *Convivio* ('Sì come dice lo Filosofo nel principio della Prima Filosofia, tutti li uomini naturalmente desiderano di sapere' ['As the Philosopher says at the beginning of the First Philosophy, all men by nature desire to know'], *Conv.* I, i, 1). In this simile, the pilgrim, with a movement that is both forward-driven and errant, wanders forward 'from house to house', mistaking each stage for the 'inn' that is his final goal; similarly, the soul mistakes different earthly attachments for the supreme good. Rather than by the tension between the two conflicting drives of

---

[27] Ibid., p. 32.   [28] Ibid., p. 31, quoting Brooks, *Reading for the Plot*, p. 109.
[29] Elena Lombardi, *The Syntax of Desire: Language and Love in Augustine, the Modistae, Dante* (Toronto: University of Toronto Press, 2010), p. 161.

Freud's masterplot ('pleasure principle' and 'death drive'), the narrative is here shaped by the self-divisions of a single drive, when the soul 'is distracted by the very desire that also serves as necessary catalyst and propeller for its forward motion'.[30] As the foremost narrative theorist in Dante studies, Teodolinda Barolini, notes, 'This view of life as a struggle along the pathway of desire...profoundly informs the *Commedia*'s narrativity'.[31] Dante's narrative is shaped by the view that the many stops and starts along the way are as many turning points that can either lead to one's final destination or lead astray.

Barolini contends that this passage from *Convivio* constitutes 'virtually a blueprint for the *Commedia*'.[32] The second and third chapters of this monograph especially sympathize with her appreciation of the forward-oriented perspective of the pilgrims depicted in the *Convivio*, for whom the 'road of life' appears 'new and never travelled' (*Conv.* IV, xii, 15), and who, like the purging souls of *Purgatorio*, 'are repeatedly shown to be neither *esperti* nor *dottrinati*, but rather strangers in a strange land'.[33] This is the perspective of the living, who do not yet know the end and meaning of their existence and thus do not share the retrospective vantage point of the dead and of those who, like Dante, write about them in the past tense. Although the forward perspective of a pilgrim is very important in Dante's poem (as discussed in Chapter 2 of the present monograph), and relevant to both *personaggio* and *poeta* (Chapter 3), it actually remains atypical in Dante's oeuvre, where it arguably constitutes a late discovery on its author's part. The passage anticipates an important aspect of the *Commedia* but, for a blueprint, it lacks a most fundamental element. Let us trade our pilgrims for a good merchant and propose another passage from *Convivio* that contains a defining feature of Dante's masterplot: creative retrospection. Here Dante is talking about the journey of the noble soul:

> E fa come lo buono mercatante, che, quando viene presso al suo porto, essamina lo suo procaccio e dice: 'Se io non fosse per cotal cammino

---

[30] Teodolinda Barolini, *The Undivine 'Comedy': Detheologizing Dante* (Princeton, NJ: Princeton University Press, 1992), p. 104. Barolini is comparing here the passage from *Convivio* to the path of 'l'anima semplicetta che sa nulla' in *Purg.* XVI, 85–93.
[31] Barolini, *Undivine 'Comedy'*, p. 104.   [32] Ibid., p. 100.
[33] Ibid., p. 101. The scholar's emphases allude to the soul in *Convivio* IV, xii, 16 ('la sua conoscenza prima è imperfetta, per non essere esperta né dottrinata') and to Virgil's words in *Purg.* II, 61–3 ('Voi credete | forse che siamo esperti d'esto loco; | ma noi siam peregrini come voi siete').

passato, questo tesoro non avre'io e non avrei di ch'io godesse ne la mia cittade, a la quale io m'appresso'; e però benedice la via che ha fatta.

[It acts like the good merchant who, as he draws near to his port, examines his profits and says: 'If I had not made my journey along this road, I would not have this treasure, nor would I have anything in which to take delight in my city, to which I am drawing near'; and so he blesses the way he has taken.]   (*Conv.* IV, xxviii, 12)

As one of the prototypes for the *Commedia*'s many wayfarers, the 'good merchant' of *Convivio* appears surrounded by the metaphors of journey by sea and by foot that pervade the imaginative universe of Dante's poem.[34] The merchant has reached the safety of the haven he was aiming for, can take stock of his profit, and assess his journey from the new vantage point. The value of his travels, in his eyes, depends on their outcome. Like the narrator of the *Commedia*, the merchant can reassess his path from a new perspective whose domain is the present tense. In the merchant's case, this revaluation is so radical that its effects are registered on the syntax of his speech: the past does not appear to him in the historic indicative of storytelling but is transfigured into subjunctive and conditional counterfactuals ('Se io non fosse...passato', 'non avre'io', 'non avrei' ['If I had not made my journey', 'I would not have', 'nor would I have']). These hypotheticals, however, do not offer positive alternatives to what his path could have been, for better or for worse, but, rather emphatically, they foreclose them. From the merchant's present perspective, the suggestion that the past could have gone differently is voiced as a strong impossibility (in triple negatives—'Se io *non*', '*non* avre'io e *non* avrei'). His use of counterfactuals is more akin to the syllogisms of logic: their effect is to reinforce the chain of cause and effect that links his past to the position of safety from which he is judging it. That path, in the merchant's speech, led him to his present position as though by an irresistible narrative necessity. After the merchant finishes his speech, Dante rounds off his character's teleological storyline with the merchant's benediction of the journey. The author's stage directions seem straightforward here: *because of* the sentiment expressed in his speech (*però*), the merchant blesses his past. And yet despite this causal connective of ordinary narrative where pasts are logically the cause of presents, the merchant's speech has been all but ordinary. Imperceptibly, the past has been transformed into

---

[34] Barolini, *Undivine 'Comedy'*, pp. 112–31.

something different. The merchant has literally *bene-dicted* the past, performatively voiced it into being good.[35]

Blessing the past, cursing the past, any operation of revaluation of the past that is predicated upon reinterpreting its historical significance from a new vantage point is the province of Dante's masterplot. The masterplot need not always be as performative as it is in the merchant's story or as Manuele Gragnolati has demonstrated it to be in the creation of a new author in the *Vita nova*—nevertheless, it is important to be aware of its performative potential.[36] Dante's masterplot operates, at its most abstract, by splitting linear time into *old* and *new*, *before* and *after*, *then* and *now*, *past* and *present*, *beginning* and *end*, and giving the *new*, the *after*, the *now*, the *present*, and the *end* hermeneutic precedence over the *old*, the *before*, the *then*, the *past*, and the *beginning*. For Dante's masterplot, it makes little difference whether previous experiences are now considered negatively or positively; the point is that they are reinterpreted from a new vantage point. It also makes little difference from what angle the past is considered, whether biographical, literary, spiritual, etc.; so long as they can be placed in a linear narrative, previous stages are always available for revaluation. In its crudest form, Dante's masterplot consists in this *divide et impera* of narrative time for the purposes of controlling interpretation.

How does the masterplot work and why is it so persuasive? The teleological narrative model imitates and harnesses, through a variety of tactics, one fundamental principle of storytelling. Brooks calls it 'the necessary retrospectivity of narrative: that only the end can finally determine meaning'.[37] This principle can be seen at work in most narrative texts, from the microcosm of a sentence, where 'only when all the words, one after the other, are uttered in time is the sentence completed and meaningful';[38] to the macrocosm of a

---

[35] For the theory of performativity in language, see J. L. Austin, *How to Do Things with Words* (Oxford: Clarendon Press, 1962). A similar dynamic between benediction and counterfactual thinking is also found in the previous paragraph of *Conv.* IV, xxviii, 11. A merchant's life, as represented in the two other occurrences of *Convivio*, is far from simple: 'li miseri mercatanti che per lo mondo vanno' laden with riches experience anxiety every day on their job (*Conv.* IV, xiii, 11). Moreover, one's assessment of one's life is compared to that of the 'falso mercatante' who uses different measures according to whether he is buying or selling, 'sì che 'l numero e la quantità e 'l peso del bene li pare più che se con giusta misura fosse saggiato, e quello del male meno' (*Conv.* I, ii, 9). Positive experiences, in this view, are easily overestimated.

[36] Manuele Gragnolati, 'Authorship and Performance in Dante's *Vita nova*', in *Aspects of the Performative in Medieval Culture*, ed. Manuele Gragnolati and Almut Suerbaum (Berlin, New York: de Gruyter, 2010), pp. 123–40, and *Amor che move*, pp. 17–34.

[37] Brooks, *Reading for the Plot*, p. 22.

[38] Lombardi, *Syntax of Desire*, p. 4. Lombardi's book recognizes the structural importance of this pattern when she compares it to Dante's dynamics of desire.

complete work 'as the sentences flow toward the poem's ending in order to give it meaning';[39] indeed, Dantists have clearly recognized the importance of different levels of end-determinacy in the very structure of the *Commedia*.[40] Even outside of literature, 'the structuring power' of the end to 'retrospectively give...order and significance' plays an important part in understandings of life itself, which, like all narrative, is most intelligible when complete.[41] This idea of end-determined meaning pervades all areas of human experience and, as such, is not Dante's invention—if anything, a personal epiphany. The idea is at least as old as the fabulous dialogue between Solon and King Croesus, when the Athenian sage rejected claims that his life could be described as 'happy' by stating that 'before he comes to his end it is well to hold back and not to call him yet happy but only lucky'.[42] One can only judge a life from its endpoint. As one French essayist wrote, the last day of a life is veritably 'the master day'.[43]

The narrative principle of end-determinacy becomes the greatest ally of Dante's masterplot. If it is true, as Frank Kermode writes in *The Sense of an Ending*, that '[w]e cannot, of course, be denied an end; it is one of the great charms of books that they have to end',[44] it is equally true that nothing prevents writers from mimetically multiplying ends within the confines of their works. Having taken care to punctuate his storytelling into binary *befores* and *afters*, *olds* and *news*, *pasts* and *presents*, Dante harnesses the end's capacity to determine meaning and grants it to his various fictional *afters*, *news*, and *presents*. Such turning points take the shape of as many endings from which revaluation in retrospect becomes possible. It is no wonder,

---

[39] Freccero, *Poetics of Conversion*, p. 216. Freccero links the way in which 'Dante's poetic history derives its significance retrospectively from its ending' to 'the spiritual evolution of his protagonist'.

[40] See references to Elena Lombardi and John Freccero in the two notes above. Dante's conception of syntax and narrative is often related to Augustine's discussion of time in the *Confessions* IV, xi, 15–17, where 'the temporal universe is described in terms of a syntactically organized sentence' (Lombardi, *Syntax of Desire*, p. 53). See, for instance, Charles S. Singleton, 'The Vistas in Retrospect', *MLN* 81.1 (1966), 55–80 (62).

[41] Brooks, *Reading for the Plot*, p. 94.

[42] The anecdote is told by Herodotus, *Historiae* I, 32 (in English as *The Histories*, trans. G. C. Macaulay, rev. Donald Lateiner (New York: Barnes & Noble Classics, 2004)). Herodotus stresses this point by telling us that Croesus only understood Solon's words when he himself ended up captive, facing execution.

[43] The expression is Michel de Montaigne's in *Les Essais*, ed. Jean Balsamo, Michel Magnien, and Catherine Magnien-Simonin (Gallimard: Paris, 2007), I, xviii, p. 81: 'C'est le maistre jour, c'est le jour juge de tous les autres: c'est le jour, dict un ancient, qui doit juger de toutes mes années passées'.

[44] Frank Kermode, *The Sense of an Ending: Studies in the Theory of Fiction* (Oxford: Oxford University Press, 1966), p. 23.

then, that fictional endpoints scan and structure Dante's oeuvre: from the *Vita nova*'s rereading of his past poetic and existential self to the *Convivio*'s practice and theory of self-exegesis, and the canon established in book II of the unfinished *De vulgari eloquentia*, which traces a literary history of the lyric culminating in the author's moral canzoni;[45] experiences which, in turn, are funnelled into the new end-all of the *Commedia*. In the poem, endpoints explode. The *Commedia* can be read as a sustained fiction that an ultimate endpoint is possible; at the same time, however, the poem's own endpoints do not cease multiplying, as Dante reports back to us from the end of his and his characters' errors, the end of life, the end of history, the end of time, each with their own significance and meaning-making power. Fictional ends matter to Dante insofar as they imitate and channel the power of real ends. They are instrumental in the retrospective revaluation of what precedes them, which is at the heart of the masterplot.

I.3 The Cases of *Vita nova* and *Commedia*

The *Vita nova* represents the first and clearest embodiment of Dante's masterplot, as indirectly evidenced by the fact that refraining from teleological language when describing its story is virtually impossible. Thematically, the *libello* has been described as 'the recollective and teleological tale of how the protagonist has successfully overcome the limits of a courtly conception of desire and transformed his love for Beatrice into a new modality';[46] Dante's book offers a 'retrospective summing up, as well as a palinodic reframing and reinterpretation, of his earlier career as vernacular love lyricist'.[47] The salient moments in this narrative—'the shift to the new "stilo" of praise; the traumatic changes surrounding Beatrice's death; the reversion to Beatrice *in morte* after flirtation with a *donna* gentile'—are as many 'turning points' in this 'Augustinian conversion story'.[48] Retrospective revaluation pervades the

---

[45] Here and throughout, this monograph adopts the spelling *Vita nova* proposed by Guglielmo Gorni: see his 'Paragrafi e titolo della *Vita nova*', *Studi di filologia italiana*, 52 (1995), 203–22. It should be noted that teleological readings of the literary histories traced in the *Convivio* and *De vulgari* are based on books that are unfinished. For the implications of unfinishedness, see Chapter 3 in this monograph.

[46] 'il racconto memoriale e teleologico di come il protagonista è riuscito a superare i limiti della concezione cortese del desiderio e a trasformare il proprio amore per Beatrice in una nuova modalità' (Gragnolati, *Amor che move*, p. 23, trans. mine).

[47] Ascoli, *Dante and the Making of a Modern Author*, p. 179.

[48] Ibid., p. 183.

youthful work not only thematically but in its very form.[49] Through the *prosimetrum*, Dante collects previously scattered lyrics and poetic fragments, linking them by means of a unifying narrative. Scholars have identified an eclectic number of models behind the *Vita nova*'s interaction between poetry and prose—from the *vidas* and *razos* of vernacular poetry to the Latin commentaries, to biblical books, or to classical poets and philosophers— while still maintaining the consensus that Dante radically innovates these traditions 'by introducing a first-person commentator identical with, though temporally successive to, a first-person author'.[50] The identity *and* temporal succession, here, are key. The autobiographical (or autofictional) narrative of the *Vita nova* proceeds mainly chronologically from the past tense of Dante's earliest memories to the present tense of the time of writing (and eventually, the future beyond).[51] This linear development shows its seams in the formal break between Dante's past poetry and his more mature perspective in prose. This is where the author first adopts a strategy that will feature prominently in the *Convivio*, in parts of the *De vulgari eloquentia*, and which also underpins, more subtly, the dual *personaggio-poeta* of the *Commedia*, as he 'formally splits himself in two: there is one "Dante" who analyses, another "Dante" who is analysed'.[52] Scholars such as Ascoli, Barolini, Picone, and Gragnolati have studied the ways in which this strategy, in the *Vita nova*, allows Dante to co-opt and performatively create for himself the authority of a medieval *auctoritas*, and the personalized and individualized identity of a proto-modern author, and have related this, more widely, to Dante's other works and the *Commedia*.[53] What is important

---

[49] Ibid., p. 179.
[50] Ibid., p. 185. For a review of the models behind the *prosimetrum*, see pp. 179–85.
[51] Teodolinda Barolini has detected in the *Vita nova* 'the presence of a double *contaminatio*, whereby the *libello* is the locus not only of a narrativized—chronologized—lyric, but also of a lyricized—dechronologized—narrative' ('Cominciandomi dal principio infino a la fine' (*V.N.* XXIII, 15): Forging Anti-Narrative in the *Vita Nova*', in *La gloriosa donna de la mente: A Commentary on the 'Vita Nuova'*, ed. Vincent Moleta (Florence: Olschki, 1993), pp. 119–40 (p. 123)).
[52] Ascoli, *Dante and the Making of a Modern Author*, p. 176. The modern scholarly construction of Dante 'poeta-personaggio' is founded on Charles S. Singleton, *Dante Studies 1. 'Commedia': Elements of Structure* (Baltimore, MD: Johns Hopkins University Press, 1954), and Contini, 'Dante come personaggio-poeta'. For a review of the issue, see Michelangelo Picone, 'Dante come autore/narratore della *Commedia*', *Nuova rivista di letteratura italiana*, 2.1 (1999), 9–26; Maria Grazia Riccobono, *Dante Poeta-Profeta, Pellegrino, Autore: Strutturazione Espressiva della Commedia e Visione Escatologica Dantesca* (Rome: Aracne, 2012), esp. pp. 11–39; Lino Pertile, '"Trasmutabile per tutte guise": Dante in the *Comedy*', in *Dante's Plurilingualism: Authority, Knowledge, Subjectivity*, ed. Sara Fortuna, Manuele Gragnolati, and Jürgen Trabant (Oxford: Legenda, 2010), pp. 164–78.
[53] See Toby Levers, 'The Image of Authorship in the Final Chapter of the *Vita Nuova*', in *Italian Studies*, 57 (2002), 6–10; Ascoli, *Dante and the Making of a Modern Author*, pp. 175–201;

for the purposes of the present volume is how Dante's strategy operates. The poet displays an acute understanding of how certain formal features (for example, in the case of the *Vita nova*, the distinction between commented text and prose commentary) have a strong hermeneutic potential (that is, the power of the commentary to interpret texts), which is capable of being imitated and harnessed in other ways in a text. Understanding this, Dante first reproduces the hermeneutic potential of the commentary-form, straightforwardly, in the form of the *libello* (through the *prosimetrum*); he then takes this one step further as he translates the distinction between poetic text and prose commentary into a temporal distinction between an *old* and a *new* self, through his innovation of the auto-commentary written by a single author at different stages of his life. The achievement of this operation is as great as its strategy is simple: the mature Dante claims for himself the right to *interpret*, a right that did not traditionally belong to him as a then-living vernacular poet but that he harnesses mimetically from the form of the commentary. The traditional authority of the commentary-form is thus appropriated by the retrospective Dante, who, for the first time in his career, claims the right to reinterpret his own past.[54]

By the time he is writing the *Commedia*, Dante does not need the form of the commentary to be able to interpret previous experiences; he has learned how to imitate its hermeneutic power fully within the confines of narrative poetry. The temporal distance between forward-living protagonist and backward-understanding narrator is no longer underpinned by a formal distinction as clear-cut as the *prosimetrum*;[55] it shapes the poem's form in more subtle ways. John Freccero has written eloquently on the relationship of the *Commedia*'s content to its form, by showing how the protagonist's forward motion and the narrator's self-reflection are embodied in the form of the terzina: 'the verse pattern and the theme' of the poem 'proceed by a forward motion that is at the same time recapitulatory', which is arguably the formal 'representation of narrative logic' in general but 'particularly autobiography'—a view of narrative and autobiography that is also held,

---

Gragnolati, 'Authorship and Performance', pp. 123–40, and *Amor che move*, pp. 17–34. As Barolini puts it, 'The shrewdness of the *Vita Nuova* in its construction of a new authorial persona cannot be overstated' (*Dante's Lyric Poetry: Poems of Youth and of the 'Vita Nuova'*, ed. Teodolinda Barolini, trans. Richard Lansing (Toronto: University of Toronto Press, 2014), p. 61).

[54] On the different functions of Dante in the *Vita nova*, see Michelangelo Picone, 'La teoria dell'*Auctoritas* nella *Vita nuova*', *Tenzone*, 6 (2006), 173–91.

[55] See esp. Amilcare A. Iannucci, 'Autoesegesi dantesca: La tecnica dell'"episodio parallelo"', repr. in *Forma ed evento nella 'Divina Commedia'* (Rome: Bulzoni, 1984), pp. 83–114; Ascoli, *Dante and the Making of a Modern Author*, pp. 301–405.

independently, by Peter Brooks.[56] Freccero's account relies on a division of labour between the past-tense narration of Dante's pilgrimage and the narrator's present-tense perspective on it, but also recognizes their continuity. What remains important in the poem, in its skeletal form, is a relative distinction between a previous experience and a successive position with the power to interpret it. In the *Commedia*, the watershed between the two is marked by the crucial experience of Dante's fictional pilgrimage through the afterlife, which allows the *personaggio-poeta* to make sense of his past existence and reorient it towards a future, the key points of which are gradually revealed to him; these include his personal exile, the historical events that are prophesied to him, the eschatological future he witnesses first-hand and is personally promised, and so forth.[57] There is no longer need for a division of labour between poetry and prose—the one expressing the past, the other interpreting it in retrospect—but the authority to reinterpret the past is conferred on the poet by the very story he is writing: in the logic of the fiction, the *poeta* has already achieved this authority by having experienced the afterlife, its encounters, and visions as *personaggio* during the fictional journey.[58] The teleological masterplot is thus justified not through a formal separation but through one main thematic division of *before* and *after* which has the journey as its watershed. The existence of this master distinction,

---

[56] John Freccero, 'The Significance of *Terza Rima*', repr. in *Poetics of Conversion*, pp. 258–71 (p. 263). Brooks relates narrative in general to autobiography in *Reading for the Plot*, pp. 4–33. Within Dante Studies, Elena Lombardi has recognized the structural importance of Freccero's 'recapitulation', and its meaning-making ability 'to integrate the beginning...into the end', for the 'syntax/desire' nexus in the *Commedia* (*The Syntax of Desire*, p. 173).

[57] The notion of Dante as pilgrim, rooted in such passages of the *Commedia* as *Purg.* II, 61–3 ('Voi credete | forse che siamo esperti d'esto loco; | ma noi siam peregrin come voi siete'), and part of a long Christian tradition that interpreted life on earth as *peregrinatio* or even exile (cf. Gerhardt B. Ladner, '*Homo viator*: Medieval Ideas on Alienation and Order', *Speculum*, 42.2 (1967), 233–59), has been variously conceptualized in Dante Studies: see Roberto Mercuri, *Semantica di Gerione: Il motivo del viaggio nella 'Commedia' di Dante* (Rome: Bulzoni, 1984); John Demaray, *Dante and the Book of the Cosmos* (Philadelphia: American Philosophical Society, 1987), pp. 1–60; Bruno Basile, 'Dante e l'idea di *peregrinatio*', in *Il tempo e le forme: Studi letterari da Dante a Gadda* (Modena: Mucchi, 1990), pp. 9–36; Julia Bolton Holloway, *The Pilgrim and the Book* (New York: Peter Lang, 1992), esp. pp. 57–84; Michelangelo Picone, '*Inferno* VIII: il viaggio contrastato', *L'Alighieri*, 9 (1997), 35–50; Peter S. Hawkins, 'Crossing over: Dante and Pilgrimage', in *Dante's Testaments. Essays in Scriptural Imagination* (Stanford: Stanford University Press, 1999), pp. 247–64 and 333–6; Catherine Keen, 'The Language of Exile in Dante', *Reading Medieval Studies*, 27 (2001), 79–102; Carlo Delcorno, '"Ma noi siam peregrin come voi siete"': Aspetti penitenziali del *Purgatorio*', in *Da Dante a Montale: Studi di filologia e critica letteraria in onore di Emilio Pasquini*, ed. Gian Mario Anselmi (Bologna: Gedit, 2006), pp. 11–30; Giuseppe Ledda, 'Immagini di pellegrinaggio e di esilio nella *Commedia* di Dante', *Annali Online di Ferrara: Lettere*, 1 (2012), 295–308.

[58] On Dante's realism and its role in directing the interpretation of the poem, see Barolini, *Undivine 'Comedy'*, esp. pp. 3–20.

however, does not prevent Dante from creating other ad hoc distinctions along the way and moving the watershed accordingly; in fact, it promotes and validates this operation by providing a model for it—a reproducible master. Compared to the 'crude' *prosimetrum* of the *Vita nova*, there are considerable advantages in not fixing the distinction in the form of the text but only evoking it mimetically and when necessary. Flexibility, subtlety, and reproducibility are all added bonuses to this strategy, while the all-important hermeneutic power of retrospection maintains its effectiveness.

When it comes to the *Commedia*, Dante's masterplot might well be pervasive and supremely influential on its readers, but in the text itself it is like the panther that is nowhere to be found but whose scent is everywhere.[59] Its constitutive elements are a handful: the distinction between *before* and *after*, a retrospective gaze, a revaluation of the previous position, and, ideally, the act of writing; yet in the *Commedia* they hardly appear together in a single quotable set of terzinas.[60] Charles Singleton's essay 'The Vistas in Retrospect', which pioneers the study of what is called here Dante's masterplot, draws attention to the various passages in the poem when the protagonist turns his gaze backward to recapitulate the journey he has undertaken. Such passages, he claims, are as many 'details of a *pattern*, of a great vista of meaning that opens up in retrospect at the pivotal point'.[61] Indeed, in the poem Dante is repeatedly caught looking back, from the entrance of Hell ('così l'animo mio, ch'ancor fuggiva, | si volse a retro a rimirar lo passo | che non lasciò già mai persona viva' ['so my mind, still in flight, | turned back to look once more upon the pass | no mortal being ever left alive'], *Inf.* I, 25-7) to the Garden of Eden ('Già m'avean trasportato i lenti passi | dentro a la selva antica tanto, | ch'io non potea rivedere ond'io mi 'ntrassi' ['Already my slow steps had carried me | so deep into the ancient forest | I could not see where I had entered'], *Purg.* XXVIII, 22-4) and (implicitly) the heights of the Empyrean ('questi, che da l'infima lacuna | de l'universo infin qui ha vedute | le vite spirituali ad una ad una' ['This man who, from within the deepest pit |

---

[59] Cf. *De vulgari eloquentia* I, xvi.
[60] Perhaps the most quotable instance of the masterplot is the poem's first proem—*Inferno* I, 1–9 will be discussed in detail at the beginning of Chapter 3.
[61] Singleton, 'The Vistas in Retrospect', p. 61, italics his. Singleton's seminal article and its implications are discussed by Freccero, 'The Significance of *Terza Rima*', pp. 262–3; Zygmunt G. Barański, 'Structural Retrospection in Dante's *Comedy*: The Case of *Purgatorio* XXVII', *Italian Studies*, 41.1 (1986), 1–23 (p. 9), and his subsequent 'Without any Violence', in *Vertical Readings in Dante's 'Comedy': Vol. 1*, ed. George Corbett and Heather Webb (Cambridge: Open Book Publishers, 2015), pp. 181–202 (p. 182); and Simon A. Gilson, 'The Wheeling Sevens', in the same volume, pp. 143–60 (p. 149).

the universe contains up to these heights | has seen the disembodied spirits, one by one'], *Par.* XXXIII, 22–4). An emblematic instance of the protagonist's backward gaze is offered by the heaven of Saturn, where Dante is able to recontextualize from his new vantage point, with a smile, our planet and the struggles and ambitions it holds ('Col viso ritornai per tutte quante | le sette spere, e vidi questo globo | tal, ch'io sorrisi del suo vil sembiante' ['With my eyes I returned through every one | of the seven spheres below, and saw this globe of ours | to be such that I smiled, so mean did it appear'], *Par.* XXII, 133–5). Earth—'l'aiuola che ci fa tanto feroci' ['The little patch of earth that makes us here so fierce'] (*Par.* XXII, 151)—appears to the protagonist's backward gaze one last time in *Paradiso* XXVII, 76–87, where the narrator's reference to 'il varco | folle di Ulisse' ['the mad track of Ulysses'] (*Par.* XXVII, 82–3) evokes the Greek hero's trademark transgression. Everything in this retrospective passage contributes to make it a set piece of unmistakable moral exemplarity and endless imitability: its position at the end of the pilgrim's journey; the fact that it contains the last occurrence of the key adjective *folle*, which challenges Dante ever since the beginning of his pilgrimage ('temo che la venuta non sia folle' ['I fear it may be madness'], *Inf.* II, 35); and the episode's obvious intertextual allusion to the traditional models of Cicero's *Somnium Scipionis* and Boethius's *De Consolatione Philosophiae*.[62] This is what Dante's masterplot does best: it produces an archetypal and reproducible narrative that tells a tale of linear moral progress. The memorable scene was widely imitated and alluded to by such poets as Ariosto and Tasso.[63]

If the masterplot shows its retrospective aspect at the end of the journey, at the beginning it reveals rather its counterpart: a desire for ends. Contrary to Zygmunt Barański's claim that '[r]ather than forcing our readerly attention upwards and "vertically", Dante normally encourages us to reflect and to look backwards "Ricorditi, ricorditi!"' (*Purg.* XXVII, 22), the two movements are not exclusive but mutually necessary.[64] Take this passage from the intensely meta-literary *Inferno* XVI:

[62] Scipio's dream is found in *De re publica* VI, 20, in *De re publica, De legibus*, trans. Clinton Walker Keynes, rev. edn (Cambridge, MA: Harvard University Press, 2000); Boethius, *De Consolatione Philosophiae*, II, vii, 3–18, in *The Theological Tractates and De Consolatione Philosophiae*, trans. Hugh F. Stewart, Edward K. Rand, and S. Jim Tester, rev. edn (Cambridge, MA: Harvard University Press, 1973).

[63] Ludovico Ariosto, *Orlando Furioso*, ed. Edoardo Sanguineti and Marcello Turchi (Milan: Garzanti, 1964), XXXIV, 71–2; Torquato Tasso, *Gerusalemme Liberata*, ed. Lanfranco Caretti (Milan: Mondadori, 1957), XIV, 9–10.

[64] Barański, 'Without any Violence', p. 9. Barański makes this general statement in a polemical context against the recent hermeneutic practice of vertical readings conflating 'verticality' with 'vectoriality' a little sophistically (nothing prescribes vertical readers to move exclusively

> Però, se campi d'esti luoghi bui
> e torni a riveder le belle stelle,
> quando ti gioverà dicere 'I' fui',
> fa che di noi a la gente favelle.
>
> [Therefore, so may you escape these dark regions
> to see again the beauty of the stars,
> when you shall rejoice in saying 'I was there,'
> see that you speak of us to others.]
>
> (*Inf.* XVI, 82–5)

We are in the seventh circle of Hell, among the violent against God, and this is 'the only time in Hell that several sinners speak harmoniously as one'.[65] Displaying the typical concern with earthly fame that characterizes Dante's infernal sodomites, these souls collectively ask the protagonist to relate their story. The way they conceive of this storytelling is strictly tense-based: Dante's retrospective position, which they anticipate, is described as the time, in the future, when the protagonist will have turned into a narrator able to use the past indicative of storytelling 'I' fui' ['I was there'] (84). Thus, in the middle of the journey, Dante already directs his text towards an ideal endpoint from which retrospective (and public) storytelling will be possible, an endpoint that still lies in the future ('when you shall rejoice...') but will be voiced in the past tense ('...in saying "I was there"'). Even more remarkably, Dante cross-contaminates fiction and textuality in what can be considered a trademark move:[66] he plants in the direct speech of a set of his fictional characters an anticipation of the last line of the cantica that contains them. In the context of the souls' appeal to Dante's future writing, their wish 'se...torni a riveder le belle stelle' ['so may you...see again the beauty of the stars'] (*Inf.* XVI, 83) appears not only verified but *reified* as the conclusion of the narrative poem *Inferno* which the reader is holding in her hands ('E quindi uscimmo a riveder le stelle' ['Then we came forth, to see again the stars'], *Inf.* XXXIV, 139), and which Dante even affects to swear on as though it were a sacred text (*Inf.* XVI, 127–8).[67] Their word is made text: retrospective

upwards). Chapter 3 will explore more in detail the structural importance of the forward movement of future tenses in proemial positions.

[65] Robert Hollander *ad Inf.* XVI, 82–5 (DDP).
[66] See Barolini, *Undivine 'Comedy'*, esp. pp. 3–20.
[67] On the medieval practice of swearing on books as seen in *Inferno* XVI, see Nicolò Crisafi and Elena Lombardi, 'Lust and Law: Reading and Witnessing in *Inferno* V', in *Ethics, Politics and Law in Dante*, ed. Catherine Keen and Giulia Gaimari (London: UCL Press, 2019).

retelling, which had been conceived from the very beginning, is accomplished through the writing of the poem, and the teleology of Dante's journey from *personaggio* to *poeta* is fulfilled.

However, as is often the case with passages that appear to exemplify the masterplot most clearly (this monograph explores a number of them), its workings are not as smooth as they seem. Since Pietro Alighieri, most commentators of the passage have pointed out that Dante's tense-based expression alludes to a speech by Aeneas, in the first book of Virgil's *Aeneid*—a quintessentially teleological epic in its own right (and a recurrent reference in the present study). Aeneas speaks as follows:

> O passi graviora, dabit deus his quoque finem.
> ...
> revocate animos, maestumque timorem
> mittite: forsan et haec olim meminisse iuvabit.
> Per varios casus, per tot discrimina rerum
> tendimus in Latium; sedes ubi fata quietas
> ostendunt; illic fas regna resurgere Troiae.

[O...you who have suffered worse, this also God will end....recall your courage and banish sad fear. Perhaps even this distress it will some day be a joy to recall. Through varied fortunes, through countless hazards, we journey towards Latium, where fate promises a home of peace. There it is granted that Troy's realm shall rise again.] (*Aeneid* I, 199, 202–6)[68]

It is the beginning of the *Aeneid*, and Aeneas is giving an inspirational speech to encourage his friends and allies to reach the end of their journey. He urges them to keep in mind the ultimate goal and justification of their wanderings: the foundation of a new Troy, which will be their resting place. The passage is a textbook case of Brooks's theory: through meanderings and dangers, a desire for closure drives the narrative to an end that gives meaning to it all. Dante renders a portion of the line 'forsan et haec olim meminisse iuvabit' ['Perhaps even this distress it will some day be a joy to recall'] (*Aeneid* I, 203) as 'quando ti gioverà dicere "I' fui" ['when you shall rejoice in saying "I was there"'] (*Inf.* XVI, 84); his future tense *gioverà* renders literally Virgil's *iuvabit*, and the past tense 'I' fui' distils the pastness of Virgil's

---

[68] Virgil, *Eclogues. Georgics. Aeneid: Books 1–6*, trans. H. Rushton Fairclough, rev. G. P. Goold, Loeb Classical Library 63, new rev. edn (Cambridge, MA: Harvard University Press, 1999).

infinitive *meminisse*. It is a touching yet restrained translation. There is no need to reproduce the semantics of Virgil's verb of memory through a one-to-one equivalent as *ricordare*. Speaking in the past tense already implies memory, and so Dante drops the verb to focus on the essentials (what matters to his narrative art): the knot between direct speech, self-narrative, and retelling the past.

Taken out of context in the commentaries of the *Commedia*, Aeneas's speech may seem confident, even bombastic, as the hero claims that a god gives an end to everything (*Aeneid* I, 199). Yet the hero's words are double-edged: on the one hand, all things have an end, a *telos* that directs their course with its logic and allows for retrospective meaning; on the other, all things are threatened by premature ends that care little about human aspirations and goals. Scholars of Virgil such as Adam Parry and Gian Biagio Conte have long appreciated the ways in which the *Aeneid* gives voice to both, apparently conflicting, narratives within the poem: on the one hand, the triumphal 'epic' march directed toward the foundation of Rome; on the other, the 'pathetic' voice of those who are fallen or left behind along the way.[69] This episode offers a typical instance of this polyphony: as soon as Aeneas's rousing pep talk comes to a close, Virgil informs us that the hero is not as confident as he looks, his doubts are concealed within him, his hope merely feigned (*Aeneid* I, 207–8). It is to this ambiguous scene that Dante chooses to relate his storytelling in the episode of *Inferno* XVI. The Florentine poet signals that his texts are as ambiguous as his maestro's. The main clause 'fa che di noi a la gente favelle' ['see that you speak of us to others'] (*Inf.* XVI, 85) depends on whether the wish 'se campi d'esti luoghi bui | e torni a riveder le belle stelle' ['so may you escape these dark regions to see again the beauty of the stars'] (82–3)—with its positive trajectory from 'dark regions' to the 'beauty of the stars'—comes to fruition. There are no guarantees that the wish will be fulfilled, and so the counterfactual draws attention to the ever-present possibility of failure.

In the body of this monograph, I offer close readings of a number of similar passages in the *Commedia*—from the proems of each cantica, to the

---

[69] Adam Parry, 'The Two Voices of Virgil's Poetry', *Arion*, 2.4 (1963), 66–80, and Gian Biagio Conte, *Virgilio: L'epica del sentimento* (Turin: Einaudi, 2002), available in English as *The Poetry of Pathos: Studies in Virgilian Epic*, ed. J. Harrison (Oxford: Oxford University Press, 2007). Cf. also R. O. A. M. Lyne, *Further Voices in Vergil's 'Aeneid'* (Oxford: Clarendon Press, 1992). On Dante trying his hand at this very Virgilian ambiguity, in the story of Marcellus (*Par.* VIII), see Chapter 2 of this monograph. I explored Virgil's narrative pluralism and its significance for Dante in a paper on 'The Two Voices of Dante's Poetry: The Affective Space in the Grand March of History' at SIS Brighton, on 5 April 2018.

encounter with Beatrice in the Garden of Eden, and to the very last canto of *Paradiso*. They may be key to the establishment of a teleological master narrative in Dante's poem and yet, despite (and because of) their function, they are contaminated by design with ambiguities, contradictions, centrifugal forces, and vulnerabilities. Reading closely key loci of the masterplot in the poem confirms the findings of the preliminary close reading of teleological language in this Introduction. Predominant though teleology is in the *Commedia*, a plurality of narratives begins to emerge on closer inspection that contrasts and deviates from its trajectory, and thus questions and complicates its message. The three chapters that follow investigate Dante's narrative pluralism by exploring three alternative narratives, which either embrace non-linear narratives (Chapters 1 and 2) or take the linearity of teleology to its extreme consequences (Chapter 3). Chapter 1, 'Paradox in the Poem', argues that the paradoxes represented in the *Commedia* provide a narrative model that undoes the hierarchy of teleology in order to involve the reader in the radical otherness of Dante's otherworld. Chapter 2, 'Alternative Endings and Parallel Lives', shows how this most retrospective and self-enclosed of poems opens up the afterlife to the affective storytelling of 'what could have been' and encourages the comparison of life stories as a reminder of the fact that, although Dante's fiction represents lives as concluded, there was a time on Earth when such lives were in progress and open to a plurality of possible outcomes. Chapter 3, 'The Future In/Out of the *Commedia*' applies this perspective to the only character in the fictional afterlife whose life is not yet concluded: the protagonist Dante. The chapter focuses on the *Commedia*'s negotiation of the anxieties associated to the open-endedness of the future beyond the composition of the poem, a time that constitutes the most inevitable blind spot in Dante's, and arguably any, act of retrospective narration. Such plurality of narratives, disseminated at strategic points throughout the text, often sounds a minor chord or a dissonant note in the predominantly major harmonies of Dante's teleological masterplot with its uplifting story of poetic development and moral improvement, redemption, emancipation, and spiritual *askesis*. Alternative narratives form the basis of what this monograph calls Dante's narrative pluralism. Dante scholars will recognize in the phrase a nod to the established critical notions of Dante's pluristylism and plurilingualism, with which narrative pluralism wishes to form an alliance.[70] Hiding in plain sight at the heart of the

---

[70] For the notion of pluristylism, see Erich Auerbach, 'Farinata and Cavalcanti', in *Mimesis: The Representation of Reality in Western Thought* (Princeton, NJ: Princeton University Press, 1953), pp. 174–202; for the notion of plurilingualism, see Gianfranco Contini, 'Preliminari sulla

Commedia, alternative narratives are as much a part of Dante's text as the teleological masterplot, encoded in the poem as deliberately as the dominant narrative, though not always as obviously. If this is indeed the case, then why are Dante's alternative narratives more likely to be overlooked by *Dantisti* and dilettanti alike? What is it that makes teleological readings of Dante so hegemonic?

I.4 Exemplariness, Credibility, Reproducibility

Of the reasons why Dante's masterplot rules supreme amongst the narrative models of the *Commedia*, only a few have to do with the poem's design, while the rest are more likely his readers' responsibility. Textual design is probed here first. It is hard to dispute that the teleological narrative, in Dante's otherworldly pilgrimage from the dark wood to the vision of God, is somewhat foundational and overarching. Indeed, the very fact that this narrative trajectory is so recognizable and adaptable to various aspects of Dante's progress—his relationship to the courtly love code, lyric canon, Beatrice, the body, earthly attachments, and so on—is one of its intended advantages. In his discussion of masterplots, narrative theorist H. Porter Abbott examines the role of recognizable types in autobiographical writing. To illustrate his point, Abbott refers to the paradigm of Augustine's *Confessions*, which 'invented the enduring form of the autobiography of a convert', whose influence on Dante is unmistakable.[71] Augustine's declared objective, Abbot argues, 'was not to demonstrate his uniqueness but to show how his experience played out *according to type*. In his case the type was that of the Christian convert, and it belonged in turn to a masterplot that involved initial ignorance, news of the right path to salvation, repeated straying, repeated guidance from others, repeated renewal of effort, hard thinking, temptation, struggle, suffering, and a climactic moment of conversion, marked by divine intervention and followed by the firm decision to

---

lingua del Petrarca', *Paragone*, 2.16 (1951), 3–26, repr. in *Varianti e altra linguistica* (Turin: Einaudi, 1970), pp. 169–92. Key studies in their wake include Zygmunt G. Barański, '"Significar per verba": Notes on Dante and plurilingualism', in *The Italianist*, 6 (1986), 5–18, repr. in '*Sole nuovo, luce nuova*'. *Saggi sul rinnovamento culturale in Dante* (Turin: Scriptorium, 1996), pp. 41–77; and *Dante's Plurilingualism: Authority, Knowledge, Subjectivity*, ed. Sara Fortuna, Manuele Gragnolati, and Jürgen Trabant (Oxford: Legenda, 2010).

[71] H. Porter Abbott, *The Cambridge Introduction to Narrative* (Cambridge: Cambridge University Press, 2002), p. 132. The classic study of conversion in Dante is Freccero's influential *Poetics of Conversion*, which is expressly rooted in the Augustinian paradigm.

renounce the old ways and take up the new.'[72] It is to Abbott's credit that his description of this type's distinctive narrative arc, in its broad strokes, could just as easily be applied to Dante's trajectory. Indeed, Dantist Anna Maria Chiavacci Leonardi independently describes the poet's story in roughly similar terms, when she writes that 'Dante raises his own personal story to the exemplary significance of events emblematic of a typical Christian: innocence, fall, divine intervention of salvation, repentance, redemption.'[73] In her account, also, the *exemplum* is conceived of in narrative terms; it is characterized and recognized not by some inherent virtue but by the arc of its story. Indeed, this recognizability is the point. As Abbott concludes, for Augustine himself autobiographical writing becomes 'a matter of "collecting" or "re-collecting" from his memory those crucial events in the story of his life that conformed to the masterplot of conversion and that allowed him to fulfill the requirements of the type at the center of that story'.[74] The same could be said about Dante. Significantly, when the poet draws a direct comparison between the personal and autobiographical nature of his *Convivio* and that of Augustine's *Confessions*, two main aspects attract his attention: the 'comedic' narrative arc of Augustine's autobiography as a process from negative to positive ('lo processo della sua vita, lo quale fu di [meno] buono in buono, e di buono in migliore, e di migliore in ottimo' ['because by the progress of his life, which proceeded from bad to good, good to better, and better to best']); and its exemplary nature ('ne diede essemplo e dottrina, la quale per [altro] sì vero testimonio ricevere non si potea' ['he gave us an example and instruction which could not be provided by any other testimony so true as this'], *Conv.* I, ii, 14).

In fictional narrative, and especially in autobiography, there is always a two-way exchange between individuality and type, the personal and the exemplary, where the one plays with and against the other, and vice versa. Much is gained from this two-way exchange. In the specific case of autobiographical narratives of conversion, the main advantage is that they confer

---

[72] Abbott, *The Cambridge Introduction to Narrative*, p. 132. Italics in the text.
[73] 'Dante eleva...la sua storia personale a significato esemplare della vicenda propria di ogni uomo cristiano: innocenza, traviamento, intervento divino di salvezza, pentimento, redenzione' (Anna Maria Chiavacci Leonardi, 'Introduzione' *ad Purg.* XXX (DDP), trans. mine).
[74] Abbott, *The Cambridge Introduction to Narrative*, p. 133. T. S. Eliot made a similar point about the *Vita nova*, a book that he claimed 'cannot be classed either as "truth" or "fiction"', since the experiences it relates 'seemed to [Dante] of some importance' not for their personal significance but for their emblematic status: 'they seemed to him to have some philosophical and impersonal value' (T. S. Eliot, 'Dante' [1929], *Selected Essays*, 3rd rev. edn (London: Faber & Faber, 1951), pp. 237–77 (p. 268)).

credibility to the writer's word. 'I can say now, I used to be bad then': in this most teleological of constructions, the convert concedes to the reader their past—characterized variously as sinful, erroneous, mistaken—but through this sacrifice they obtain that the current position, from which they judge, gets acknowledged as rightful and authoritative.[75] By fashioning one's individual story as fulfilling the requirements of the type of the convert—someone who has abandoned the error of their ways and is now righteous—a new credibility is achieved. This is the most basic practical advantage of conversion narratives and one that Dante exploits repeatedly over the course of his career. Take the story of Dante's poetic development: when the poetry written with the aim of receiving Beatrice's *saluto* is disowned, the new poetry of praise, *stilo de la loda*, gains currency (*VN* XVIII–XIX); yet in the last chapter, the *Vita nova* plans its own obsolescence in favour of a future work, promising to 'dicer di lei quel che mai non fue detto di alcuna' ['write of her that which has never been written of any other woman'] (*VN* XLII, 2). Or consider the famous case of Dante's relationship with Beatrice: the relatively marginal *donna gentile* in *Vita nova* XXXV, overshadowed by Beatrice, is reinterpreted as central as she is identified with Lady Philosophy in the *Convivio* (II, ii, 1–5); the *Commedia*, however, ostensibly disowns the *donna gentile* when Beatrice reinstates her own original pre-eminence and reproaches the protagonist for having '[taken] himself from [her] | and [given] himself to others' (*Purg.* XXX, 125–6). Without entering here into the scholarly debate over these important questions in Dante Studies,[76] it is worth drawing attention to the fact that the underlying mechanism that lends plausibility to this account at its various stages is broadly the same as that which underlies narratives of conversion such as Augustine's *Confessions* or Boethius's *Consolation of Philosophy*.[77] Narratives of conversion

---

[75] On Dante's rhetorical strategies for building authority throughout his career, see Ascoli's study *Dante and the Making of a Modern Author*. On 'the connection between conversion narratives and authority', see Ryan Szpiech, *Conversion and Narrative: Reading and Religious Authority in Medieval Polemic* (Philadelphia, PA: University of Pennsylvania Press, 2013), quote at p. 60.

[76] For the record, this thesis finds support in the view of scholars who acknowledge the discrepancies in the affaire *donna gentile*/Beatrice yet refuse to resolve them teleologically: see, for instance, Kenelm Foster and Patrick Boyde, *Dante's Lyric Poetry*, 2 vols (Oxford: Clarendon Press, 1967), II, p. 341 and *passim*; Barolini, *Dante's Poets*, p. 30; Reed Way Dasenbrock, '"Paradiso ma non troppo": The Place of the Lyric Dante in the Late *Cantos* of Ezra Pound', *Comparative Literature*, 57.1 (2005), 45–60; Ascoli, *Dante and the Making of a Modern Author*, pp. 282–3.

[77] 'The Augustinian conversion story provides a broad analogue for the various "turning points" dramatized in the *Vita nova*' (*Dante and the Making of a Modern Author*, p. 183); see, most recently, Rushworth, 'Conversion, Palinode, Traces'. Of course, as D. Bruce Hindmarsh

operate teleologically by subordinating a previous, negative, straying experience to a subsequent righteous one; and by means of this sacrifice of the past, they endow the most current position with the credibility and authority that was required to move on from the past. From a rhetorical perspective, it is only of secondary importance what the position is, or whether it is eventually abandoned, recanted, or corrected in turn; teleological subordination of previous experiences is always available to those wishing to establish the authority and credibility of their current, converted position.

Quite apart from the rhetorical advantages of conversion narratives, all masterplots, regardless of their kind, are invested in questions of credibility. H. Porter Abbott considers their persuasive power one of the defining features of masterplots in general. Recognizable masterplots, with their culturally encoded associations, can have 'an enormous emotional capital that can be drawn on in the construction of narrative'.[78] Masterplots such as the quest, the story of revenge, rise and fall, seasonal myths of death and regeneration, and the story of conversion itself are immediately recognizable and their effects often predictable. They are familiar, elicit strong affective responses, and come with pre-made moral associations. As such they fall under the heading of what Gerald Prince calls the 'pragmatics' of narrative fiction, which extend beyond the semantic and grammatical relations of the words on the page to encompass their impact on, and interaction with, 'the receiver and his or her decoding strategies' as well as 'the communicative context'.[79] In calling upon the reader to recognize and relate a narrative to other instances of the same type with their distinctive associations, masterplots paradoxically achieve more credibility than reality itself. Indeed, in many cases reality is pressured into conforming to type. For this reason, masterplots are recommended, within fiction, for the writing of bestselling novels and Oscar-winning blockbusters—as promoted by such popular or how-to books as Christopher Booker's *The Seven Basic Plots: Why We Tell Stories* and Ronald B. Tobias's *20 Master Plots and How to Build Them*—and their uses extend to such pragmatic purposes as selling products through advertisement,

---

points out in his study of spiritual autobiographies in early modern England, 'the narrative shape' of Christian narratives of conversion 'was clearly provided by the larger story of salvation history in the Bible. As in the case of Augustine, the Bible's account of fall from innocence and return provided a structure and many topoi for these spiritual autobiographies' (D. Bruce Hindmarsh, *The Evangelical Conversion Narrative: Spiritual Autobiography in Early Modern England* (Oxford: Oxford University Press, 2005), p. 8).

[78] Abbott, *The Cambridge Introduction to Narrative*, p. 42.
[79] Gerald Prince, 'The Disnarrated', *Style*, 22.1 (1988), 1–8 (7). See also his earlier 'Narrative pragmatics, message, and point', *Poetics*, 12.6 (1983), 527–36.

swinging voters through political propaganda, and winning a case in trials of justice, where credibility and reproducibility are key. Where competition is fierce, the credibility afforded by a familiar narrative can give the edge. In trials, for instance, 'the prosecution and defense strive to establish narrative credibility by aligning their representation of events with rhetorically advantageous "masterplots,"... familiar skeletal narratives with an established cultural authority'.[80] the same set of circumstances can as easily be portrayed through the archetypal narrative of the fallen woman or of the manipulating seductress.[81] The recognizability and unequivocal moral conceit afforded by masterplots are vital in these fields, where a consumer, voter, or juror's choices and actions are often decided by a given narrative's credibility. As Abbott puts it, 'To the extent that our values and identity are linked to a masterplot, that masterplot can have strong rhetorical impact. We tend to grant credibility to narratives that are structured by it.'[82] Indeed, such is their rhetorical impact that it is not rare to attribute credibility to masterplots even over the evidence of fact.

The notion that Dante's *Commedia* might contain *typical, emblematic, exemplary,* or *universal* elements is nothing new in Dante Studies.[83] This Introduction's analysis of the exemplary character of Dante's masterplot aims to draw attention to the practical effects, the pros and cons, of its use in the *Commedia*. For the post-exilic writer whose historical circumstances made credibility a scarce commodity and whose moral integrity had to be defended against a defaming sentence,[84] the teleological masterplot, with its

---

[80] Richard Walsh, 'The Pragmatics of Narrative Fictionality', in *A Companion to Narrative Theory*, ed. James Phelan and Peter J. Rabinowitz (Malden, MA: Blackwell, 2005), pp. 150–64 (p. 151).

[81] For forensic narratives and their relationship to prejudice in *Inferno* V, see Crisafi and Lombardi, 'Lust and Law'.

[82] Abbott, *The Cambridge Introduction to Narrative*, p. 42.

[83] Variously conceptualized, in modern times, this notion dates back at least as far as Leo Spitzer's pioneering essay 'Note on the Poetic and the Empirical "I" in Medieval Authors', *Traditio* 4 (1946), 414–22; for its canonical formulation, see Singleton, *Dante Studies: Vol. 1. 'Commedia': Elements of Structure*, and Contini, 'Dante come personaggio-poeta', p. 35, who acknowledges his debt to Singleton. The notion is given credit by Dante himself in his theory of the four senses in the interpretation of a text (*Conv.* II, i), also in the so-called *Epistle to Cangrande* of uncertain attribution (*Epist.* XIII, 20–2). See also Picone, 'Dante come autore/narratore della *Commedia*'; and Riccobono, *Dante Poeta-Profeta, Pellegrino*, pp. 11–39; and Pertile, 'Trasmutabile per tutte guise'. The importance of type in the exemplary masterplot of the *Commedia* is not incompatible with this monograph's view of the central role of the historical individual in Dante's oeuvre and its radical embrace of affectivity, relations, and all the memories that make up each character's 'vissuto'.

[84] Defaming crimes, such as the ones Dante was sentenced for, invalidated by law the defendant's moral integrity and thus legal credibility. See Justin Steinberg, *Dante and the Limits of the Law* (Chicago: Chicago University Press, 2013), pp. 14–52; and Crisafi and Lombardi, 'Lust and Law'.

surplus of credibility and integrity, offers invaluable benefits. These practical advantages have been highlighted by Albert Russell Ascoli and Justin Steinberg, respectively, in their studies of Dante's quest for authority and control of his works' reception. As Ascoli argues, 'the depersonalising, or rather, the de-historicizing of Dante himself' accomplished in the *Commedia* is an effective rhetorical strategy that 'permits him to transcend those personal and historical attributes that impede his access to authority', including his juridically invalidated credibility and vulnerable moral status as an exile.[85] Type, in Dante's case, is valued both for its capacity to obscure personal circumstances and for its intrinsic ability to promote credibility.

There are drawbacks to this strategy. While masterplots in general have an inherent rhetorical power, and teleological masterplots specifically are perfectly engineered to produce narrative credibility and authority by subordinating previous experiences to a new decisive endpoint, they can sometimes go overboard in their outcomes. The very qualities that render Dante's masterplot so rhetorically effective are the ones that can make its influence disproportionate in the reception of the *Commedia*. The dominant narrative risks becoming overly domineering, and its credibility becomes so powerful that it is difficult to distinguish it from the textual mechanisms that constitute it. 'Masterplots can be rendered stereotypically as well', Abbott reminds us, '[i]n such cases all we see is the masterplot'.[86] It is no minor tribute to the masterplot's authority and effectiveness as a rhetorical strategy that teleological language and arguments figure overwhelmingly among Dante scholars. The fact that the teleological trajectory of the poem is so immediately recognizable helps make it endlessly reproducible. However, if the metaphorical discourse underpinning the *Commedia* consists in the pilgrim's progress toward a final revelation, this does not necessarily make all endpoints revelatory. Blanket-reading linearity into the entire *Commedia*; ordering its events hierarchically into teleological *before* and *after*; and proposing normative interpretations in the name of resolution and coherence, all risk caricaturing its author's *modus scribendi*. The *Commedia* certainly exerts special control over its own reception by

---

[85] Ascoli, *Dante and the Making of a Modern Author*, p. 316; Justin Steinberg, *Accounting for Dante: Urban Readers and Writers in Late Medieval Italy* (Notre Dame, IN: Notre Dame University Press, 2007), pp. 16, 145–69. It should be noted that Gennaro Sasso finds a conflict between two archetypal self-narratives in Dante's works—the fallen sinner on his way to redemption versus the righteous exile—in *Le autobiografie di Dante* (Naples: Bibliopolis, 2008), as discussed in the last section of this Introduction.

[86] Abbott, *The Cambridge Introduction to Narrative*, p. 45.

imitating and harnessing the interpretative power of endpoints and exploiting the credibility of emblematic narratives. At the same time, however, it also sets limits and proposes alternatives to this strategy by embedding in the text paradoxes, detours, parallel lives, and open-ended futures that counteract its teleological linearity, complicate its moral message, and safeguard what it risks bullying. Because these narratives are less predicated on the authority and reproducibility created by Dante's masterplot, his narrative pluralism is often eclipsed by a dominant narrative that has been escalated from authoritative to authoritarian. As the body of this book shows, however, each of these alternative narratives demands, and teaches, a kinder style of interpretation. Before we explore their methods in the following chapters, then, let us consider the role of interpretation in Dante's writings more generally.

I.5 Reading Hermeneutic Writing

As readers of the *Commedia* we are in a privileged position. From our vantage point we are granted a power that is most jealously guarded by Dante over the course of his literary career: the power to interpret his writings. How are we to use this power? And, given that Dante's writings are so concerned with interpretation, what are we to do with his own interpretations? Are we to respect them or to subvert them?

In Dante's writings interpretation is thematized, dramatized, or merely implied, and it invariably underpins the structure of his narratives. Indeed, Dante's narratives can be said to share a constitutive common nature, which we may call, with Roland Barthes, *hermeneutic*. In his seminal *S/Z*, ostensibly a structural analysis of a single short story by Balzac, Barthes identifies two fundamental ways in which 'classical narratives' unfold through time: the *proairetic* and the *hermeneutic* code.[87] The *proairetic* code corresponds to the forward-oriented logic of action and is most obvious in 'narratives that give precedence to happenings':[88] a typical example is that of a thriller where the succession of the action constantly spurs us to read on. The story of the pilgrims from *Convivio* (Section I.2 above) is emblematic of this code, since they move forward stage by stage, 'di casa in casa', their outcome

---

[87] Roland Barthes, *S/Z*, trans. Richard Miller (New York: Noonday Press, 1974), p. 30. See Hannah Freed-Thall, 'Adventures in Structuralism: Reading with Barthes and Genette', in *The Cambridge Companion to Narrative Theory*, ed. Matthew Garrett (Cambridge: Cambridge University Press, 2018), pp. 61–71 (p. 65).

[88] Brooks, *Reading for the Plot*, p. 18. See Brooks's discussion of Barthes therein, pp. 18–20.

unknown. The *hermeneutic* code, on the other hand, is based on interpreting an outcome that is known from the start: an obvious example is a detective story where we are presented with a murder but are motivated in our reading by our desire to discover who committed it and why. The story of the merchant from *Convivio* is emblematic of the hermeneutic code, since he is not concerned with the outcome of his journey (it is a fait accompli) but rather with its significance. The distinction between the two codes can thus be summed up with Prue Shaw's concise phrase, 'We live forward, but we understand backwards'.[89] In this light, the question that occupies the merchant of *Convivio* does not regard actions but their understanding: it is not 'What will happen next?' but 'How do I interpret what just happened?'. The issue, in other words, is one that occupies Dante throughout his literary career. The meaning and interpretation of the past are so deeply interwoven in the fabric of Dante's writings that it takes a special awareness on his readers' part to take his interpretations as critically as any other existing part of the text.

Dante's attention to hermeneutic questions is well known and covers a variety of areas: literature, biography, history, theology, philosophy, and more. Not only is it directed at Dante's own writings,[90] but it also looks outward to the reading and hermeneutic practices that characterized the literary cultures of his age.[91] 'Exegesis was central to the medieval literary experience,' writes Zygmunt Barański, 'and in the *Commedia* Dante called his readers to this in ways which would have been immediately recognisable.'[92] A seminal work in the study of Dante's relationship with medieval hermeneutics is Erich Auerbach's masterful 'Figura'. Auerbach famously argued that what was born as a relatively niche interpretative practice for understanding the relation of the New Testament to the Old

---

[89] Prue Shaw, *Reading Dante: From Here to Eternity* (New York: Liveright, 2014), p. 134.
[90] See, for instance, Gianfranco Contini, 'Introduzione alle Rime di Dante', repr. in *Un'idea di Dante*, pp. 3–20; Iannucci, 'Autoesegesi dantesca'; Barolini, *Dante's Poets*; Zygmunt G. Barański, 'Dante commentatore e commentato: Riflessioni sullo studio dell'iter ideologico di Dante', *Letture classensi*, 23 (1994), 9–39, and 'Dante Alighieri: Experimentation and (Self-)exegesis', in *The Cambridge History of Literary Criticism. Volume II: The Middle Ages*, ed. Alastair Minnis and Ian Johnson (Cambridge: Cambridge University Press, 2005), pp. 561–82; Albert Russell Ascoli, 'Auto-commentary: Dividing Dante', in *Dante and the Making of a Modern Author* (Cambridge: Cambridge University Press, 2008), pp. 175–226.
[91] See Barański's essays collected in *'Sole nuovo, luce nuova': Saggi sul rinnovamento culturale in Dante* (Turin: Scriptorium, 1996) and *Dante e i segni: Saggi per una storia intellettuale di Dante Alighieri* (Naples: Liguori, 2000); Steinberg, *Accounting for Dante*; and, most recently, Elena Lombardi, *Imagining the Woman Reader in the Age of Dante* (Oxford: Oxford University Press, 2019).
[92] Barański, 'Experimentation and (Self-)exegesis', p. 576.

Testament—figural interpretation—came to have a profound impact on 'the interpretation of history in the Middle Ages and even often play[ed] a role in the way that everyday realities of the period [were] understood'.[93] For Auerbach, this was most notable in Dante's *Commedia*. According to the scholar, Dante creatively incorporated figural hermeneutics in his poem, where 'they are decisive for its entire structure'.[94] 'Figural interpretation', wrote Auerbach, 'creates a connection between two events or persons in which one signifies not only itself but also the other'.[95] As Auerbach argued, this interpretative practice can be seen as structuring the fictional universe of his *Commedia*. In figures such as Virgil, Cato, and Beatrice, for instance, 'the literal meaning and historical reality of [the] character do not contradict that figure's deeper meaning. Rather they figure it. Historical reality is not annulled by this deeper meaning. Rather it is confirmed and fulfilled by it.'[96] In figural hermeneutics, Auerbach believed to have found 'the historical foundation' of his claim that Dante was first and foremost a 'poet of the earthly world', for whom earthly experience in its historicity and concreteness did not constitute a mere shadow of the spiritual realities in which it was to be ultimately resolved but had its own dignity and autonomy.[97] Auerbach's work remains an essential point of reference for Dantists who agree (and disagree) with this view.[98]

For the purposes of the present study, Auerbach's contribution is invaluable for three main reasons. First of all, by pioneering the study of medieval interpretative practices and models, Auerbach underlined the historical role of interpretation in the design of Dante's *Commedia*. In his view, figural hermeneutics actively shaped the poem by being dramatized in such characters as Virgil, Cato, and Beatrice. At the same time, this model for interpretation can also be applied to 'la struttura a due tempi del poema', whereby the narrator reinterprets his earthly attachments and the journey he undertook as a character.[99] Thus, if for Barthes a poem such as the *Commedia* can be called

---

[93] Erich Auerbach, 'Figura' [1938], in *Time, History, and Literature: Selected Essays of Erich Auerbach*, ed. James I. Porter, trans. Jane O. Newman (Princeton, NJ: Princeton University Press, 2014), pp. 65–113 (p. 103).
[94] Ibid., p. 105.   [95] Ibid., p. 96.   [96] Ibid., p. 111.
[97] Ibid., p. 110. The expression 'poet of the earthly world' comes, of course, from the title of his 1929 monograph *Dante: Poet of the Secular World*, trans. Ralph Manheim (Chicago: University of Chicago Press, 1961); 'earthly' is arguably a more accurate translation for *irdisch* than 'secular'.
[98] Manuele Gragnolati makes Auerbach the starting point of his *Experiencing the Afterlife* (p. xi). For a 'theologizing' critique of Auerbach, see John Freccero, 'Infernal Irony: The Gates of Hell', repr. in *Poetics of Conversion*, pp. 93–109 (pp. 103–4).
[99] Riccobono, *Dante Poeta-Profeta, Pellegrino, Autore*, p. 12.

hermeneutic by virtue of its 'structural retrospection' and search for meaning,[100] for Auerbach *figura* constitutes the historical foundation of this inherently hermeneutic character.

Auerbach's 'Figura' is not only instrumental in putting hermeneutics at the heart of the *Commedia*'s storytelling. The essay also offers an early critique of teleological interpretations of Dante, complete with its own alternative model. Auerbach's defence of the dignity of the historicity, concreteness and earthly qualities of the *figura*, was originally motivated by his wish to balance out or counter allegorist interpretations of the Old Testament that denied the reality and truthfulness of the events depicted therein and replaced them instead with a 'spiritual and extra-historical' meaning supposedly dictated by the New Testament. Just like teleological readings of Dante, spiritualist interpretations subjugated the Old to the New.[101] Thus, in the *Commedia*, since Virgil the pagan poet was prior to Virgil poet-prophet and leader-guide, his historical character was to be superseded by its allegorical interpretation. However, as another master of narrative puts it, 'Reality can have metaphorical content; that does not make it less real.'[102] For Auerbach, restoring the reality and autonomy of Old Testament events, like restoring the historical dignity of Virgil, represented an antidote to the tendency to split history into old and new, and automatically subjugate the former to the latter on grounds of chronology. Auerbach's *figura* (as Chapter 2 shows) offered a more unresolved and paradoxical model instead: the old pointed to the new, but it did not have to be subordinated to it; although the spiritual world was to succeed the earthly, it did not thereby supersede its meaning.

In this respect, Auerbach's 'Figura' provides a cautionary tale of the dark side of teleological interpretations. As Avihu Zakai and David Weinstein have argued, the Jewish scholar's essay in defence of the historical aspect of figures and of the continuity between Old and New Testament was conceived in response to 'the European crisis' of the thirties.[103] The goal of

---

[100] Barański's phrase: 'Structural Retrospection in Dante's *Comedy*'.
[101] Auerbach's understanding of this problem was markedly temporal: he thought of the 'two poles of the figure' as successive and 'part of the ongoing flow of historical life'. 'Figura', p. 96. See also his 'Typological Symbolism in Medieval Literature' [1952], in the same volume, pp. 114–23 (esp. p. 116).
[102] Salman Rushdie, *Midnight's Children* [1981] (London: David Campbell, 1995), p. 255.
[103] Avihu Zakai and David Weinstein, 'Erich Auerbach and His 'Figura': An Apology for the Old Testament in the Age of Aryan Philology', *Religions*, 3 (2012), 320–8. The expression 'European crisis' is Auerbach's own and dates from after the war: Erich Auerbach, 'Introduction: Purpose and Method', in *Literary History & Its Public in Late Latin Antiquity and in the Middle Ages* (Princeton, NJ: Princeton University Press, 1965), p. 6.

'Figura', conceived in Germany but completed after Auerbach's exile in Turkey in 1936, was polemical: to confute Aryan philology's attempts to eradicate the Old Testament from the Christian canon and literary tradition of Europe. While this tale is specific to the circumstances of the publication of 'Figura', when much was at stake, I believe it is important to be aware of the potential for violence that is latent in any teleological reading. Even at a hermeneutic level, a quest for authority comes at the cost of marginalizing other voices and can thread the line of authoritarianism (as Albert Russell Ascoli has warned Dantists),[104] while an interpretative desire for 'the so-called total interpretation' (as Gianfranco Contini put it)[105] risks cancelling differences and deviancies and turning totalitarian.[106] The dark side of teleology thus comes to light in its problematic relationship with the 'otherness' it inevitably chooses to leave behind, silence, or sacrifice in the name of its ultimate aim.

I.6 'The good' and 'the other things'

While the *Epistle to Cangrande* inaugurates the critical tradition of interpreting the poem in terms of the trajectory of its plot, it also puts it in the context of competing narratives.[107] A *comedia*, the epistle declares, 'is a certain kind of poetical narration which *differs from all others*':

---

[104] On the relationship between authority and authoritarianism in the Dantean project, see Ascoli's important reflections in *Dante and the Making of a Modern Author*, pp. 61–4, which also explores the question of otherness in Dante.

[105] 'La cosiddetta lettura totale' (Gianfranco Contini, 'Filologia ed esegesi dantesca', repr. in *Un'idea di Dante*, pp. 113–42 (p. 114), trans. mine).

[106] On the appropriation of Dante at the hand of the totalitarian fascist regime, see Lino Pertile, 'Dante e la Shoah', in *The Oxford Handbook of Dante*, pp. 651–67; I reflected on this issue, and its consequences, on the digital pages of Jacobin Italia: 'Defascistizzare Dante', *Jacobin Italia*, 2 June 2021 <https://jacobinitalia.it/defascistizzare-dante/> [accessed 29 June 2021]. Jonathan Druker makes a similar point by applying Adorno and Horkheimer's analysis to Primo Levi's reading of Dante to show the potential for violence and intolerance inherent in post-Enlightenment rationality (Jonathan Druker, *Primo Levi and Humanism After Auschwitz* (New York: Palgrave Macmillan, 2009), pp. 35–54). I am very grateful to my anonymous reader at OUP for this insightful reference.

[107] The authenticity of the *Epistle* is debated; without taking sides, I here treat the epistle as evidence of an early reading of the *Commedia*. On the issue of its authenticity, see Lino Pertile, 'La Comedìa tra il dire e il fare', in *Sotto il segno di Dante: Scritti in onore di Francesco Mazzoni* (Florence: Le Lettere, 1998) pp. 233–47; Mirko Tavoni, 'Il titolo della *Commedia* di Dante', *Nuova rivista di letteratura italiana*, 1.1 (1998), 9–34; Zygmunt G. Barański, ' "Comedìa": Dante, l'*Epistola a Cangrande* e la commedia medievale', in *Chiosar con altro testo: leggere Dante nel Trecento* (Florence: Cadmo, 2001), pp. 41–76; and Alberto Casadei, 'Il titolo della *Commedia* e l'*Epistola a Cangrande*', in *Dante oltre la 'Commedia'* (Bologna: Il Mulino, 2013), pp. 15–43.

Differt ergo a tragedia in materia per hoc, quod tragedia in principio est admirabilis et quieta, in fine seu exitu est fetida et horribilis.... Comedia vero inchoat asperitatem alicuius rei, sed eius materia prospere terminatur.... Et per hoc patet quod Comedia dicitur presens opus. Nam si ad materiam respiciamus, a principio horribilis et fetida est, quia Infernus, in fine prospera, desiderabilis et grata, quia Paradisus.

[It differs, then, from tragedy in its subject-matter, in that tragedy at the beginning is admirable and placid but at the end of issue is foul and horrible.... Whereas comedy begins with sundry adverse conditions, but ends happily.... And from this it is clear that the present work is to be described as a comedy. For if we consider the subject-matter, at the beginning it is horrible and foul, as being Hell, but at the close it is happy, desirable, and pleasing, as being Paradise.]   (*Ep.* XIII, 29 and 31)

Sad beginnings, happy endings. The narrative trajectory of Dante's *poetica narratio* is illustrated by the author of the epistle through a semantic shift from negative to positive: from 'asperitatem' to 'prospere'; from 'horribilis et fetida' to 'prospera, desiderabilis et grata'. The pattern was well established in the *auctoritates* backing up the epistle, John of Garland and Hugh of Pisa,[108] and was clearly common currency with Dante's early commentators.[109] The terms used to characterize beginnings and endings in the epistle correspond roughly to their distribution across the three canticas of the *Commedia*: negative terms are prevalent in the *Inferno* and positives in the *Paradiso*. Listing them here from negative to positive: *orribile* ['horrible'] occurs ten times in *Inferno*, three in *Purgatorio*, and not at all in *Paradiso*; *asperitate* ['harsh circumstances'] and its cognates occur five times in *Inferno*, three in *Purgatorio*, and not at all in *Paradiso*; the positive (*am*)*mirabile* ['admirable'], in contrast, never occurs in *Inferno* but appears once in *Purgatorio*, and

---

[108] '[T]ragedia est carmen gravi stilo compositum incipiens a gaudio et terminans in luctu'; 'comoedia est carmen iocosum incipiens a tristicia et terminans in gaudium' (John of Garland, *Poetria magistri Johannis Anglici de arte prosayca metrica et rithmica*, ed. Giovanni Mari, in *Romanische Forschungen*, 13 (1902), pp. 883–965 (p. 918)); 'Item comedia a tristibus incipit sed cum letis desinit, tragedia e contrario.... Unde in salutatione solemus...optare tragicum principium et comicum finem, idest bonum et letum principium et bonum et letum finem' (Uguccione da Pisa, *Derivationes*, ed. Enzo Cecchini and Guido Arbizzoni (Florence: SISMEL-Edizioni del Galluzzo, 2004), O 11 17). Cf. Carlo Paolazzi, *Dante e la 'Comedia' nel Trecento: Dall'"Epistola a Cangrande" all'età di Petrarca* (Milan: Vita e Pensiero, 1989), p. 86.

[109] Variations on this narrative definition are featured in the introductory notes to *Inferno* by Jacopo della Lana, Pietro Alighieri (all three redactions), Guglielmo Maramauro, Benvenuto da Imola, Filippo Villani. The relationship between these commentaries and the *Epistle to Cangrande* is debated.

ten times in *Paradiso*. Although *fetido* ['foul'] and *prospero* ['happy'] are never used in Dante's oeuvre and *desiderabile* ['desirable'] only occurs in *Convivio*, the semantic field of desire, as is known, grows exponentially across the three canticas.[110] The adjective *quieto* ['calm'] is alone in being evenly distributed, with four occurrences in *Inferno* and *Paradiso* and six in *Purgatorio*. Dante's linguistic choices in the *Commedia*, then, seem to match narrative expectations of a medieval reader of comedies. Indeed, at various stages in the poem Dante describes the trajectory of his journey through the same trick of semantic shifts from negative to positive. The protagonist uses this dynamic antithesis in the middle of *Inferno* to characterize his pilgrimage ('Lascio lo *fele* e vo per *dolci pomi*' ['I leave *bitterness* behind for the *sweet fruits*'], *Inf.* XVI, 61); the narrator employs it at the beginning of *Purgatorio* to express a gear shift in subject matter ('Per correr *miglior acque*...lascia dietro sé *mar* sì *crudele*' ['To run its course through *smoother water*...leaving that *cruel sea* behind'], *Purg*. I, 1 and 3); and at the top of *Paradiso* to recapitulate his astounding trajectory ('ïo, che al *divino* da l'*umano*, | a l'*etterno* dal *tempo* era venuto, | e di *Fiorenza* in *popol giusto* e *sano*' ['I, who had come to *things divine* from *man's estate*, | to *eternity* from *time*, | from *Florence* to a *people just and sane*'], *Par*. XXXI, 37–9).[111] Consider the noun *asperitatem* ['harshness'], which the *Epistle to Cangrande* refers to comedic beginnings, and which has no precedents in the traditional descriptions of a comedy.[112] It occurs as early as the first canto of *Inferno* as part of a whole host of negative adjectives used to describe the dark wood in which Dante finds himself: *oscura* ['dark'] (*Inf*. I, 2), *selvaggia* ['savage'], *aspra* ['harsh'], *forte* ['dense'] (5), and *amara* ['bitter'] (7). As Luca Azzetta notes in his commentary to the *Epistle to Cangrande*, 'readers would have been able to deduce that the poem had to have a positive ending already from *Inferno* I, 8–9'.[113] This very passage, however, also presents the earliest suggestion that there are alternative ways of reading Dante's poem:

---

[110] See Lino Pertile, *La punta del disio: Semantica del desiderio* (Fiesole: Cadmo, 2005), pp. 19–23.
[111] On the *hysteron proteron* used here and the rhetorical figure's relation to the *Commedia*'s structural retrospection, see Singleton, 'The Vistas in Retrospect', p. 64.
[112] So vouches Claudia Villa, in her commentary to Dante Alighieri [?], 'Epistola a Cangrande', ed. Claudia Villa, in *Opere*, ed. Marco Santagata, 3 vols (Milan: Mondadori, 2011–14), III, p. 1588.
[113] 'Che poi l'esito del poema dovesse essere positivo, il lettore poteva già arguire da *Inferno* I, 8–9' (Luca Azzetta, in Dante Alighieri, 'Epistola XIII', ed. Luca Azzetta, in *Le Opere*, vol. V. *Epistole, Egloge, Questio de aqua et terra*, ed. Marco Baglio, Luca Azzetta, Marco Petoletti, Michele Rinaldi (Rome: Salerno, 2016), pp. 271–487 (p. 362), trans. mine).

> Tant'è amara che poco è più morte;
> ma per trattar del ben ch'i' vi trovai,
> dirò de l'altre cose ch'i' v'ho scorte.
>
> [It is so bitter death is hardly more so.
> But to set forth the good I found
> I will recount the other things I saw.]
>
> (*Inf.* I, 7–9)

This programmatic statement has elicited a number of different interpretations over the course of the centuries.[114] As is generally acknowledged, its rhetorical construction turns on an antithesis between '[il] ben' ['the good'] (8) and 'l'altre cose' ['the other things'] (9), deceptively straightforward terms that reward a closer look. Whereas the context of *Inferno* I does not shy away from adjectives and nouns that carry negative associations, as we have seen, in this terzina the phrase used to describe the negative pole of the antithesis is not negative per se. '[L]'altre cose', in fact, are only understood negatively by the reader relative to their position with respect to '[il] ben'. They are otherwise neutral and without moral judgements, but through their rhetorical positioning they get moralized and hierarchically subjugated: they become a generic negative to which '[il] ben' is opposed. These lines replicate, *in nuce*, the mechanism of Dante's masterplot. That the distinction between *good* and *evil* is the result of a rhetorical operation, not a given state of affairs, is even subtly reflected in the verbs used. There is in fact a qualitative difference in how Dante writes about something morally connoted and how he writes about everything else. Whereas he can simply *dire* 'l'altre cose' neutrally, '[il] ben' requires *trattare*, a more self-conscious rhetorical treatment, a process of extraction from an experience that is otherwise neutral. Embedded in the very first lines of the *Commedia* is the desire to treat in writing the positives in the journey, which works— transparently here—by turning something as neutral as 'other things' into something negative, simply by its relative positioning. Anticipated in this microcosm is not only the dominant narrative model of the *Commedia* but also a trace of the otherness it inevitably leaves behind. By focusing on the plurality of narratives within the poem that offer alternatives to its hegemony, this monograph sheds light on the alternatives which are often

---

[114] The explanations proposed are in line with those reviewed by Francesco Mazzoni, *Saggio di un nuovo commento alla 'Divina Commedia': 'Inferno' Canti I–III* (Florence: Sansoni, 1967), pp. 51–5. See, more recently, Nicola Fosca ad *Inf.* I, 8 (DDP).

sanitized through Dante's teleological masterplot, or through his readers' tendency to take its hermeneutic model too literally.[115] More recently, the critical practices of scholars like Manuele Gragnolati (*Amor che move*) and Elena Lombardi (*The Wings of the Doves*) have provided a model for resisting the masterplot's influence, by opening Dante's text to anti-teleological interpretations or by providing multi-angled readings that revel in the text's undecidability. Gennaro Sasso can be credited with a more in-depth analysis of the conflict between two contrasting, and in his view irreconcilable, 'autobiographies of Dante': on the one hand, 'the story of the radical and extreme sinner that only the intervention of divine grace is able to direct... on the path of salvation'; on the other, the counterstory 'of the virtuous citizen', unjustly exiled and therefore righteous from the outset.[116] As the work of these scholars shows, critiquing the teleological masterplot and exploring alternative narratives allow a new picture of Dante and the *Commedia* to emerge. Dante will appear here not so much as an authoritative genius, master of a grand narrative encompassing his life and works, but as a writer opening his text to experiences of vulnerability, failure, and circumstance, accepting and even welcoming their role in life and in the poem. The term *masterplot* itself, which at first will have put off some readers because of its gendered, potentially violent, connotations of mastery and manipulation, will gradually be recontextualized and understood as part of this author's interest in a whole host of other narratives; it will hopefully be discarded like Wittgenstein's ladder after the reader has considered the narrative pluralism that lies at the heart of the *Commedia*. Attending to Dante's use of narrative, it becomes evident that the fabric of the poem is woven with alternative storylines that run alongside, detour from, or otherwise resist the dominant teleological and retrospective narrative. Dante Studies as a field has tended to overlook them or to order them in some new hierarchy, thereby replicating once more the dynamics of the masterplot. The structural role of alternative narratives in the poem, however, is precisely to counter the hegemonic appetite for conclusive and cannibalizing interpretations. As will become increasingly evident over the course of this volume,

---

[115] See Barolini, 'Dante's Sympathy for the Other'. Barolini concludes her essay by reflecting on the last adjective of the *Commedia*: 'the multiplicity, difference, and sheer otherness embodied in the "altre stelle"—an otherness by which [Dante] is still unrepentantly captivated in his poem's last breath' (p. 194).
[116] Gennaro Sasso, *Le autobiografie di Dante* (Naples: Bibliopolis, 2008), p. 85. For a response to Sasso's thesis and an argument for the textual and cultural conditions for a possible harmonization of the two 'autobiographies', see Elisa Brilli, *Firenze e il suo profeta: Dante fra teologia e politica* (Rome: Carocci, 2012), pp. 324–54.

what is at stake when talking about the narrative pluralism of Dante's *Commedia* is the interpretation of the poem and of its world. Yet the critique of teleological readings proposed here can also be taken more generally as an exposé of a human temptation to iron out paradoxes and difficulties (in fiction as much as in life), and a little paean to the role of poetry in continually presenting us with the creases.

1
Paradox in the Poem

In her study on the formal workings of Dante's narrative poem, Teodolinda Barolini begins her discussion of *Paradiso* with what she identifies as the root problem of the last cantica, 'the temporality of narrative'.[1] The *Paradiso* sets out to thematize a realm that lies beyond time, yet narrative cannot follow so freely in this transcendence. With its every step, narrative 'creates time and difference in a context where [Dante] wants to create eternity and unity'.[2] The temporal nature of narrative stands as a serious structural limit to *Paradiso*'s mimetic possibilities. Yet although it is true, as Barolini writes, that 'if the problem of time in narrative afflicts most narrators…, it afflicts Dante in the *Paradiso* more than most',[3] this is not merely by virtue of the gap between the cantica's matter and the inescapable temporal dimension of narrative, language, and indeed human experience. The problem inherent in this gap is not exclusive to the *Paradiso*; it plays an important part in any attempt to represent eternity, be it in a fourteenth-century narrative poem, a postmodern novel, or the latest theory of the multiverse in quantum physics. What makes the problem of time in narrative a more critical one for Dante than for most writers of eternity is the special case of his masterplot. By virtue of the masterplot, narrative time in the *Commedia* is not simply a neutral, value-free order where the simultaneity of eternity is ready to be laid out linearly in a text that has a *before* and an *after*. Narrative time in the *Commedia* is, rather, a hierarchy, where the *after* takes precedence over the *before*. The question, then, is not simply how Dante can represent a dimension beyond time in the temporal medium of narrative but how he can surmount this already impossible task *given his masterplot*, which grants the endpoint authority over what precedes it.

This is the question that I will explore in the present chapter, which identifies, analyses, and interprets paradoxes in the *Commedia*. The inclusion of

---

[1] Teodolinda Barolini, *The Undivine 'Comedy': Detheologizing Dante* (Princeton, NJ: Princeton University Press, 1992), p. 166. For Barolini's discussion of time, see specifically pp. 166–74.
[2] Ibid., pp. 171–2.   [3] Ibid., p. 171.

paradox in the main timeline of the *Commedia* raises one of the most significant narrative challenges to Dante's teleological masterplot and the hermeneutic assumptions it promotes. The challenge lies in the fact that the specific truths that the fiction of *Paradiso* is concerned with require a kind of narrative where they can coexist without being subordinated to one another. However, since the only way they can coexist in a text is chronologically, Dante needs to undo his own meticulous, persuasive work of ordering time into a hierarchy—the teleological masterplot—so that the ability to represent temporally two or more contradictory elements without subordinating them or ordering them in a new hierarchy may be restored to the text. The narrative model that emerges from this need, as I show over the course of this chapter, takes the shape of paradox. The chapter explores different models of paradox in Dante's medieval cultural context and their implications, before investigating Dante's use of paradoxes from minute textual details to longer-range correspondences across different canticas. I will argue that paradoxes in the *Commedia* call readers out for their reliance on the comfort of Dante's masterplot and the ordered cosmos it may be associated with, in order to express and perform something of the irreducible otherness of the poem's universe.

1.1 Paradox in the Middle Ages: Scholastic Theology and Mystical Writings

To say that the world Dante lived in was rife with paradoxes is not a statement specific to the Middle Ages but a truism about any world. So argues historian Caroline Walker Bynum in her retrospective account of her academic career, titled 'Why paradox?' Faced with evidence of a complex and often contradictory period, the historian asks herself, 'How could medieval people have held those funny, incompatible beliefs and done such silly, incompatible things?' Her answer is simply, 'So do we'.[4] We are free to disagree with Walker Bynum's view of the world as intrinsically paradoxical; and indeed, as a literary critic rather than a historian or a philosopher, it will be wiser for me to suspend my judgement on what lies outside the text. But from the vantage point of the verifiable words on the page, a literary critic can examine the paradoxes that are an integral part of many of the writings

---

[4] Caroline Walker Bynum, 'Why Paradox? The Contradictions of my Life as a Scholar', *The Catholic Historical Review*, 98 (2012), 433–55 (435).

that circulated or were composed in Dante's times. In this Section I will thus briefly examine two traditions that engaged with the same paradoxes that are found in *Paradiso*: scholastic theology and mystical writings.

Paradox was arguably 'the starting point' of the scholastic method.[5] Oral disputations and written works of theology and philosophy agreed in this practice. Each article of Thomas Aquinas's *Summa theologiae* and *Quaestiones disputatae* sets up a theological problem in statements and counterstatements, and takes the move from there.[6] The declared aim of the scholastic method is to solve the contradictions arising from these statements. It is true, as Denis Janz argues, that the resolution achieved often takes the form of 'another yes and no which can be held simultaneously because of a distinction Aquinas makes in his response';[7] but if the paradox can be said to endure, it can equally be said to never have been there in the first place. Paradox is only ever the appearance of paradox. The solution is a reminder that if you look at it closely enough (or from a higher perspective), it isn't really paradoxical after all.

There are many passages in the *Paradiso* where Dante follows the scholastic method, endorsing its view of paradox as merely the semblance of paradox. The most evident of these is in the heaven of the *spiriti sapienti*, where Aquinas makes an appearance not simply as an intertextual source but as a character in the fiction.[8] The core of *Paradiso* XIII consists in the fictional Thomas's explication of a paradoxical riddle with the method characteristic of his historical counterpart. As the character explains, a contradiction arises from Dante's faith that Adam and Christ were the only two people in whom human nature was ever perfect, and Thomas's own assertion, a few cantos earlier, that Solomon was second to none in his wisdom

---

[5] Denis R. Janz, 'Syllogism or Paradox: Aquinas and Luther on Theological Method', *Theological Studies*, 59 (1998), 3–21 (15). Janz makes a compelling case that 'Aquinas cannot be accused of solving paradox' (p. 19) by stressing the importance of the reminders, ubiquitous in his writings, of the ultimately incomprehensible nature of God. The moments in the *Paradiso* that follow Aquinas's method of solving (apparent) paradoxes often present similar reminders (*Par.* XIII, discussed below, is such a case).
[6] Thomas Aquinas, *Summa theologiae*, in *Opera Omnia iussu impensaque Leonis XIII P. M. edita* (Rome: Typographia Polyglotta, 1882–), vols. 4–12 (1888–1906), available in English as *Summa theologica*, trans. Fathers of the English Dominican Province, 5 vols (Allen, TX: Christian Classics, 1948). Out of seven *Quaestiones disputatae* and twelve *Questiones de quodlibet*, only one has been published in the ongoing *Editio Leonina*; collectively, they are available online as part of the Corpus Thomisticum, <http://www.corpusthomisticum.org/iopera.html>.
[7] Janz, 'Syllogism or Paradox', p. 15.
[8] For clarity's sake, I refer to the fictional character simply as Thomas to distinguish him from the historical Thomas Aquinas.

('a veder tanto non surse il secondo', *Par.* X, 114). After seventy lines of scholastic arguments, syllogisms, and objections, Thomas makes a qualification: the verb 'surse' in his sentence does not apply to human beings in general but should be understood narrowly as referring to kings ('solamente respetto | ai regi,' *Par.* XIII, 107–8). With this qualification—*distinzion* is the theologian's technical term (lines 109 and 116)[9]—the paradox ceases to be. In Thomas's words,

> Con questa distinzion prendi 'l mio detto;
> e così puote star con quel che credi
> del primo padre e del nostro Diletto.
>
> E questo ti sia sempre piombo a' piedi,
> per farti mover lento com'uom lasso
> e al sì e al no che tu non vedi:
> ché quelli è tra li stolti bene a basso,
> che sanza distinzione afferma e nega
> ne l'un così come ne l'altro passo.
>
> [Take my words, along with this distinction
> and they can stand alongside your beliefs
> concerning the first father and the One we love.
>
> And let this always be as lead upon your feet
> to make you slow, just like a weary man, in moving,
> whether to say yes or no, unless you see both clearly.
>
> For he ranks low among the fools
> who, without making clear distinctions,
> affirms or denies in one case or another.]
>
> (*Par.* XIII, 109–17)

The *distinzion* allows the two contradictory statements to resolve their differences and discover that they can coexist without contravening Aristotle's principle of non-contradiction.[10] As Thomas liberally puts it, 'my

---

[9] The term 'distinzione' and its cognates occur four times in the heaven of the *spiriti sapienti* (*Par.* XI, 97; XII, 142; XIII, 109, 117), most notably in the hendiadys identifying Thomas with the discriminating power of his discourse ('fra Tommaso e 'l discreto latino', XII, 142). In *Monarchia* III, iv, 5 Dante mentions distinction ('distinctionem') in the context of a list of logical fallacies.

[10] Aristotle, *Metaphysics* IV, 3–6, 1005a–1001 1b, in *Metaphysics*, trans. Hugh Tredennick and George Cyril Armstrong, 2 vols, rev. edn (Cambridge, MA: Harvard University Press, 2014); see Thomas Aquinas's commentary *Sententia Super Metaphysicam*, 5–15, available in English as *Commentary on the Metaphysics of Aristotle*, trans. John P. Rowan, 2 vols (Chicago:

words...can stand alongside your beliefs' (109–10): Solomon is the wisest king *and* Adam and Christ are the most perfect men. The function of Thomas's discursive reasoning is to bring into view what the form of paradox was hiding from view, 'perché paia ben ciò che non pare' ['to make quite clear what still remains obscure'] (91). In this view, paradox is an obscure, partial, preliminary form. The natural consequence of the solution of a paradox is the shedding of its paradoxical outer shell.

Scholastic practice, then, has an ambivalent relationship with paradox, on the one hand accepting and even seeking out its appearance, on the other undermining its reality. Implicit in this practice is the tendency to treat paradox as solvable. When, for instance, the historical Thomas Aquinas commented on such passages as the Pauline paradox, 'for my power is made perfect in my weakness' (2 Corinthians 12:9), he carefully distinguished between the power of Paul's reason and the strength of his body.[11] 'This interpretation', as Denis Janz explains, 'introduces a distinction and thereby essentially translates the paradox into a straightforward assertion.'[12] The paradox's solution thus implies a *dissolution*: a translation of the content of the original paradox into another form: the form of discursive reasoning. In this exegetical practice, the paradoxical form is only a temporary stage on the path that leads eventually to discursive form. When thus conceived, paradox is bound to time not simply in the general way of all language but in a specific way, its content always waiting to be teased out and unfolded in the time it takes to give an explanation. The time that is unique to this view of paradox, then, is teleological: paradox always looks forward to its end.

The teleology intrinsic in the scholastic method of dealing with paradoxes undoubtedly plays an important role in the *Paradiso*. One of its advantages is that the theological discussions by Beatrice and other characters are often the driving narrative force of the last cantica. The promise of explanation entices curious readers to read on, accompanying the protagonist on his progress toward the ultimate revelation.[13] The promise of

---

Regnery, 1964); reprinted in one volume with revisions as *Commentary on Aristotle's Metaphysics* (Notre Dame, IN: Dumb Ox Books, 1995).

[11] Aquinas, *Summa theologiae* I.ii, q. 55, a. 3 ad 3; see also II.ii, q. 123, a. 1 ad 1. A similar exegetical practice is applied to various passages from Matthew: see Janz, 'Syllogism or Paradox', pp. 17–18.

[12] Janz, 'Syllogism or Paradox', p. 17.

[13] '[T]he satisfaction of each doubt increases both his knowledge and his desire to know' (Lino Pertile, '*Paradiso*: A Drama of Desire', in *Word and Drama in Dante: Essays on the 'Divina Commedia'*, ed. John C. Barnes and Jennifer Petrie (Dublin: Irish Academic Press, 1993), pp. 143–80 (p. 161)). Elena Lombardi elaborates on Pertile's point in her *The Wings of the*

explication, however, also has some drawbacks. One critic who thought ill of it was Benedetto Croce. For Croce, doctrinal explications in the *Paradiso* made for tedious poetry; what was worse, they also had a terrible influence on the ensuing scholarship, where explicating Dante's doctrine became very popular with Dantists. Croce disparagingly termed such interpretations *allotrie* ['extrinsic'], claiming that they forsook the words on the page for some context extrinsic to it, which they risked eclipsing by sheer volume of scholarly erudition: 'theology subjugates poetry and reduces it to its tool, and, in the end, it acts as though it did not exist'.[14] In Croce's terms, extrinsic interpretations resolve the paradoxes of *Paradiso* by laying out their content through paraphrase or commentary; indeed, they give the impression that these paradoxes are always waiting to be teased out through commentaries. The price of the formal translation from poetry to prose, which aggrandizes the interpreter as it belittles the text, is the poem itself. The poem is treated as merely a step in the process of its explication.

Before I argue why this is not the case with the *Paradiso*, I will turn to the other model of paradox considered in this section: the tradition of mystical writings and visions. In the years of Dante's lifetime, this tradition includes an enormous variety of genres, from the apocalyptic fictions of Uguccione da Lodi, Giacomino da Verona, and Bonvesin de la Riva to the religious lyrics of Iacopone da Todi and the mystical theology of Bonaventure and Meister Eckhart.[15] What these very different texts have in common, and what distinguishes them from scholastic theology, is their emphasis not on systematic, discursive, rational understanding but on 'experiential

---

Doves: Love and Desire in Dante and Medieval Culture (Montreal: McGill-Queen's University Press, 2012), p. 125.

[14] '[L]a teologia...si assoggetta la poesia e la riduce a suo strumento e, in fondo, fa come se non esistesse' (Benedetto Croce, *La poesia di Dante* (Bari: Laterza, 1921), p. 3).

[15] The relationship between Dante and these authors has been studied. For Uguccione, Giacomino, and Bonvesin, see Manuele Gragnolati, *Experiencing the Afterlife: Soul and Body in Dante and Medieval Culture* (Notre Dame, IN: Notre Dame University Press, 2005); for Francis and Iacopone, see Paolo Canettieri, *Iacopone e la poesia religiosa del Duecento* (Milan: Rizzoli, 2001); for Bonaventure, see Étienne Gilson, *The Philosophy of St. Bonaventure*, trans. Illtyd Trethowan and F. J. Sheed (London: Sheed & Ward, 1938); Franco Ferrucci, *Le due mani di Dio: Il cristianesimo e Dante* (Rome: Fazi, 1999), pp. 58–9, and Zygmunt G. Barański, *Dante e i segni: Saggi per una storia intellettuale di Dante Alighieri* (Naples: Liguori, 2000); for Meister Eckhart, Rubina Giorgi, *Dante e Meister Eckhart: Letture per il tempo della fine* (Salerno: Ripostes, 1987), and Heinrich Fels, 'Dante und Meister Eckhart', *Deutsches Dante-Jahrbuch*, 27 (1948), 171–87. William Harmless, *Mystics* (Oxford: Oxford University Press, 2008), p. 229, lists at least twelve literary genres that can be included in the wide category of 'mystical writings'.

knowledge'.[16] The very epistemology of these writings is not merely based on reason but—so these texts claim—on experience. At the level of content, this means simply that these writings all purport in various ways to describe an experience (vision literature and journeys to the afterlife are a case in point). At the level of form, more interestingly, it means that in reverence to that purported experience, mystical accounts often feel compelled to forego the scholastic allegiance to Aristotle's principle of non-contradiction and rational and logical discourse. Indeed, one of the ways in which these fictions manage to craft textually the impression of a real, out-of-the-text mystical experience is by emphasizing in their rhetorical choices the distinctive, untranslatable gap between such transcendent experience and human language. Different genres will opt for different strategies to convey that fundamental strangeness. The apocalyptic writings of Uguccione, Giacomino, and Bonvesin largely confine the strangeness of the experience to their content, focusing on the description of the wonders of the afterlife; on the other hand, the poetry of Iacopone and the mystical writings of Bonaventure and Eckhart entrust that strangeness to their form, making extensive use of defamiliarizing rhetorical devices, such as oxymora, anacolutha, adynata, which constitute the language of paradox.[17] Witness the following excerpt from the penultimate stage of Bonaventure's *Itinerarium mentis in Deum*:[18]

> dum mens nostra contemplatur in Christo Filio Dei, qui est imago Dei invisibilis per naturam, humanitatem nostram...mirabiliter exaltatur, ... ineffabiliter unitam, videndo simul in unum primum et ultimum, summum et imum, circumferentiam et centrum, *alpha et omega*, causatum et causa, Creatorem et creaturam, librum scilicet *scriptum intus et extra*; iam pervenit ad quandam rem perfectam....

---

[16] Mysticism 'is a domain of religion that deals with the search for and the attainment of a profound *experiential knowledge* of God or of ultimate reality. It takes its literary form in mystical texts' (William Harmless, *Mystics*, p. 263, my italics).

[17] On the importance of these rhetorical figures in mystical writings, see the densely written Carlo Ossola, 'Apoteosi ed ossimoro: Retorica della "traslazione" e retorica dell'"unione" nel viaggio mistico a Dio: Testi italiani dei secoli XVI–XVII', in *Mistica e retorica: Studi*, ed. Franco Bolgiani (Florence: Olschki, 1977), pp. 46–103; Massimo Baldini, *Il linguaggio dei mistici* (Brescia: Queriniana, 1986), pp. 47–54; Manuela Colombo, *Dai mistici a Dante: Il linguaggio dell'ineffabilità* (Florence: Nuova Italia, 1987); Giovanni Pozzi, 'L'alfabeto delle sante', in *Scrittrici mistiche italiane*, ed. Giovanni Pozzi and Claudio Leonardi (Turin: Einaudi, 1988), pp. 21–42 (pp. 38–9).

[18] Bonaventure, *Journey of the Soul into God: Itinerarium Mentis in Deum*, ed. Philotheus Boehner, trans. Zachary Hayes (Saint Bonaventure, NY: Franciscan Institute Publications, 2002), pp. 130–1.

[our mind has already reached something perfect when it contemplates our humanity so remarkably exalted and so ineffably united in Christ, the Son of God, who is by nature the image of the invisible God; and when, at the same time, our mind sees in a single glance the first and the last, the highest and the lowest, the circumference and the center, the *Alpha* and the *Omega*, the caused and the cause, the creator and the creature, that is, *the book written within and without*...]

The text centres on a series of antitheses. Bonaventure goes in quick succession through time, hierarchy, space, language, causation, and creation, but chooses to divide each concept up in the simplest constitutive paradoxes, each bound together by the copulative conjunction *et*. The fictional seams are not hidden but brought into view: the text does not tackle paradoxes directly but draws our attention to the narrative frame afforded by the mind that experiences them ('mens nostra contemplatur' ['our mind...contemplates'], 'videndo' ['when [it] sees']); further, both the naming of God as 'alpha et omega' and the comparison of the book stress the textual nature of this attempt to gesture at the ineffable. No discursive explanation follows; before we could get it, some kind of perfection has *already* been reached ('iam pervenit ad quandam rem perfectam').[19] The paragraph from which this quotation is taken ends with the simple statement of what the culminating step of the soul's journey into God consists of: the day of rest ('dies requiei'). The chapter again does not describe it directly but performatively ends on this meditation that the rest is silence.

Much is at stake in bringing form into view as Bonaventure's passage does. The scholastic method is based on the premise that it is possible to defuse the strangeness of paradox by translating its content into familiar discursive reasoning, thereby dissolving what is strange about its form. But mystical writings take the opposite route. They dare the reader to face the content in all its irreducible strangeness, to take the text seriously even though, especially though, it is strange. By drawing attention to the text's strangeness, they are able to prevent textuality from disappearing from under the reader's eyes. This is where the scholastic method of dealing with paradox is arguably more deceptive than that of mystical writing.[20] For all

---

[19] Dante may have been inspired by Bonaventure's use of the adverb *iam* at the end of his own *Paradiso*: 'ma già volgeva il mio disio e 'l *velle*' (*Par.* XXXIII, 143). On Dante's 'final time-defying' construct there, see Barolini, *Undivine 'Comedy'*, p. 257.

[20] As New Critic Cleanth Brooks, discussed below, writes, 'there is a sense in which paradox is the language appropriate and inevitable to poetry. It is the scientist whose truth requires a

its appeals to clarity, discursive language does not actually escape the problems inherent in every text—how could it possibly?—it merely disowns them with a magic trick. I mentioned the role of this trickery in attempts to describe eternity that, however well explained, still fall into time. In contrast, mystical paradox reminds us that something as alien as eternity can never be accounted for textually unless it is expounded in a form that is founded on antinomies joined together by the conjunction *et*, such as 'the first and the last', 'the *Alpha* and the *Omega*'. The unignorable strangeness of the form is the way, and possibly the only way, in which the text can gesture towards its own irreducible alterity from something as radically foreign to human language as eternity. The paradoxical form of mystical writings has this one advantage then: its claim is not to *describe* the content of the paradox but to *perform* its paradoxicality; not to describe eternity but to perform the fact that eternity, like paradox, does not obey Aristotle's principle of non-contradiction. By wearing its own insufficiency on its sleeve, mystical paradox manages to perform, rather than vainly purport to describe, the radical otherness that can only be gestured toward and never accommodated in a text.

Paradiso learns important lessons from the paradoxes of scholastic theology and mystical writings. Dante uses paradoxes according to the scholastic model when he employs explanations in the fiction to push the narrative forward. In contrast, when he needs to point beyond the text to an experience that transcends humanity, he follows the mystical model. But for the reader who wishes to resist teleology in her reading of the *Paradiso*, it is mystical paradox that can provide a valid alternative. This claim can be justified by looking at the hermeneutic problem identified above, arising from readings that effectively forsake the poetry of *Paradiso* in order to explicate it in commentaries and paraphrases; these readings seem to find a justification in the scholastic model of paradox whereby a text can be explained by another—the scholar's—text. It is important to notice here that in the only instances where Dante himself follows the scholastic model, he is doing so in order to push his narrative forward—through the drama of doubts and answers, and the plot of unfolding, increasing knowledge—not to abandon it altogether; his aim is not to consume the *Paradiso* but to fuel the writing of more of it. It is significant, then, that in the only glimpses we have

---

language purged of every trace of paradox; apparently the truth which the poet utters can be approached only in terms of paradox' (*The Well-Wrought Urn: Studies in the Structure of Poetry* (New York: Harcourt Brace, 1947) p. 3).

of Dante ever reaching for meaning beyond his text, this is not for the sake of another text but for experience. The *locus classicus* is the famous terzina of the first canto of *Paradiso*:

> Trasumanar significar *per verba*
> non si poria; però l'essemplo basti
> a cui esperïenza grazia serba.
>
> [To soar beyond the human cannot be described in words. Let the example be enough to one for whom grace holds this experience in store.]
>
> (*Paradiso* I, 70–2)[21]

Dante is known for often declaring the ineffability of his experience, only to then proceed to write about it, and I will discuss instances of this tactic more extensively in Subsection 1.4.3 of this chapter. Suffice it to say, for now, that, in contrast to the usual pattern, the terzina quoted offers a rare example of Dante ostensibly standing by his own declaration of ineffability and actually letting go, in the lines immediately following, of what he originally set out to represent. His appeal to experience exhausts the description but also makes sure to affirm the impossibility of any description after his own aborted one. In this, Dante follows the mystical model, though perhaps with an agonistic twist that is characteristic of its author.

It is time to return to the quotation with which this section opened. Caroline Walker Bynum was discussing the difficulties of analysing the paradoxes of the Middle Ages in her academic writings. I am no closer to answering the question of whether these paradoxes are inherent in the world itself, a question that I said I should bracket in favour of the analysis of the text. However, in light of this discussion of the traditions of medieval scholastic theology and mystical writing I have made a distinction between

---

[21] The idea is also expressed in *Par*. III, 37–9 ('a' rai | di vita etterna la dolcezza senti | che, non gustata, non s'intende mai'); X, 74–5 ('chi non s'impenna sì che là su voli, | dal muto aspetti quindi le novelle'); and see also the sonnet 'Tanto gentile', 11 ('ch'intender no la pò chi no la prova'). As Anna Maria Chiavacci Leonardi comments, 'Dalla Scrittura (*Ps*. 33, 9; *Apoc*. 2, 17), l'idea passò...nei testi mistici, tra i quali Bernardo, Riccardo di San Vittore e Bonaventura, tutti autori noti a Dante. Ricordiamo l'*Epistola ad Severinum de charitate*...dove l'anima nell'estasi si immerge in Dio "gustando ciò che nessuno conosce se non chi lo riceve"' (Anna Maria Chiavacci Leonardi, *ad Par*. III, 38–9). See also Bernard of Clairvaux, *Liber de diligendo deo* (Turnhout: Brepols, 2010), XV, 39: 'Asserant hoc si qui esperti sunt. Mihi, fateor, impossibile videtur'.

two kinds of paradox.[22] Whereas mystical paradox keeps the emphasis on its form, making its insufficiency unignorable, discursive reasoning (be it that of the scholastic method or contemporary academic writing) introduces a phantomatic distinction between form and content, only to identify the latter with the world beyond the text, thus bypassing the bracketing that is the starting point of a formal analysis of the text's workings on its own terms. Before discussing paradox in the poem, then, it may be useful to keep this methodological practice in mind as we consider Cleanth Brooks's words on the language of paradox: '[it] is the scientist whose truth requires a language purged of every trace of paradox; apparently the truth which the poet utters can be approached only in terms of paradox'.[23] In what follows, I will explore paradox in the *Paradiso* without dissolving it in the name of a supposed content beyond the page but rather standing by its bond. As I will argue over the course of the chapter, paradoxes and paradoxical forms are employed in the *Commedia* for their ability to neutralize the hierarchizing machinery of the teleological masterplot and thus to convey something of the unfamiliar, irreducible otherness that makes up the content of the *cantica*. The next section begins with the smallest possible form that paradox can take in language: the rhetorical figure of oxymoron.

1.2 Oxymoron as 'compact verbal paradox'

Oxymoron can be defined as a figure of speech whereby two words with contradictory meanings are coupled in one phrase; the etymology of oxymoron is itself an example of the term, as it is made up of two Greek adjectives meaning 'pointed' and 'foolish',[24] with connotations comparable to those that an English speaker may perceive in the antonyms 'sharp' and 'dull'. The affinities between oxymoron and paradox are evident, and indeed it is commonplace to define the one in terms of the other, either by calling

---

[22] In the first two chapters of his *Cultural Thematics* (New Haven, CT: Yale University Press, 1976), T. K. Seung argues for an interaction between an 'Augustinian' (i.e. either/or) and a 'Pseudo-Dionysian' (i.e. both/and) logic as a context for Dante's own alternation of models of paradox. Thank you to my second anonymous reader at OUP for pointing me toward this monograph.
[23] Brooks, *The Well-Wrought Urn*, p. 3.
[24] The Ancient Greek ὀξύμωρος is a compound of ὀξύς ('sharp, keen, pointed') and μωρός ('dull, stupid, foolish').

the oxymoron a compressed, 'compact or succinct form of verbal paradox',[25] or by noting that 'the structure of paradox is similar to that of oxymoron, which unites two contradictory concepts into a third'.[26] The affinity between the two figures extends to the assumptions that accompany them. Most definitions of oxymoron stress the fact that the contradiction between the two terms is only so *in appearance*. The *Princeton Encyclopedia of Poetry and Poetics*, for instance, defines it as a 'figure of speech that yokes together two *seemingly* contradictory elements'.[27] We have seen how a comparable assumption was problematic in the scholastic view of paradox. Nonetheless, it is certainly fruitful to think about some of the oxymora that we find in the *Commedia* as just a trick of the poetry. In *Inferno* XIV, for instance, the protagonist encounters those who were violent against God. These damned are punished in the seventh circle, where fiery rain falls down on them like snow on windless mountains while scorching the sands on which they lie naked, sit, or run, each according to their prescribed punishment. Dante lingers on the description of their torment:

> Sanza riposo mai era la tresca
> de le misere mani, or quindi or quinci
> escotendo da sé l'arsura fresca.
>
> [Ever without repose was the rude dance
> of wretched hands, now here, now there,
> slapping at each new scorching cinder].
>
> (*Inf.* XIV, 40–2)

On first encountering this terzina, readers will probably trip over the phrase 'arsura fresca'. Early commentators and the majority of modern ones clear up the misunderstanding, in the scholastic-explicative mode, by glossing

---

[25] Marvin K. L. Ching, *A Linguistic Analysis of Compact Verbal Paradox in Literature: A Semantic Interpretation of the Oxymoron*, Ph.D. dissertation, Florida State University (1975), p. 11.
[26] 'Paradox' in *The Princeton Encyclopedia of Poetry and Poetics*, ed. Roland Greene and others, 4th edn (Princeton, NJ: Princeton University Press, 2012), p. 996. See also 'Oxymoron' in David Mikics, *New Handbook of Literary Terms* (New Haven, CT: Yale University Press, 2007), p. 219: 'The oxymoron is related to the paradox'.
[27] 'Oxymoron' in *The Princeton Encyclopedia of Poetry and Poetics*, p. 988; 'A figurative...combination of two *seemingly* contradictory words' (Raymond W. Barry and A. J. Wright, *Literary Terms: Definitions, Explanations, Examples* (San Francisco: Chandler Pub. Co., 1966), p. 64); 'A figure of speech (rhetorical antithesis) which combines two *seemingly* contradictory or incongruous words' ('Oxymoron' in *Dictionary of World Literary Terms: Forms, Techniques, Criticism*, ed. Joseph T. Shipley, new rev. edn (London: Allen & Unwin), 1970); 'uniting (not opposing, as in antithesis) contrary and incompatible-*seeming* terms or states' (Brian Vickers, *In Defence of Rhetoric* (Oxford: Clarendon Press, 1989), p. 498).

the adjective *fresca* not as 'fresh' and 'cool' but as 'recent' or 'new', thus returning the reader to the torment of the damned shaking off the falling flames, only to see them constantly renewed.[28] And yet our misunderstanding, originating from the double meaning of *fresca* (both 'cool' and 'new') and its punning oxymoron with *arsura* ('hot'), is precisely what awakes us to a more empathic appreciation of the painful torments experienced by the violent against God. The fiery rain burns *hotter* when it is *freshly* fallen: the effect, and precise poetic purpose, of the oxymoron defeat paraphrasis. If we then look back on the preceding terzinas, we see that the ground for the punning oxymoron 'arsura fresca' has been set in the line '*piovean* di *foco dilatate falde*' ['broad flakes of fire showered down'] (29) representing a rain of fire, and in the following comparison of that fiery rain to snow, 'come di neve in alpe sanza vento' ['as snow falls in the hills on windless days'] (30). Both images play on the same trick of enhancing the contrast between the antonyms cold/wet and hot.

This kind of oxymoron I call 'poetic', as we generally expect to find it in poetic language.[29] The 'poetic oxymoron' does not purport to describe some essential or intrinsic property of the object it describes—fire is not revealed to be actually cold—but aims, rather, at presenting it vividly and freshly to the reader's imagination through a conspicuous rhetorical trick. The experience of reading this text is first one of surprise, then of pleasure. Surprise derives from the unfamiliar form, pleasure from the realization that one has been duped by the poet. The ensuing cognitive dissonance has the aim of involving the reader in a comprehension of the text that is not automatic. It is yet another expressive trick in the poet's bag, a *coup de théâtre* that, while representing the world under a particular light, does not really make any ontological claims about its inherent nature. Heat remains hot, rain remains cool.

There are a number of 'poetic oxymora' in the *Commedia*: they are used to express the inexhaustible hunger of the she-wolf in the first canto of *Inferno* 'che di tutte brame | sembiava *carca ne la sua magrezza*' ['all hide and bones, | seemed charged with all appetites'] (*Inf.* I, 49–50);[30] the

---

[28] The commentators that call 'arsura fresca' an oxymoron are Manfredi Porena, Giuseppe Giacalone, and Nicola Fosca *ad Inf.* XIV, 40–2 (DDP). Porena also comments on the pun, as do Gabriele Rossetti, Ernesto Trucchi, and Daniele Mattalia, *ad loc.*
[29] For an argument for the relationship of the oxymoron to poetic language, see Yeshayahu Shen, 'On the Structure and Understanding of Poetic Oxymoron', *Poetics Today*, 8.1 (1987), 105–22.
[30] 'La lupa, che fa perdere a Dante la speranza di salire il colle…è descritta con un ossimoro (carca…magrezza)' (Nicola Fosca, *ad Inf.* I, 49–54 (DDP)).

duplicitousness of the fraudulent Sinon who, though Greek, pretended he had defected to the Trojans in order to be able to betray them to the Greeks ("l falso Sinon greco di Troia' ['false Sinon, the lying Greek from Troy'], *Inf.* XXX, 98-9);[31] the bittersweetness of nostalgia, called 'il *memorar presente*' ['that memory now'] (*Purg.* XXIII, 117); and the rose of the blessed that Dante finds in the Empyrean heaven, which is called '*pacifica oriafiamma*' (literally, 'battle banner of peace') to highlight the fact that its triumph was achieved not in the conventional sense, through warfare, but by spreading peace (*Par.* XXXI, 127).[32] Purgatorial punishments, painful yet productive and ultimately leading to bliss, constitute a special case. These are described by the purging souls as '*buon dolor*' ['blessed sorrow'] and '*dolce assenzo d'i martiri*' ['sweet wormwood in the torments'] (*Purg.* XXIII, 81 and 86). Keeping in mind the productive outcome of their pain and martyrdom, the souls are able to teleologically contextualize their suffering and see it as *buono* and *dolce*.[33]

When thinking of oxymora in poetic language, similar examples will spring to mind. After Dante, the oxymoron enjoyed great fortune in Renaissance and baroque poetry, both in Italy and abroad, especially with the spread of Petrarchism,[34] so much so that Teodolinda Barolini calls Dante's antitheses in *Purgatorio* XXIII 'Petrarchism *avant la lettre*'.[35] Petrarch is celebrated for turning the oxymoron inward to express the psychological contradictions of his tormented self. He will remember Dante's

---

[31] 'E adotta sottili artifici retorici' such as 'quella specie di ossimoro che è l'espressione *greco da Troia*' (Giuseppe Giacalone, *ad Inf.* XXX, 98–9 (DDP)). See also Emilio Bigi, *Il canto XXX dell'Inferno*' (Florence: Le Monnier, 1963).
[32] Both Nicola Fosca and Robert Hollander comment on the oxymoron (*ad Par.* XXXI, 127 (DDP)).
[33] The commentators H.F. Tozer, Umberto Bosco and Giovanni Reggio, Anna Maria Chiavacci Leonardi, and Nicola Fosca note the oxymoron (*ad loc.*, DDP). The entire canto is dedicated to spelling out the apparent paradox of pleasure in the punishment, which is explained and resolved later: 'E non pur una volta questo spazzo | girando, si rinfresca nostra pena: | io dico *pena*, e dovria dir *sollazzo*, | che questa voglia a li alberi ci mena | che menò Cristo *lieto* a dire "*Eli*"'. The concept of productive pain in the *Commedia* has been explored by Manuele Gragnolati in *Experiencing the Afterlife* and *Amor che move: Linguaggio del corpo e forma del desiderio in Dante, Pasolini e Morante* (Milan: Il Saggiatore, 2013).
[34] See 'Oxymoron' and 'Paradox' in *The Princeton Encyclopedia of Poetry and Poetics*, p. 988 and p. 996 respectively.
[35] Teodolinda Barolini, *Dante's Poets: Textuality and Truth in the 'Comedy'* (Princeton, NJ: Princeton University Press, 1984), p. 50.

'arsura fresca' in his *Rerum vulgarium fragmenta*, where he writes the *ballata mezzana* 'Quel foco ch'i' pensai':[36]

> Quel *foco* ch'i' pensai che fosse spento
> dal *freddo* tempo et da l'età men *fresca*,
> *fiamma* et martir ne l'anima *rinfresca*.
>
> [That *fire* which I thought had been extinguished
> by the *cold* times and by an age less *fresh*
> renews the *flame* and suffering of my soul.]
>
> (*Rerum vulgarium fragmenta* LV, 1–3)

Here the refrain of Petrarch's *ballata* sees Dante's punning oxymoron and, agonistically, doubles it over the two words *fresca* and *rinfresca*, having insinuated the connotation of 'cold' into the reader with the astutely placed adjective *freddo*. We may notice that in contrast with Dante's ultimately literal description, the fires, flames, colds, and renewals in Petrarch are entirely metaphorical; something which may have led Barolini to claim about Dante's oxymora that their 'rigour is foreign to the lyric experience'.[37] Yet Petrarch's use of antitheses here, although metaphorical, expresses an experience of internal contradiction which remains all too real, and resists resolution. No amount of teleological contextualization can explain away Petrarch's pleasant pain in the *Rerum vulgarium fragmenta* in a comparable way as the 'blessed pain' or 'sweet wormwood in the torments' of *Purgatorio* XXIII.[38]

There is a different kind of oxymoron in the *Commedia* that has less to do with ornament and poetic language but purports to tackle directly the contradictions intrinsic in the object it seeks to represent. Unlike the antinomies of the 'poetic oxymoron', the contradictions yoked together in this kind of oxymoron can never be fully accounted for or revealed to be only apparent. The famous terzinas of Bernard's prayer to the Virgin that opens

---

[36] Petrarch, *Il Canzoniere*, ed. Gianfranco Contini (Turin: Einaudi, 1964); English translation: Petrarch, *Canzoniere*, ed. and trans. Mark Musa (Bloomington, IN: Indiana University Press, 1996). See also *Rerum vulgarium fragmenta* XXXVII, 49–50: 'Lasso, se ragionando *si rinfresca* | quel' *ardente* desio' ['Alas, if talking this way can renew | that ardent wish of mine'].

[37] Barolini, *Dante's Poets*, p. 50.

[38] For a recent exploration of paradoxes and teleological endpoints in Dante and Petrarch, see Manuele Gragnolati and Francesca Southerden, 'From Paradox to Exclusivity: Dante and Petrarch's Lyrical Eschatologies', in *The Unity of Knowledge in the Pre-Modern World: Petrarch and Boccaccio between the Middle Ages and Renaissance*, ed. Igor Candido (Berlin: De Gruyter, 2018).

the last and most paradoxical canto of the *Paradiso* are an example of just this kind of oxymoron:

> Vergine Madre, figlia del tuo figlio,
> umile e alta più che creatura,
> termine fisso d'etterno consiglio,
>   tu se' colei che l'umana natura
> nobilitasti sì, che 'l suo fattore
> non disdegnò di farsi sua fattura.
>   Nel ventre tuo si raccese l'amore,
> per lo cui caldo ne l'etterna pace
> così è germinato questo fiore.
>
> [Virgin Mother, daughter of your Son,
> more humble and exalted than any other creature,
> fixed goal of the eternal plan,
>   you are the one who so ennobled human nature
> that He, who made it first did not disdain
> to make Himself of its own making.
>   Your womb relit the flame of love—
> its heat has made this blossom seed
> and flower in eternal peace.]
>
> (*Par.* XXXIII, 1–9)

There is no way to paraphrase the oxymora in the first line of Bernard's prayer:[39] if you talk about Mary in the Christian tradition, the fact that she is both virgin *and* mother, both mother *and* daughter of her own son *and* father, even when glossed, remains unresolvedly paradoxical. The paradox does not belong to poetry any more than it does to prose. As commentators Anna Maria Chiavacci Leonardi and Siro Chimenz highlight, the paradox in these terzinas is not a matter of embellishment but of fact: 'there is not any rhetoric in them, because these antitheses are a fact'[40] and 'here they are not an artifice of style, because the antithetic nature lies in the fact itself'.[41] For all his claims of factuality, however, Chimenz does not refrain from

---

[39] These oxymora, of course, have a long tradition in religious writings before Dante. Erich Auerbach discusses this tradition in the context of the *Paradiso* XXXIII in his article 'Dante's prayer to the Virgin (*Paradiso* XXXIII) and earlier eulogies', *Romance Philology*, 3.1 (1949), 1–26.

[40] 'Non vi è in esse alcuna retorica, perché tali antitesi sono un fatto' (Anna Maria Chiavacci Leonardi, *ad Par.* XXXIII, 1 (DDP), trans. mine).

[41] 'Qui non sono artificio di stile, perché l'antiteticità è nel fatto stesso' (Siro A. Chimenz, *Il canto XXXIII del 'Paradiso'* (Rome: Signorelli, 1951), p. 4, trans. mine).

reproaching this canto for being merely verbal and excessively artificial: 'it opens with a weak periphrasis and continues with an antithesis that results in a play on words, the contrivedness of which I will not dwell on'.[42] In a similar contradiction, Daniele Mattalia can claim that these are 'conceptual antitheses fixed in verbal dyads that betray a taste for conceits' even as he simultaneously holds that they state 'what is humanly impossible as natural and normal'.[43] So which is it? Are these oxymora empty wordplay or do they reflect essential facts?

It is the defining property of this particular kind of oxymoron that we find in the *Commedia*—which I call 'literal oxymoron'—to be both at the same time. Within the fiction, it purports to be a faithful, non-rhetorical, literal description of reality; at the level of the text, however, they remain what they are, rhetorical figures. Indeed, they flaunt their own artifice. The antitheses on which these terzinas are structured are in fact the sole mark of poetic language in a passage that is otherwise notable for its plainness.[44] As Erich Auerbach points out, 'this famous text, in its basic structure', is simply 'a rigid composition of dogmatic statements'.[45] The language of the passage is especially lacking in metaphors.[46] When an image does appear—and it is the most hackneyed symbol of poetry conceivable: a flower[47]—it is not actually a metaphor but the 'literal' *rosa dei beati*, the rose-shaped amphitheatre where all the blessed are seated, which Bernard sees in front of him

---

[42] 'Si apre con una fiacca perifrasi e continua con un'antitesi che si risolve in giuoco di parole, di cui non starò a sottolineare l'artificio' (ibid., p. 5, trans. mine).

[43] 'antitesi concettuali fissate in diadi verbali di gusto scopertamente concettoso', and 'l'umanamente impossibile come naturale e normale' (Daniele Mattalia (1960), *ad Par.* XXXIII, 1 (DDP), trans. mine).

[44] I agree on this point with Anna Maria Chiavacci Leonardi, Siro Chimenz (*ad loc.*, DDP), and Erich Auerbach, who all remark on the 'plainness' of Dante's lines compared to the Marian tradition and the eulogies that are among his sources: 'Il mistero è espresso in vari modi in tutti i più noti testi mariani, dogmatici o liturgici ("mater semper virgo"; "genuisti qui te fecit" ecc.), ma nessun luogo può competere con questo nudo verso dantesco, che col suo ritmo alto e la sua sobrietà assoluta – fatta di quattro parole – fa risuonare il grande mistero in apertura del canto finale del poema.' (Anna Maria Chiavacci Leonardi, *ad Par.* XXXIII, 1 (DDP)); 'l'espressione dantesca non fa che scolpire in termini essenziali…, senza alcuno degli ornamenti e commenti che accompagnano i passi analoghi della tradizione mariana, l'inconcepibile miracolo' (Chimenz, *Il canto XXXIII del 'Paradiso'*, p. 4).

[45] Auerbach, 'Dante's prayer to the Virgin', p. 25.

[46] Mario Fubini points out the dearth of images in the passage: 'le antitesi si sciolgono in un'immagine, una delle rare immagini dell'orazione' (*Due studi danteschi* (Florence: Sansoni, 1951), p. 68).

[47] For the smack-in-the-face poeticity of the *fiore* (in rhyme with *amore*), witness Umberto Saba's memorable lines 'M'incantò la rima fiore | amore, | la più antica, difficile del mondo' ('Amai', *Mediterranee* (Milan: Mondadori, 1946)).

in the Empyrean heaven.[48] In this general dearth of recognizable marks of poetic language, the oxymora stick out all the more as rhetorical figures.

The self-evident literariness of the 'literal oxymoron' is another of Dante's 'techniques of verisimilitude'.[49] With a trademark move, explained by Teodolinda Barolini, Dante draws attention to the self-contradictory nature of his fiction but imputes it to the self-contradictory nature of the content it is describing. By so doing, he creates the illusion of the existence of a content beyond the text. On Dante's terms, if 'Vergine madre' *appears* to be a trope, it is not because the *Paradiso* is a poetic text that uses this poetic convention but because the reality it is describing is intrinsically paradoxical: Mary is actually both a virgin and a mother. To paraphrase Barolini, if in this passage Dante is candid in highlighting the artifice of his rhetorical figures, he is, however, far from candid in his goal, which is to displace onto Mary—here a character of the fiction—concerns that in fact belong to his poetic text.[50]

If we read Dante's 'literal oxymora' in this light, it will appear that they are paradoxical on a further level than that of their self-contradictory content. Their paradox consists in the fact that, by making their fictionality obvious, they manage to gesture towards what lies beyond the fiction. Not by chance, Dante's own metapoetic statements in the *Commedia* often take precisely the form of oxymoron. These are the 'oxymoronic formulations'[51] of the 'ver c'ha faccia di menzogna' ['a truth that bears the face of falsehood'] (*Inf.* XVI, 124), of the 'non falsi errori' ['errors…not false'] (*Purg.* XV, 117), of the 'cosa incredibile e vera' ['a thing incredible but true'] (*Par.* XVI, 124). With these metapoetic oxymora Dante openly declares the work that all his 'literal oxymora' undertake for him covertly: 'literal oxymora' such as 'Vergine madre', 'liberi soggiacete' [literally, 'you are freely subject'] (*Purg.* XVI, 80), and 'primavera sempiterna' ['eternity of spring'] (*Par.* XXVIII, 116)[52] illusionistically hold together reality and fiction; they

---

[48] Fubini highlights the words 'così' and 'questo' that give literality to the image of the flower: 'Bernardo torna con lo sguardo al mondo che è suo e due semplice parole, un *così* e un *questo*, bastano a darci il senso di quella familiarità' (Fubini, *Due studi danteschi*, p. 68). For apparent metaphors that are revealed to be literal, see also the ladder ('*escalina*') that Arnaut Daniel gestures towards in the Provençal passage of *Purgatorio* XXVI, 140–7; Dante will see the literal 'scaleo' in *Paradiso* XXI, 29. It is important to bear in mind, however, that the textual tradition of these lines is debated.
[49] Barolini, *Undivine 'Comedy'*, p. 16.   [50] Ibid., p. 187.   [51] Ibid., p. 60.
[52] Robin Kirkpatrick's description of the effect of these lines bears witness to the mechanism of the self-evident paradox pointing beyond the fiction that I am trying to describe: the sentence 'is so evident a paradox as to be emblematic in its force, inviting one to countenance,

contrive to gesture to a 'reality' beyond the poetic text by the very act of wearing their artifice on their sleeve. By being blatantly contradictory, incomplete, unsatisfying, even frustrating as fiction, they point to a truth beyond themselves. They are, in all the ambiguity of the oxymoron, *true fictions*.

Teodolinda Barolini has written eloquently on Dante's illusionism—the 'literal oxymora' that appear in the *Commedia* certainly have a place among Dante's 'techniques of verisimilitude'.[53] But I would like to conclude this section with the claim that the task Dante entrusts to his 'literal oxymoron' goes beyond this very important function. It is my claim that 'literal oxymora' are an instance of the paradoxes that provide Dante's text with an alternative narrative model capable of resisting the hegemony of the teleological masterplot. If in the narrative of the masterplot 'the truth' is located at the endpoint of the text, where the meaning of previous statements is interpreted retrospectively, the narrative alternative of the 'literal oxymoron' locates the truth altogether beyond the text. This is the pinnacle of Dante's illusionism. Just like the masterplot, in fact, the narrative model of paradox is itself a product of the fiction. Just like the masterplot, this fiction works by inventing a dualism between truth and falsehood; but whereas the masterplot entrusts truth and falsehood to the hierarchy of time, which identifies *before* with falsehood and *after* with truth, the paradoxical narrative model displaces them respectively onto *inside* and *outside* of the fiction. It is important to keep in mind here that what gives these categories their truth value is not a given 'reality' outside of the fiction but the fiction itself, which, of course, obeys the same laws of before-and-after or fiction-and-reality of all human language. By distracting the reader with an artificial, illusionistic distinction between a false fiction and the truth beyond it, Dante's text is actually once more appropriating the categories of *truth* and *falsehood* for its own agenda. These forms are oxymoronic 'non falsi errori': they are fictional (insofar as they are rhetorical tricks), and at the same time they are literal (if we buy into the fiction); they point our attention to the text and its workings by being so blatantly rhetorical, and at the same time they point to the truth beyond it through the trick of their own insufficiency. At Dante's illusionistic bidding, *fiction* and *reality*, rather than *before* and *after*, are now laden with falsehood and truth. When paradox is represented, the hierarchy

in reason, the discrepancy between time and eternity' (Robin Kirkpatrick, *Dante's 'Paradiso' and the Limitations of Modern Criticism* (Cambridge: Cambridge University Press, 1978), p. 166).
[53] Barolini, *Undivine 'Comedy'*, p. 16.

of time is neutralized; when the hierarchy of time is neutralized, paradox can be represented. Paradox affords the *Commedia* an alternative narrative model to represent the kinds of 'truth' that the teleological model, by virtue of its hierarchizing power, renders unrepresentable. Countering that power with paradox, Dante sacrifices Aristotle's principle of non-contradiction in order to free up a neutralized time that he can then have at his disposal in the writing of his fiction. This narrative model can be seen at work in the microcosm of the *Commedia*'s oxymora and related paradoxical figures, certainly, but it is also active over a more extended range, as I will show in the next section.

1.3 Long-range Paradox in the *Commedia*

The narrative model of paradox can be useful for a 'lettura a lunghe campate' of some of the long-range contradictions in the *Commedia*.[54] This is arguably the textual range where the pressure of the teleological masterplot is felt more strongly, due to the narrative imprint of the protagonist's progression through the three realms that acts as an ordering principle for a hierarchical interpretation of the poem. Read teleologically, episodes in the *Inferno* are recontextualized in view of successive revelations in the *Purgatorio* and *Paradiso*, with the second cantica also often read in light of the last. In this section, I will offer instead an example of a deteleologized interpretation of the long-range symmetries in the *Commedia*.

Take the following passage from *Inferno* XX. As Robert Hollander points out, it is 'probably the tercet in the canto that has caused the most debate'.[55] Indeed, Virgil could be said to tease the readers themselves, as he mocks Dante with two rhetorical questions:

> Ancor se' tu de li altri sciocchi?
> Qui vive la pietà quand'è ben morta;
> chi è più scellerato che colui
> che al giudicio divin passion comporta?

---

[54] I borrow the phrase from Paolo Cherchi and Selene Sarteschi, 'Il cielo del Sole: Per una lettura della *Commedia* a "lunghe campate"', *Critica del Testo*, 14.2 (2011), 311–31.
[55] Robert Hollander, *ad Inf.* XX, 28–30 (DDP).

[Are you still witless as the rest?
Here piety lives when pity is quite dead.
Who is more impious than one who thinks
that God shows passion in his judgement?]
(*Inf.* XX, 27–30)

The passage is yet another instance in the dynamics of pity and piety that run throughout the *Commedia*. In this context, the meaning of the highly compressed one-liner 'Qui vive la pietà quand'è ben morta' is clear to all commentators: when Dante appears to be moved by the infernal punishment of the diviners and sorcerers, Virgil remarks that it is more pious not to feel any pity toward them. What is less clear—and has been the cause of the ensuing critical debate—is everything else. Does Virgil's 'Qui' ['Here'] refer to Hell in general, or is it limited to this *bolgia*? And consequently, should 'colui | che al giudicio divin passion comporta' be taken to refer to the sorcerers and diviners themselves, whose activity impiously assumes that God's judgement 'admits of passion', that is, can be affected by external, and more specifically human, agency?[56] Or should it be taken to refer to Dante, whose compassion for the damned appears to question divine justice?

Although early commentators unanimously accepted the latter interpretation, they soon puzzled over the evident contradiction with the other passages in *Inferno* where Dante,[57] and even Virgil himself,[58] unequivocally show compassion for the damned. Conversely, the competing interpretation that the sorcerers are impious in believing that God 'admits of passion'

---

[56] Hollander's translation quoted here seems to side with this interpretation. Teodolinda Barolini, 'True and False See-ers in *Inferno* XX', *Lectura Dantis*, 4 (1989), 42–54 (p. 45): '[Virgil] concludes his rebuke with another fierce question, impugning those who, like the diviners, attempt to render the divine will inactive: "chi è più scellerato che colui | che al giudicio divin passion comporta?"'
[57] See Johannis de Serravalle, *ad Inf.* XX, 25–30 and Cristoforo Landino, *ad* 25–30 (DDP); Benvenuto da Imola, *ad* ll. 28–30 (DDP) offers the same interpretation while holding that Virgil is talking about the soothsayers in particular, not all the damned. For the contradiction with Dante's compassion elsewhere in the *Inferno*: 'come si spiegherebbe tanta severità nel volere qui applicato un principio generale che dovrebbe essere applicato a tutto l'Inferno, se Virgilio avea piú volte lasciato che Dante sentisse la guerra della pietà e ne mostrasse gli effetti, come dinanzi a Francesca, a Ciacco, a Pier della Vigna, a Brunetto Latini, ad altri tre Fiorentini, e questo senza fargliene mai rimprovero, non solo, ma talvolta anche assecondandolo, come per i tre Fiorentini (*Inf.* XVI, 13–18), e partecipando lui stesso al sentimento di riverente pietà, come per Pier della Vigna, per Diomede e Ulisse? (*Inf.* XIII e XXVI)' (Enrico Mestica, *ad Inf.* XX, 28–30 (DDP)).
[58] Siro A. Chimenz, *ad Inf.* XX, 28–30, lists Virgil's displays of compassion at *Inf.* IV, 19–21 and 43; V, 109–11; XIII, 50–4 and 84; XIV, 1–3; XVI, 10–18 and XXIX, 1–30 (DDP).

(championed by Ernesto Parodi in a 1908 article)[59] has been found inconsistent at worst[60] and strained at best,[61] typically bringing to bear the apparent contradiction with a passage from *Paradiso* to disprove it.[62] Made cautious or hermeneutically despairing by the debate, many recent commentators have chosen not to take a stance or to confess to the dilemmas in taking one.[63]

It is true, as these critics lament, that the text of the passage is already particularly cryptic;[64] yet long-range contradictions beyond the confines of the cantica complicate the issues it raises even further. The idea that questioning the dispositions of divine justice may be impious is explicitly rejected by Beatrice in *Paradiso* IV;[65] and the notion that God is not affected by good deeds, wishes, and prayers is openly contradicted by the eagle of justice in *Paradiso* XX.[66] In both instances, the comparison with *Inferno* XX is supported by striking formal parallels. Thus, if one appeals to internal consistency as a hermeneutic criterion, teleology seems to offer a solution to the contradiction inherent in the two passages. In this case, the interpreter's task seems to be to give priority to the passage of the last cantica over its infernal counterpart and find a way to interpret the former in light of the latter. However, if, faced with these hermeneutic difficulties, one takes

---

[59] Ernesto G. Parodi, 'La critica della poesia classica del ventesimo canto dell'*Inferno*', in *Atene e Roma*, 11 (1908), 183-95. Among the commentators, this interpretation has its advocates in Mestica, Steiner, Scartazzini-Vandelli, V. Rossi, Chimenz, Comparetti, Chiavacci Leonardi, Hollander (*ad loc.*, DDP).

[60] Manfredi Porena and Daniele Mattalia, *ad Inf.* XX, 29-30 (DDP).

[61] Attilio Momigliano, *ad Inf.* XX, 29-30 and Natalino Sapegno, *ad* 28-30 (DDP).

[62] 'Prima di tutto non è vero che la predizione del futuro sia uno sforzare i destini segnati da Dio (cfr. *Par.* XVII, 37-45)' (Manfredi Porena, *ad Inf.* XX, 29-30 (DDP)). The passage he refers to denies that prescience involves determinism, as following: 'La contingenza, che fuor del quaderno | de la vostra matera non si stende, | tutta è dipinta nel cospetto etterno: | necessità però quindi non prende | se non come dal viso in che si specchia | nave che per torrente giù discende.'

[63] These commentators include Grandgent, Grabher, Provenzal, Momigliano, Sapegno, Fallani, Giacalone, Bosco-Reggio, Pasquini-Quaglio (*ad loc.*, DDP); Pietrobono offers a third interpretation, also based on referring the terzina, restrictedly, to the diviners (*ad loc.*, DDP).

[64] Attilio Momigliano, *ad Inf.* XX, 29-30 (DDP). It is interesting that Momigliano uses here the word 'oscuro', as the fiction of the *Commedia* does attribute obscurity to the infernal language of the *porta dell'inferno*: 'queste parole di colore oscuro' (*Inf.* III, 10).

[65] The passage in question is the famous terzina 'Parere ingiusta la nostra giustizia | ne li occhi d'i mortali, è argomento | di fede e non d'eretica nequizia' (*Par.* IV, 67-9). The paradox that 'giustizia' may appear 'ingiusta' in *Paradiso* is formally mindful of the paradox that the 'pietà' should be dead in order to be truly alive in *Inferno*.

[66] I am referring to the lines '*Regnum celorum* vïolenza pate | da caldo amore e da viva speranza, | che vince la divina volontate' (*Par.* XX, 94-6). The formal parallels are discussed right below. See also *Purg.* VI, 28-46, where Virgil himself maintains that God is affected by prayers (so long as they do not come from pagans).

paradox as a narrative model, the criterion of internal consistency has to be set aside and the tension between passages of the *Inferno* and the *Paradiso* becomes an irreducible starting point. Compare the passage quoted above with its vertical counterpart, *Paradiso* XX:

> *Regnum celorum* vïolenza pate
> da caldo amore e da viva speranza,
> che vince la divina volontate:
>   non a guisa che l'omo a l'om sobranza,
> ma vince lei perché vuole esser vinta,
> e, vinta, vince con sua beninanza.
>
> [Regnum celorum suffers violence
> from fervent love and living hope.
> These conquer the very will of God,
>   not as man may master man, but conquer it
> because it would be conquered, and,
> once conquered, itself conquers by its goodness.]
>
> (*Par.* XX, 94–9)

The parallel between this passage of *Paradiso* XX and its infernal counterpart is evident.[67] The eagle talks of a violence that affects and overcomes both the realm of Heaven and the very will of God, thereby effectively paraphrasing the words of the 'scellerato…| che al giudicio divin passion comporta' (*Inf.* XX, 29–30) as interpreted by Parodi and others. The verb *pate* ['suffers'], used by the eagle, is an etymological match for Virgil's *passion* ['passion']; both cast God in a theologically tricky position of passivity to human agency. The contradiction lies in the fact that whereas in *Inferno* this divine possibility is refuted as an impiety, in *Paradiso* it is authoritatively affirmed.

The keyword, then, is *passion*. In his essay '*Passio* as passion', which also discusses the passage from *Paradiso* XX, Erich Auerbach traces the semantic and cultural development of the term *passio* from its etymological roots of passive suffering to a Christian idea of suffering as a redemptive activity, and beyond. What is unprecedented about this paradoxical concept of

---

[67] For more structural connections between the vertical cantos *Inferno* XX, *Purgatorio* XX, and *Paradiso* XX, see Claudia Rossignoli, 'Prediction, Prophecy, and Predestination: Eternalising Poetry in the *Commedia*', in *Vertical Readings in Dante's 'Comedy': Volume 2*, ed. George Corbett and Heather Webb (Cambridge: Open Book Publishers, 2016), pp. 193–215.

passio, in Auerbach's view, is its distinctive capacity to 'move between two poles that stand in opposition to one another.'[68] The Passion of Christ, for Auerbach, provides a model for Christians, whose 'goal was not to withdraw from the world as a way of avoiding suffering and passion. Instead they intended to prevail over the world precisely by suffering.'[69]

A similar model of suffering can be seen as emerging behind the irreducibly paradoxical lesson of *Inferno* XX and *Paradiso* XX. Not only does this paradoxical understanding make up the substance of the eagle's speech on God's will as prevailing over the world by being prevailed upon ('vince lei perché vuol esser vinta, | e, vinta, vince con sua beninanza' ['but conquer it | because it would be conquered, and, | once conquered, itself conquers by its goodness'], *Par.* XX, 98–9), but it also informs the interesting correlation between the two passages of *Inferno* and *Paradiso*. From the nudge to Christ's Passion in the keywords *passion* and *pate*, to the biblical allusion to his advent in the line '*Regnum celorum* vïolenza pate' lifted *verbatim* from Matthew 11:12 ('regnum caelorum vim patitur et violenti rapiunt illud' ['the kingdom of heaven suffereth violence, and the violent take it by force']), the text alternatingly affirms in *Inferno* and *Paradiso* first what is called, in theological terms, God's impassibility and then its opposite, God's passibility. And indeed Dante's poem offers a complete representation both of the inflexibility of God's justice and the openness of his mercy, expressed, as Teodolinda Barolini observed, with Dante's trademark 'alternating strategy', whereby the poet seeks to 'accommodate synchronic paradox to the unfolding diachrony of his text'.[70] Such an understanding of the long-range contradictions of the *Commedia* is only possible if one takes them at their word. The narrative model of paradox thus helps us resist the teleological reading that makes internal contradiction a justification for its hierarchical ordering of the text in value-laden views of *before* and *after*.

1.4 Coexistence of Narrative Models of Teleology and Paradox

The seamless alternation between different narrative models is the most striking mark of Dante's narrative pluralism. Although the proportion of

---

[68] Erich Auerbach, '*Passio* as passion' [1941], in *Time, History, and Literature: Selected Essays of Erich Auerbach*, ed. James I. Porter, trans. Jane O. Newman (Princeton, NJ: Princeton University Press, 2014), pp. 165–87 (p. 179).
[69] Auerbach, '*Passio* as passion', p. 170.   [70] Barolini, *Undivine 'Comedy'*, p. 193.

text devoted to the various models varies as the story progresses, there is no definitive shift from one model to another, no forthright abjuration of one in the name of another. Indeed, the very idea that there should be a palinode is imparted by the dominant model of the teleological masterplot, which, as I have shown, is internal to the fiction. In practice, the *Commedia* remains agile in its alternation of the various models, and it demands similar agility from its readers to the very end. The coexistence of the different narrative models is the subject of the following three subsections, which centre on the last canto of the poem, *Paradiso* XXXIII, in order to show three seamless ways in which the *Commedia* catches the reader in the act of experiencing and performing its paradoxes.

1.4.1 Teleological Plot and Paradoxical Content

The last canto of *Paradiso* is possibly the most forward-driven of the *Commedia*. At the level of the plot, it contains the fulfilment of the desire that fuels the protagonist's journey, the desire that moves everyone to their ultimate end. The whole of *Paradiso*, if not the entire *Commedia*, has been anticipating and building up to this moment; the plot of the poem is even recapitulated once more in Bernard's speech, where it is described as one continuous movement leading up to the vision of the 'ultima salute':

> Or questi, che da l'infima lacuna
> de l'universo infin qui ha vedute
> le vite spiritali ad una ad una,
>   supplica a te, per grazia, di virtute
> tanto, che possa con li occhi levarsi
> più alto verso l'ultima salute.
>
> [This man who, from within the deepest pit
> the universe contains up to these heights
> has seen the disembodied spirits, one by one,
>   now begs you, by your grace, to grant such power
> that, by lifting up his eyes,
> he may rise higher toward his ultimate salvation.]
>   (*Par.* XXXIII, 22–7)

The two terzinas sum up the *Commedia*'s basic plot from beginning to end, which are arched from the prominent rhyme-words 'infima lacuna | de l'universo' ['deepest pit | the universe contains'] to the 'ultima salute' ['ultimate salvation']. In reading these lines, the readers' desire to make sense of the sentence and its syntax suspensefully draws them forward to the last words, which point towards the story's impending and ultimate vision of God. About a hundred lines later, the final vision of God—it seems inevitable to use such rich adjectives as 'final' and 'ultimate' when discussing it—will appear at the end of the book, in a textual place that is structurally decisive, establishing once and for all the meaning of the entire work. The solidarity between plot and structure, in the microcosm of these lines as well as in the poem as a whole, is very significant here; it can be appreciated all the more if we consider that this solidarity is built into the poem deliberately by its author. The protagonist's desire for the end of his journey and the reader's desire for the ending of the book join forces and overlap to bring the narrative to its climax. The 'end' of the *Paradiso*, in all its connotations of 'conclusion', 'aim', 'fulfilment', is where both the protagonist's and the reader's desire are fulfilled, where the ultimate meaning of the journey and the text lies.[71] Indeed, so persuasive is the teleological masterplot at work here that no discussion of *Paradiso* XXXIII can resist including the charged descriptors 'final', 'last', 'ultimate', 'end'. In this, one follows in the wake of Dante's own crafty appropriation of these words in his last canto.[72] Teleology is most powerful at the *telos* of the *logos*: right at the end of the text.

And yet, for all its unequivocal teleological investment, *Paradiso* XXXIII is also the canto of paradox and the narrative model associated with it. The canto begins with the oxymora quoted above that portray Mary in a paradoxical language that aims to neutralize the hierarchy of time. The 'action' of the canto consists in the vision of three great philosophical and theological paradoxes: the problem of the one and the many (represented as a book binding together the quires scattered throughout the universe, 85–93), the mystery of the Trinity (three circles of different colours and the same size, 115–20), and the mystery of the Incarnation (our human image

---

[71] Elena Lombardi has explored the relationship between desire and syntax in her *The Syntax of Desire: Language and Love in Augustine, the Modistae, Dante* (Toronto: University of Toronto Press, 2007), to which I am indebted in this discussion.
[72] Blurring the lines between fiction and text, the word 'fine', its synonyms, and their cognates appear repeatedly in the last canto of the *Commedia*: 'termine' (3), 'ultima salute' (27), 'fine di tutt' i disii' (46), 'l'ardor del desiderio in me finii' (48), 'quasi tutta cessa mia visione' (61), and then, antonymically, 'valore infinito' (81); I disagree with Teodolinda Barolini, then, when she claims that *Paradiso* XXXIII 'den[ies] beginnings and endings' and 'evades narrative distinctions' (*Undivine 'Comedy'*, p. 252); in the recurrence of 'fine' and its synonyms Dante seems rather to parade them—teleology is never defeated.

inscribed inside one of the circles, 127–31). In the text, these mysteries appear—as they must—in temporal succession. In a trademark move, Dante is perfectly aware of the problem of representing eternity in a time-bound text and tries to displace the textual problem onto his fiction:

> Non perché più ch'un semplice sembiante
> fosse nel vivo lume ch'io mirava,
> che tal è sempre qual s'era davante;
> ma per la vista che s'avvalorava
> in me guardando, una sola parvenza,
> mutandom'io, a me si travagliava.
>
> [Not that the living Light at which I gazed
> took on other than a single aspect—
> for It is always what It was before—
> but that my sight was gaining strength, even as I gazed
> at that sole semblance and, as I changed,
> it too was being, in my eyes, transformed.]
>
> (*Par.* XXXIII, 109–14)

These lines explain the successive appearance of the three mysteries as the phenomenological perception of Dante; in the central line of the terzinas, the object of the vision is expressly said to remain, in itself, unchanged and beyond temporal succession ('for It is always what It was before', 111). Around this line, however, the subjective change of perception is expressed with words that subtend progress, a teleological development leading to a definitive vision. The verb 's'avvalorava' ['was gaining strength'] (112) that refers to Dante's sight, in fact, signifies improvement, refinement. Its temporality is fully teleological, suggesting a hierarchy between the visions. As has often been the case in the *Paradiso*, the more Dante sees, the stronger his senses become ('my sight was gaining strength', 'as I changed', 112 and 113); the stronger they become, the more clearly he is able to see ('that sole semblance |…was being, in my eyes, transformed', 113–14). The last canto is but a dramatization of this paradisiacal ploy of increased sight, with its three successive visions apparently getting closer and closer to the transcendent 'truth'.

It may be helpful to think back to the scholastic model of paradox discussed above, whereby the content of a paradoxical statement can be explained in another form as one's understanding of it matures. In this positivistic understanding of paradox contradictions are only such in appearance and can be dissolved into a non-paradoxical form. As I have shown in discussing *Paradiso* XIII above, this practice of solving paradox is often dramatized in the *Commedia*'s narrative of doubts, questions, and answers through which Dante reaches greater and clearer knowledge, and thus drives the narrative forward. In part, this is also the case in the last canto of *Paradiso*. In the threefold vision described there, however, the three mysteries are never explained in a non-paradoxical form, but Dante simply abandons each vision in turn for the next one. Thus, although the entire episode of the final vision is constructed as a progressive path toward increased sight and understanding, in practice it remains but a succession of unexplained mysteries. The teleological model is at work in the ploy of improving vision, serving its narrative function as it drives forward the narrative; it gives a sense of developing 'action', appealing to a readerly desire for a plot, as we are led to believe that where there is improvement of understanding, the reader is getting closer to a final 'truth'. Yet at the same time, even as the verb 's'avvalorava' suggests otherwise, the fiction soberly reminds us that there is no hierarchy between the coexistence of the one and the many, the coexistence of three in one, and the coexistence of the divine and the human. The three visions represent three different mysteries of the same God, and these remain in paradoxical tension with one another. They remain, in other words, equivalent—unteleologized. Once more, Dante manages readerly expectations that time should carry a hierarchy, an expectation that he himself has planted in his readers and that he now successfully counteracts with the alternative model of paradox.

1.4.2 The 'Time' of Antanaclasis

The last of the three visions of *Paradiso* XXXIII offers the final example of paradox counteracting time. The object of the vision is the mystery of the Incarnation, which appears to Dante as our human image painted in the same colour as the circle of the Trinity in which it is inscribed.[73] The terzinas that portray this vision suspensefully withhold the syntactic resolution of the sentence until the fifth line, where the image contained in the circle— the 'nostra effige'—is finally revealed:

---

[73] On the hermeneutic model offered by the paradox of the incarnation, see Guy P. Raffa, *Divine Dialectic: Dante's Incarnational Poetry* (Toronto: University of Toronto Press, 2000).

>Quella circulazion che sì concetta
>pareva in te come lume reflesso,
>da li occhi miei alquanto circunspetta,
>   dentro da sé, del suo colore stesso,
>mi parve pinta di nostra effige:
>per che 'l mio viso in lei tutto era messo.

>[That circling which, thus conceived,
>appeared in you as light's reflection,
>once my eyes had gazed on it a while, seemed,
>   within itself and in its very color,
>to be painted in our likeness,
>so that my sight was all absorbed in it.]

>   (*Par.* XXXIII, 127–32)

The syntax of the sentence comes to rest on the image of 'our likeness', which Dante finds at the peak of his vision of the Trinity, while the most paradoxical aspect of the vision described—the fact that our image is visible in the circle even though it is 'del suo colore stesso'—is easily skipped over by the reader eager to find out the content of the protagonist's vision. What Dante has seen is something impossible to see, a visual paradox, an image that can somehow be discerned though not discernible from its background.[74] Dante parodies the attempt to understand such an image rationally, with the celebrated simile of the geometer wholly bent on squaring the circle and failing to make sense of it rationally (133–6). He then returns once more to the paradoxical image he has crafted:

>tal era io a quella vista nova:
>veder voleva come si convenne
>l'imago al cerchio e come vi s'indova.

>[such was I at that strange new sight.
>I tried to see how the image fit the circle
>and how it found its where in it.]

>   (*Par.* XXXIII, 136–8)

---

[74] Several commentators have noted the impossibility of the image: Raffaello Andreoli, *ad Par.* XXXIII, 127–32; G. A. Scartazzini, *ad* l. 130; Giacomo Poletto, *ad* ll. 127–32; Carlo Steiner, *ad* ll. 130–1; Carlo Grabher, *ad* ll. 127–32; Ernesto Trucchi, *ad* ll. 127–32; Emilio Pasquini and Antonio Quaglio, *ad* ll. 127–31; Anna Maria Chiavacci Leonardi, *ad* ll. 130. Nicola Fosca, *ad* ll. 127–32 (DDP). See also Mirko Tavoni, 'La visione di Dio nell'ultimo canto del *Paradiso*', in *Dire l'indicibile: Esperienza religiosa e poesia dalla Bibbia al Novecento*, ed. Cesare Letta (Pisa: Edizioni ETS, 2009), pp. 65–112 (p. 82 and *passim*).

The vision that appears to the protagonist is the visual equivalent of the rhetorical figure of 'antanaclasis'. As the antanaclasis requires one to recognize two different meanings in two words that look identical—as Dante does when punningly pairing *ombra* (shadow) and *ombre* (souls) in *Purgatorio* XXVI, 7–9[75]—so here readers are asked to discern two different images in the same colour. Dante is neither new to this trope nor to its visual equivalent; indeed, he often couples them in the same canto. 'Visual antanaclases' are found, for instance, in the image of the indiscernible 'perla in bianca fronte' ['so faint a pearl on a pallid forehead'] of *Paradiso* III, 14, used to represent the souls' deceptively insubstantial appearance in the heaven of the moon;[76] or in the simile of the hoar frost that is mistaken for snow in *Inferno* XXIV, 4–5 ('la brina in su la terra assempra | l'imagine di sua sorella bianca' ['when the hoar frost copies out upon the fields | the very image of her snowy sister']). All these instances filter the image through the eyes of a viewer inside the fiction; however, whereas the sameness of the two images in the previous cantos is revealed to be a misperception, the paradoxical colour identity of the circle and our human image in *Paradiso* XXXIII does hold up to Dante's scrutiny. The protagonist in the fiction finds that the last vision he sees is not an apparent antanaclasis but a literal one that resists resolution. Between the first two antanaclastic images and the one in *Paradiso* XXXIII, then, there is the same qualitative difference that we find between the poetic and literal oxymora: one is a figure of speech that can be explained away; the other points to an irreducible reality.

There is more to the last vision of *Paradiso* XXXIII. With the visual antanaclasis, it expresses the mystery of the Trinity not through a rhetorical figure that takes place in time but through an image, which in the fiction is non-temporal, simultaneous. This is, of course, a fictional, mental, and

---

[75] 'e io facea con l'*ombra* più rovente | parer la fiamma; e pur a tanto indizio | vidi molt'*ombre*, andando, poner mente' (*Purg.* XXVI, 7–9).

[76] John Freccero calls this an 'anti-image'. As he comments, '[The] comparison is obviously self-defeating' and 'irreducibly literary' (*Poetics of Conversion*, pp. 212–13). Teodolinda Barolini relates visual image and antanaclasis (in the form of a *rima equivoca*) in her discussion of *Paradiso* III: 'The image of the pearl on a white forehead ("perla in bianca fronte" [*Par*. III, 14]) visually relays the idea of subtle shades of difference within an overarching unity (in this case the whiteness that encompasses both pearl and forehead), as, in the linguistic sphere, do the rhyme words "vòto" ("empty") and "vóto" ("vow"): here the same sound encompasses two different meanings' (*Undivine 'Comedy'*, p. 182). Guy P. Raffa affords a similar insight with regard to *Inferno* XXIV, the canto with the highest density of *rime equivoche*: 'The repetition of the word *piglio* (21, 24) is the third instance of equivocal rhyme in the opening verses of canto XXIV. These examples of poetic doubling, two words which look and sound the same but have different meaning, reinforce the image of doubling, the hoar frost that is mistaken for snow' (*Divine Dialectic*, p. 41).

entirely impossible image. Its impossibility, however, does not exactly take place on the page in the same way as that of oxymora and paradoxes, which are verbal and immediately recognizable as paradoxes; instead, it relies on the reader to try to construct in her imagination a vision that is impossible to see. The insistence on the verbs of seeing in these lines is not another technique of verisimilitude but aims to invite the reader to imitate the protagonist in imagining an impossibility. It is important to notice at this point that the language of the last vision refrains from overtly paradoxical figures of speech such as oxymoron. Yet although the perfectly 'normal' expression 'dentro da sé, del suo colore stesso' is immediately intelligible, it is impossible to conceive the image it is describing. It is indeed true, as Robin Kirkpatrick matter-of-factly points out, that the imagery of the last canto does not contain a 'sequence of paradoxes or of "clues" but a conspicuously normal presentation of colours, shapes, numbers and consequences'.[77] The paradox, in fact, does not lie in the 'conspicuously normal' words it uses but one step removed, in the impossible image they encourage the reader to construct in her imagination.

The visual antanaclasis functions by asking the reader to perform the impossibility that an oxymoron more blatantly depicts in words. Both tropes declare their own fictionality, but the oxymoron is immediately recognizable on the page, while the visual antanaclasis takes a second longer to register. That second is a time that does not extend on the page in the same way as the swift but recognizable juxtaposition of words of the oxymoron but elapses within the reader, who is asked to try to construct an impossible image, inevitably fails, and returns to the image. This very movement is dramatized in the plot of the lines quoted (127–38), which move from the impossible circle to the failing geometer, and back. The reader, similarly to the protagonist, experiences what the 'paradoxicality' of the hypostatic union of the human and divine nature of Christ feels like; she experiences it not in the time of the words on the page but in the time it takes her to

---

[77] Kirkpatrick, *Dante's 'Paradiso'*, p. 150. Kirkpatrick sees 'the stable phrase', as he calls it, as a characteristic feature of the poetry of the *Paradiso*. Cf. also the introduction to his translation of Dante's *Inferno* (London: Penguin, 2006), which stresses the importance of 'plain style and syntax' in the *Commedia* (p. ciii). On Dante's plain language see also T. S. Eliot, 'Dante' [1929], *Selected Essays*, 3rd rev. edn (London: Faber & Faber, 1951) pp. 237–77, p. 252; Giuseppe Ledda's comments on the 'parole...nude' of *Purgatorio* XXXIII, 100–1 ('*Tópoi* dell'indicibilità e metaforismi nella *Commedia*', *Strumenti Critici*, 83.1 (1997), 117–141, pp. 139–40); and Elena Lombardi on the 'chiare parole e...preciso | latin' of *Par.* XVIII, 34–5 (*The Syntax of Desire*, pp. 143–4).

realize that the image is impossible.[78] In a discursive text, meaning is created through a string of words that are read in time; but in the last canto of the *Paradiso* time is contracted and so the reader is given responsibility for taking over the function that time has in a text. Meaning then takes place not in the time of the text but in the time it takes the reader to imagine the impossible circle, and fail.

1.4.3 The Ineffability Topos

It is not by chance, then, that the dialectics between words and their failure are one of the great themes of the *Commedia*. We have already encountered this leitmotif in the celebrated terzina from the first canto of the *Paradiso*, where Dante declares the impossibility of putting into words the experience of transcending one's human limitations. The narrator of the *Commedia* cites a series of obstacles to the writing of his poem: the insufficiency of the protagonist's senses, the failure of his memory to retain what he did see and hear, and the inadequacy of language to express the little that he managed to retain.[79] Indeed, as the author declares in the first canto, the subject of the last cantica is not Heaven per se but only the portion that the narrator still remembers: 'quant'io del regno santo | ne la mia mente potei far tesoro' ['as much of the holy kingdom | as I could store as treasure in my mind'] (*Par.* I, 10–11). There is a noticeable shift, here, from the ineffability of the *Inferno* and *Purgatorio*. In the first canto of *Inferno*, the narrator attributes the inability to 'ridir' how he came to the dark wood to a drowsiness which is temporary, personal, and morally charged ('io non so ben ridir com'i' v'intrai, | tant'era pien di sonno a quel punto' ['How I came there I cannot really tell, | I was so full of sleep'], *Inf.* I, 10–11). In contrast, in the parallel canto of *Paradiso*, the lines,

---

[78] In his monograph, Guy Raffa takes precisely the mystery of the incarnation as the quintessential symbol of Dante's paradoxical poetics: by means of his 'incarnational dialectics', Dante promotes a paradoxical, "both-and" way of reading his poetry—a hermeneutics that serves, in turn, as a model for thinking and being in the world' (Raffa, *Divine Dialectic*, p. 4).

[79] Dante draws a distinction between conceptual and linguistic 'ineffabilitadi' in *Conv.* II, iii, 14–15; see Ledda, '*Tópoi* dell'indicibilità e metaforismi nella *Commedia*', p. 128. For the most recent review of the occurrences of the different ineffability topoi in the *Commedia*, see Giuseppe Ledda, 'Teologia e retorica dell'ineffabilità nella *Commedia* di Dante', in *Le teologie di Dante*, ed. Giuseppe Ledda (Ravenna: Centro Dantesco dei Frati Minori Conventuali, 2015), pp. 261–92.

> e vidi cose che ridire
> né sa né può chi di là su discende.
> [He who comes down from there
> can neither know nor tell what he has seen.]
>
> (*Par.* I, 5-6)

make use of the impersonal subject *chi* and the gnomic present tenses *sa*, *può*, and *discende*. The inability to *ridir* Heaven is not personal and transient but universal and definitive, a structural problem; the allusion contained in these lines to Paul's own inability to tell his experience of the afterlife (2 Corinthians 12:2-3) serves as an authoritative reference for Dante's statement. This is the first instance in the cantica of a staple of the poetry of the *Paradiso* and one of its distinguishing features: the so-called 'ineffability topos'. The bibliography expressly dedicated to the subject is considerable;[80] but virtually all scholars of the *Paradiso* have to confront the paradox of a cantica that routinely states the inexpressibility of Heaven even as it devotes 4,758 lines of poetry to its expression.

This is, of course, a paradox;[81] and like the other paradoxes of the *Commedia* it tempts scholars to take sides when it comes to interpreting it. This is especially evident in the case of *Paradiso* XXXIII, a canto whose movement is articulated over three successive professions of ineffability, each contradicted in turn by the following description of the three mysteries.[82]

---

[80] Cf. Luigi Tonelli, *Dante e la poesia dell'ineffabile* (Florence: Barbera, 1934); Francesco Tateo, 'Il tema dell'ineffabile', in *Questioni di poetica dantesca* (Bari: Adriatica, 1972), pp. 173-200; Peter S. Hawkins, 'Dante's *Paradiso* and the dialectic of ineffability', in *Ineffability: Naming the Unnamable*, ed. Peter S. Hawkins and Anne Howland Schotter (New York: AMS Press, 1984), pp. 5-21; Colombo, *Dai mistici a Dante*; Steven Botterill, '"Quae non licet homini loqui": The Ineffability of Mystical Experience in *Paradiso* I and the "Epistle to Can Grande"', *Modern Language Review*, 83.3 (1988), 332-41; Claire E. Honess, 'Expressing the Inexpressible: The Theme of Communication in the Heaven of Mars', *Lectura Dantis*, 14-15 (1994), 42-60; Angelo Jacomuzzi, 'Ond'io son fatto scriba', in *L'imago al cerchio e altri saggi sulla 'Divina Commedia'* (Milan: Angeli, 1995), pp. 29-100 and 'Il topos dell'ineffabile nel *Paradiso*', ibid., pp. 78-113; Giuseppe Ledda, *La guerra della lingua: Ineffabilità, retorica e narrativa nella 'Commedia' di Dante* (Ravenna: Longo, 2002); Giuseppe Polimeni, 'Grammatica e stile dell'ineffabile: Spitzer legge Dante', in *Leo Spitzer: Lo stile e il metodo*, ed. Ivano Paccagnella and Elisa Gregori (Padua: Esedra, 2010), pp. 371-9. For the 'inexpressibility topos' in the Latin Middle Ages, see Ernst Robert Curtius's concise section in *European Literature and the Latin Middle Ages*, trans. Willard R. Trask (London: Routledge & Kegan Paul, 1953), pp. 159-62.

[81] David Mikics comments on this in his entry on the subject: 'the inexpressibility topos often carries with it an automatic paradox' ('Inexpressibility topos', in Mikics, *New Handbook of Literary Terms*, p. 156).

[82] The three inexpressibility topoi proper are 'Da quinci innanzi il mio veder fu maggio | che 'l parlar mostra, ch' a tal vista cede, | e cede la memoria a tanto oltraggio' (*Par.* XXXIII, 55-7), 'Omai sarà più corta mia favella, | pur a quel ch'io ricordo, che d'un fante | che bagni ancor la

As with the other ineffability topoi of the *Paradiso*, scholars are generally divided into those who place the emphasis on the 'negative' moment of the profession of ineffability and those who stress, rather, the 'positive' moment of expression.[83] Take the following famous terzina:

> Da quinci innanzi il mio veder fu maggio
> che 'l parlar mostra, ch'a tal vista cede,
> e cede la memoria a tanto oltraggio.
>
> [From that time on my power of sight exceeded
> that of speech, which fails at such a vision,
> as memory fails at such abundance.]
>
> (*Par.* XXXIII, 55–7)

In interpreting this and the similes that follow, 'cataphatic' scholars hark back to the literary tradition of the ineffability topos as grounds for dismissing the claim of ineffability as a rhetorical convention set to play up the difficulty inherent in the subject matter and thus show off the author's prowess;[84] conversely, 'apophatic' scholars take the topos at its word and seek to show how the *Paradiso*'s language 'breaks down'[85] and surrenders to 'silence'.[86] One can see how each reading might appeal to a specific interpretation of the *Commedia*, by promoting an image of its author as, say, proud proto-modern layman or awed Christian mystic. Although the two interpretations may be at odds in their ideological stance, in this case they share a methodological assumption: they take for granted some kind of determining relationship between what the fictional narrator says and the way the *Commedia* should be interpreted, even as they disagree over the

---

lingua a la mammella' (106–8), and 'Oh quanto è corto il dire e come fioco | al mio concetto! e questo, a quel ch'i' vidi, | è tanto, che non basta a dicer "poco"' (121–3), to which perhaps the 'per tal modo | che ciò ch'i' dico è un semplice lume' (89–90). The canto also refers twice to the inadequacy of the senses and intellect (139, 142) and once more to the failure of memory (94–6).

[83] The two moments are sometimes referred to as 'apophatic' and 'cataphatic', borrowing the Greek forms used in Pseudo-Dionysius the Areopagite, *De mystica theologia*, ch. 3. See Harmless, *Mystics*, p. 101, and Paul Rorem, *Pseudo-Dionysius: A Commentary on the Texts and an Introduction to their Influence* (New York and Oxford: Oxford University Press, 1993), pp. 194–205.

[84] Emblematic of this position is James Miller: 'His fallback to speechless wonder is playfully ironic: what the ineffable topos is meant to signal here is, as usual, the very opposite of what it literally means' ('Introduction: Retheologizing Dante', in *Dante and the Unorthodox: The Aesthetics of Transgression*, ed. James Miller (Waterloo, ON: Wilfrid Laurier University Press, 2005), pp. 1–62 (p. 2)). On the rhetorical tradition of the topos, cf. Ernst Robert Curtius's contribution, noted above, and Giuseppe Ledda's analysis of the ineffable in the *Inferno*, which he relates to traditional hyperbole ('Teologia e retorica dell'ineffabilità nella *Commedia* di Dante', p. 283).

[85] Miller, 'Introduction: Retheologizing Dante', p. 2.

[86] See, for instance, Hawkins, 'Dante's *Paradiso* and the dialectic of ineffability', p. 9.

sense of the relationship by taking the ineffability topos as either 'playfully ironic' or in earnest.[87] In doing this, both camps are engaging in what Teodolinda Barolini calls 'theologizing':[88] judging the fiction in terms promoted by the fiction itself and which do not necessarily reflect the workings of the text. This may seem perhaps more evident in the case of the 'apophatic' readers. It is particularly misleading, for instance, to talk about the language of the *Paradiso* 'breaking down', as this overlooks the fact that the *Paradiso* uses some of the plainest language of the poem when it is at its most paradoxical, as my analysis of the visual antanaclasis has aimed to show;[89] it is even more perplexing to insist on the 'silence' of language in the face of the evidence that, for all the ineffability of the mysteries of the last canto, the text does go on to represent them for a further number of lines. 'Cataphatic' readings, on the other hand, may seem to show a more sophisticated understanding of the text, insofar as they take into account the fact that the narration continues after the profession of ineffability. These readings typically use this as evidence for interpreting the ineffability ironically, as a clever wink to the reader. And yet, in so doing such readings are no less subject to the guidelines embedded in the fiction than their 'apophatic' counterpart. In explaining the narrator's profession of ineffability as ironic in light of the poetry that follows it, 'cataphatic' readings base their interpretation on the criterion of temporal hierarchy promoted by the fiction of the *Commedia*. The teleological prejudice can be distinctly perceived in James Miller's discussion of the topos:

> [Dante] has trained us through nearly a hundred cantos…to read the temporary 'failure' of his words as a cue for the imminent triumph of speech over silence—the ecstatic silence that paradoxically gives rise to the inexhaustible 'effability' of the Sacred Poem![90]

Miller's temporal expressions 'temporary failure', 'imminent triumph', and 'gives rise to', and his discounting of the ineffability as a mere 'cue' for what follows it, order the succession of ineffability and 'effability' in a teleological

---

[87] Miller, 'Introduction: Retheologizing Dante', p. 2. Robin Kirkpatrick also notices the irony 'that the inexpressibility topos elicits from [Dante]…some of his most highly wrought and complex poetry' but does not share Miller's conclusions ('Introduction', in Dante, *Paradiso*, trans. Robin Kirkpatrick (London: Penguin, 2007), p. lix).
[88] Barolini, *Undivine 'Comedy'*, p. 17.
[89] The adjectives 'plain' and 'simple', along with 'stable' and 'normal', are Robin Kirkpatrick's. For his insistence on the plain style of the *Paradiso* see n. 77 above.
[90] Miller, 'Introduction: Retheologizing Dante', p. 2.

hierarchy where the former points to the latter and is superseded by it. From the present monograph's perspective, however, the interpretation of the ineffability topos in the *Paradiso* must take the move from this fact that, formally, the narrator's professions of inexpressibility take turns on the page with poetic acts of expression. It is precisely this formal alternation, repeated three times in *Paradiso* XXXIII, that offers itself as a starting point for its interpretation. If this alternation is not teleologized but read instead in light of the narrative of paradox, it might be helpful in understanding the workings and meaning of the professions of ineffability of the *Paradiso*. Dante's insistence on alternating them with demonstrations of effability, in other words, is not to be ordered in a teleological hierarchy that privileges one side of the paradox or the other, but the two should, rather, be read simultaneously, as equals in a neutralized time. Only then can the nuances of the fiction be understood. It is true that there is value in taking the narrator seriously and acknowledging that 'when Dante confesses the inadequacy of his words, he means what he says';[91] but, equally, there is also value in taking him seriously when he then describes the indescribable. If one follows through the 'automatic paradox' that 'ineffability carries with it' to its implications,[92] it will be evident that the narrative model that I have analysed over the course of this chapter is particularly relevant for understanding such disclaimers. By not taking for granted the hierarchy of teleological time, the paradoxical model can help make sense of the ineffability topos as a reminder of inexpressibility whenever something is actually expressed; just as the representations of the *Paradiso* act as a counter-reminder whenever the ineffable is professed. Witness the terzina already quoted:

> Da quinci innanzi il mio veder fu maggio
> che 'l parlar mostra, ch'a tal vista cede,
> e cede la memoria a tanto oltraggio.
>
> [From that time on my power of sight exceeded
> that of speech, which fails at such a vision,
> as memory fails at such abundance.]
>
> (*Par.* XXXIII, 55–7)

While it is somewhat absurd to take seriously the narrator's statement that "l parlar...cede' to the point of claiming that the poem is 'stopped in its

---

[91] Kirkpatrick, 'Introduction' to *Dante's 'Paradiso'*, p. lx.
[92] David Mikics, cited in n. 81 above.

tracks..."a tanto oltraggio";[93] it is also misleading to cite the fact that the poem continues for another eighty-eight lines as evidence that the statement is entirely ironic. The *oltraggio* Dante speaks of here is not expressed qua content, in the shape of a perfectly rational description of the mystery of the one and the many that follows this terzina. Rather, the *oltraggio* is performed in the very poetic act of going beyond the ineffability topos with words. The coexistence and equivalence of ineffability and effability, in a paradoxical model, are what accomplish this performance. The cataphatic representation does not delete or surpass the apophatic topos teleologically but works together with the apophatic moment to perform the paradox of its *oltraggio*. It is not the *representation* of the *oltraggio* that expresses something of its essence but its *performance* in the paradoxical alliance of ineffability and effability that exceeds the laws of human expression and thus captures an essential aspect of the mystic 'reality' it is pointing towards.

The paradoxical alternation between ineffability topos and continued poetic expression takes advantage of paradox's ability to neutralize teleological time. The paradoxical model frees up time as a building block in the narrative construction of the *Paradiso*, and thus opens up for Dante the possibility of expressing an essential trait of the transcendent, excessive, *oltraggiosa* 'reality' that is the subject matter of the *Paradiso*.[94] This 'reality' is not put into words directly—by expressing the ineffable qua content (which is impossible)—but indirectly—by performing the paradoxical form of ineffability which is then left for the reader to experience. Just like the oxymoron, the long-range paradox, and the visual antanaclasis, the ineffability topos and its blatant contradiction through more writing hold together two unresolved antinomies. In doing this, they create a brief illusionistic experience of the aspects of Dante's vision that resist Aristotle's principle of non-contradiction inherent in discursive reasoning. Indeed, the coexistence of the ineffability topos and its contradiction can be read as thematizing the paradoxical workings of the formal devices analysed in this

---

[93] Hawkins, 'Dante's *Paradiso* and the dialectic of ineffability', p. 16. On this *oltraggio*, see Lino Pertile, *La Punta del Disio: Semantica del desiderio nella 'Commedia'* (Fiesole: Cadmo, 2005), pp. 247–63.

[94] Erich Auerbach wrote eloquently of excess as a distinctive character of Dante's universe, which he considered 'richer, deeper, and more dangerous than pagan antiquity's culture of the person, for it inherited from the Christian religion out of which it sprang and which it finally overcame a sense of disquiet and a drive towards excessiveness' (Erich Auerbach, *Dante: Poet of the Secular World*, trans. Ralph Manheim (Chicago: University of Chicago Press, 1961), p. 176). As James I. Porter notes, for Auerbach Dante's poem is exemplary of a world that is 'driven not simply by a need for more, but by a need for "too much," for excess (*das Zuviel*)' ('Introduction', in *Time, History and Literature*, p. xxviii).

chapter. These rhetorical tricks all draw attention to the non-discursive form of the text and, by apophatically declaring its insufficiency, make the reader focus on the words of the *Paradiso* even as they cataphatically point beyond them.

1.5 The Role of the Reader

In this chapter I have shown the ways in which the fiction of the *Commedia* manages meaning by divesting of value the antinomies *before/after* and attributing it instead to the binary *fiction/reality*. These two sets of antinomies are the building blocks, respectively, of the teleological masterplot and the narrative model of paradox. Dante's teleology makes meaning by placing the 'truth' of the fiction at the end of a string of words that are read in time; paradox, on the other hand, neutralizes the hierarchy of time so as to make it possible to express self-contradictory truths in a sequence of words without having to resolve an earlier contradictory statement in light of a new one. Meaning, therefore, is no longer entrusted to the time of the text, which is neutralized, but to the time it takes the reader to make rational sense of a paradox and fail. The reader's desire for meaning is thus used to create an illusionistic perception of 'depth' in a text that is otherwise a two-dimensional fiction unfolding through time. Similarly to a painting in perspective, the *Commedia* depicts a distinction between *fiction* and *reality* on the surface of the fiction itself. Paradox thus makes the reader focus closely on the words on the page, while simultaneously exploiting their professed inadequacy and the reader's own desire for meaning to illusionistically conjure up the third dimension where the truth of the text purportedly lies.

The representation of the Trinity that opens the heaven of the sun inhabited by the *spiriti sapienti* will shed light on the hermeneutic process associated with reading the paradoxes of the *Paradiso*. Depictions of the Trinity in the *Commedia* invariably involve a fictional observer, through the eyes of whom this greatest of mysteries is seen:[95]

---

[95] Representations of the Trinity other than the one of *Paradiso* X discussed here are found at *Purg.* III, 34–6, where it is hubristically searched by 'our reason'; *Par.* XIII, 55–60, where it is mirrored in the creation; *Par.* XIII, 25–7, *Par.* XIV, 28–33 and *Par.* XXXI, 28–30, where it is sung or contemplated by the blessed, and *Par.* XXXIII, 115–20 and 124–38.

> Guardando nel suo Figlio con l'Amore
> che l'uno e l'altro etternalmente spira,
> lo primo e ineffabile Valore
> quanto per mente e per loco si gira
> con tant'ordine fé, ch'esser non puote
> sanza gustar di lui chi ciò rimira.
>
> [Gazing on His Son with the Love
> the One and the Other eternally breathe forth,
> the inexpressible and primal Power
> made with such order all things that revolve
> that he who studies it, in mind and in space,
> cannot but taste of Him.]
>
> (*Par.* X, 1-6)

The two terzinas of *Paradiso* X introduce the semantic field of sight from the very first word, 'Guardando' ['Gazing'] (1), which describes the self-reflexive gaze of the Father into the Son in the loving relationship of the Holy Spirit. The syntax of the terzinas is a masterpiece of suspense. Readers do not find out who the subject of the verb 'Guardando' is until the third line 'lo primo e ineffabile Valore' ['the inexpressible and primal Power'] (3); then they do not get the main clause's verb, 'con tanto ordine fé' ['made with such order'], until two lines later (5); even then, the resolution of the syntax is delayed once again, as the adjective 'tanto' ['such'] (5) commits readers to the consecutive clause 'ch'esser non puote | senza gustar di lui' ['that he who studies it...cannot but taste of Him'] (5-6). The grammatical subject and syntactic resolution of this clause are postponed, one last time, until the end of the terzina, in the relative clause 'chi ciò rimira' [literally, 'those who gaze on it'] (6). On these three words the sentence comes to rest. They are a *coup de théâtre*: they turn the reader's attention on the reader, who suddenly recognizes herself as she who gazes, the person holding the whole sentence, and the universe it describes, in her view; and sure enough, Dante goes on to address her as reader in the following lines ('Leva dunque, lettore, a l'alte rote | meco la vista', *Par.* X, 7-9). Rearranging her understanding of the sentence as a series of nested and concentric Chinese boxes, and her position in it, the reader will recognize this representation as a circular *mise en abyme*: here we are, in our universe, reading a work of fiction where we find ourselves represented as we contemplate the God that looks over all of this. The seamless transition between the fiction of the text and the reality of the reader has at its hinge the discovery that a reader, in which you may recognize yourself, is the grammatical subject of the sentence.[96] The person responsible for joining the world of the fiction and that of reality, giving the text its third dimension, is the real reader. The moment she recognizes herself in 'chi ciò rimira', she will have done for Dante the dirty work of welding together fiction and reality, thus setting the seal on the *Commedia*'s narrative illusionism.

The narrative model of paradox requires the reader's collaboration even more than the teleological masterplot, which can count on the inherent temporality of the text in order to charge it with value. It is the reader who, through the act of holding together two contradictory elements and joining them in her mind, creates the illusion of a reality beyond the fiction, where meaning lies. Without a reader mindful enough to experience the performance of the contradiction, paradox is not merely incomplete but a risky poetic strategy, lending itself easily to partial readings that privilege any one aspect over others. Just like the representations of the Trinity in the *Commedia*, the ultimate paradox always needs someone to gaze on it in wonder.

---

[96] Eugenio Montale will remember this syntactic construct in his 'L'anguilla', *La bufera e altro* (Venice: Pozza, 1956). The last lines of the poem, 'puoi tu | non crederla sorella?', reveal the second person 'tu' to have been the grammatical subject of the sentence all along, with a similar recognition/estrangement effect.

2
Alternative Endings and Parallel Lives

Dante's masterplot—his personal take on the Christian narrative of 'innocence, straying, saving divine intervention, repentance and redemption'[1]—finds its most authoritative and purest formulation halfway through the *Commedia*, in Beatrice's speech in the Garden of Eden (*Purg.* XXX, 109–45). At this stage, the pilgrim has already undertaken the first three steps of the journey; the canto then ends on the word 'pentimento'. The last step of redemption, we are led to imagine, does not lie too far ahead.

However, in contrast with the exemplary trajectory of this life story, its plot is, unexpectedly, hijacked. Beatrice retells the momentous facts of Dante's life in the most straightforward possible order, in the indicative mood of storytelling, but two aberrant conditional sentences make an appearance:

> Non pur per ovra de le rote magne,
> che drizzan ciascun seme ad alcun fine
> secondo che le stelle son compagne,
> ma per larghezza di grazie divine,
> che sì alti vapori hanno a lor piova,
> che nostre viste là non van vicine,
> questi fu tal ne la sua vita nova
> virtüalmente, ch'ogne abito destro
> *fatto averebbe* in lui mirabil prova.
>
> [Not only by the working of the wheels above
> that urge each seed to a certain end
> according to the stars that cluster with them,
> but by grace, abundant and divine,
> which rains from clouds so high above
> our sight cannot come near them,

---

[1] Anna Maria Chiavacci Leonardi, 'Introduction' to *Purg.* XXX (DDP).

> this man in this new life potentially was such
> that each good disposition in him
> *would have come* to marvelous conclusion.]
> (*Purg.* XXX, 109–17, italics mine)

Everything in the syntax of these three terzinas—from the suspenseful 'Non pur' / 'ma' (109–11) construct and parallel relative clauses it sustains ('che drizzan', 110; 'che sì alti vapori hanno', 113) to the adverbial clause of result 'tal' / 'che' (115–16)—conspires to delay the disclosure of what Dante was indeed like in his youth. But at the turn of the line, when readers might expect such disclosure to be finally made, it is further deferred by the five-syllable-long word 'virtüalmente' ['potentially' (116)] on which the whole sentence pivots. The three terzinas do not describe what Dante *was* but what he *could have been*, in the conditional ('fatto averebbe' ['would have come'], 117). Spreading out before the reader's eyes is a glimpse of an alternative future, a potential life of marvellous exploits that the protagonist has so far, however, failed to realize.

And so Dante has had to go instead through his personal take on the Christian narrative of conversion, which Beatrice promptly rehearses to her Edenic audience. The pilgrim has had to fall after her death and consequently be saved by journeying through the otherworld; now, he must repent. The second conditional sentence reinstates the inevitable course of his life with the syllogistic necessity of a *reductio ad absurdum*:

> Alto fato di Dio *sarebbe rotto*,
> *se* Letè *si passasse* e tal vivanda
> *fosse gustata* sanza alcuno scotto
>   di pentimento che lagrime spanda.
>
> [*Broken would be* the high decree of God
> *should* Lethe *be crossed* and its sustenance
> *be tasted* without payment of some fee:
>   his penitence that shows itself in tears.]
> (*Purg.* XXX, 142–5, italics mine)

God's high fate cannot possibly be broken; therefore Dante must repent. The conditional's function, here, is to restore narrative necessity and exorcize the very alternatives that the first conditional conjured up.

But why does Dante, at the moment of giving his masterplot its most definitive statement, put it under the pressure of an alternative storyline? If one takes the fiction of the *Commedia* seriously, one soon realizes that such an alternative threatens the work that envisions it. Had Dante lived his virtuous life, he would not have carried out the journey that culminates in the writing of the *Commedia* itself. Through this brief narrative detour, then, Dante exposes the conditions of possibility of his autobiographical masterplot as such. As John Freccero puts it, 'the exigencies of autobiography' place 'a radical discontinuity into the sequence of a life, thanks to which one can tell one's life story as though it were true, definitive, concluded'.[2] Indeed, it is thanks to a radical discontinuity such as that of Dante's sin and conversion that one can tell one's life story at all. The fact that the protagonist's life could have gone differently *then* highlights what makes it significant *now*.

In the following canto, Beatrice asks Dante to identify the moment of discontinuity. When Dante confesses that 'Le presenti cose | col falso lor piacer volser miei passi' ['Things set in front of me, | with their false delights, turned back my steps']—that is, took his life off course—(*Purg.* XXXI, 34–5), Beatrice tells again a contrasting, alternative story. But this time she does not phrase it in terms of what Dante *could* have done but of what he *should* have done:

> sì udirai come in contraria parte
> mover *dovieti* mia carne sepolta.
>
> [Then you shall hear just how my buried flesh
> *should have* directed you to quite a different place.]
>
> (*Purg.* XXXI, 47–8, italics mine)

The verb *dovere* ['should have'] (48), here and three more times over the next four terzinas,[3] expresses the moral imperative of the straight path Dante should have taken even as it obscures the narrative exigency of the

---

[2] John Freccero, 'The Significance of *Terza Rima*', in *Dante: The Poetics of Conversion*, ed. Rachel Jacoff (Cambridge, MA: Harvard University Press, 1986), pp. 258–71 (p. 265). Peter Brooks notices similar radical discontinuities in Rousseau's autobiographical writing: 'There are many... contrivances of finality and endstop in the *Confessions*: conversion, fall (from childhood, from grace, into authorship, into publicity, etc.), and even simulacra of death.... There is a repeated insistence on special experiences and unique moments that open and close epochs in Rousseau's life, as if in an attempt to demarcate and stabilize the passage of life and time. As Sartre claimed, in order to narrate one's life one must become one's own obituary' (Peter Brooks, *Reading for the Plot: Design and Intention in Narrative* (New York: Knopf, 1984), p. 33). Fredric Jameson analyses comparable disruptions as necessary for creative thinking, in his study of classic utopian writing and science fiction *Archaeologies of the Future: The Desire Called Utopia and Other Fictions* (London and New York: Verso, 2005), esp. pp. 10–21 and 211–33.

[3] 'qual cosa mortale | *dovea* poi trarre te nel suo disio? | Ben ti *dovevi*...levar suso', 'Non ti *dovea* gravar le penne in giuso' (*Purg.* XXXI, 53–6 and 58, italics mine).

straying path he did in fact take. Straight and straying, in this case, have two interchangeable meanings depending on whether one views them from a narrative or moral standpoint: the biographical errancy is as necessary to Dante's narrative as the righteousness is to his moral message, and vice versa.

It is evident, then, that even in this key moment of the masterplot, where uniformity is most expected, the centrifugal tendencies of alternative storylines play a structural role. Insofar as the fiction of the *Commedia* purports to be a truthful narrative of past events, it recounts them as they happened; insofar as it purports to be a moral narrative, it represents them as they should have happened. Bridging the gap between these two modes of discourse—which are normative inasmuch as they are determined, in the fiction, by historical facts and a moral order—the alternative stories and parallel lives that are the subject of the present chapter explore the realm of possibility throughout the *Commedia*. They open up a creative and imaginative space at the heart of the poem that is structural to its pluralistic narrative thinking.

It is not by chance that in the few other instances when Dante imagines alternatives to his own life story, these are couched in the context of discussions of how heavenly influences determined his personal destiny, a question which Dante examines at greater length in *Purgatorio* XVI and *Paradiso* VIII and refers to throughout his text. The quotation above, where Dante gives credit to claims of a positive astral influence on his life by having them confirmed by Beatrice's authority, is not the first time that we hear about his own blessed potential. In *Inferno* XV, Brunetto Latini introduces the theme when he famously tells his former student:

> *Se* tu segui tua *stella*,
> non puoi fallire a glorïoso porto,
> se ben m'accorsi ne la vita bella.
>
> [[*If* you follow] your *star*
> you cannot fail to reach a glorious port,
> if I saw clearly in the happy life.]
>
> (*Inf.* XV, 54–6, italics mine)

His words and hypothetical construct are echoed by the narrator himself in *Inferno* XXVI:

> e più lo 'ngegno affreno ch'i' non soglio,
> perché non corra che virtù nol guidi;

sì che, *se stella* bona o miglior cosa
m'ha dato 'l ben, ch'io stessi nol m'invidi,
  [and more than is my way, I curb my powers
    lest they run on where virtue fail to guide them,
  so that, *if* friendly *star* or something better still
  has granted me its boon, I don't misuse the gift.]
                              (*Inf.* XXVI, 21–4, italics mine)

Lastly, they are repeated once more by the narrator in *Paradiso* XXII:

O gloriose *stelle*, o lume pregno
di gran virtù, dal quale io riconosco
tutto, qual che si sia, il mio ingegno,
  con voi nasceva e s'ascondeva vosco
quelli ch'è padre d'ogne mortal vita,
quand'io senti' di prima l'aere tosco;
  e poi, quando mi fu grazia largita
d'entrar ne l'alta rota che vi gira,
la vostra region mi fu sortita,

  [O glorious *stars*, O light made pregnant
with a mighty power, all my talent,
whatever it may be, has you as source.
  From you was risen and within you hidden
he who is the father of all mortal life
when first I breathed the Tuscan air.
  And afterward, when I was granted grace
to enter the high wheel that keeps you turning,
it was your zone to which I was assigned.]
                              (*Par.* XXII, 112–20, italics mine)

The word *ingegno* ['talent'] (113) looks back to the comparable passage in *Inferno* XXVI, while *stelle* ['stars'] (112), *grazia* ['grace'] (118), and *rota* ['wheel'] (119) allude to Beatrice's Edenic speech of *Purgatorio* XXX. For the purposes of this chapter, the first thing to notice about these three passages is that—from the prophecy of a damned soul and the narrator's hesitant pledge to Beatrice's unequivocal revelation and the narrator's ultimate acknowledgement—the *Commedia* stacks on its claims of a positive heavenly influence on its protagonist's life all the authority it can progressively muster. In the face of this indubitable investment in what one must not forget is but the fictional masterplot, one should also notice that the stress is not placed so much on the certainty of Dante's brilliant future but rather on its conditional, tentative, pending status. In *Inferno* XV and XXVI this condition is expressed by the hypothetical *se*, and Brunetto's confident indicative 'non puoi fallire' ['you cannot fail'] (*Inf.* XV, 55) is further tempered by the qualification 'se ben m'accorsi ne la vita bella' ['if I saw clearly in the happy life'] (56), which should also arguably be taken with an extra pinch of salt, considering that it is voiced by a damned soul; in *Purgatorio* XXX, as I have mentioned, Beatrice puts the emphasis not on Dante's promise but on its betrayal, whereas in *Paradiso* XXII Dante merely calls on the Gemini constellation to help him live up to the strength and virtue he was imbued with at birth (straying is still very much available as a possibility). These passages offer a clear instance of Dante's narrative pluralism, as they express two narratives that are essential to the message of the *Commedia*: on the one hand, Dante the narrator is promoting the truth-claims of his masterplot of promise, betrayal, grace, and salvation—the teleological life story that granted him the authority of a prophet on all matters; on the other hand, however, he is no different from his readers in that he too is still on his way, both as a protagonist in the fiction and as a man writing the book on which all his hopes of a glorious return from exile are staked. The 'cammin di nostra vita', the path of our life, looks as open and undivinable to that man as ours does now to you and me. What is crucial to these claims of Dante's potential as they are phrased, then, is not so much their prophetic certainty (these hypotheticals will all in fact turn out to be true once the protagonist has accomplished his otherworldly pilgrimage and the author has finished the *Commedia*), but rather the existential truth that *in itinere* promises can be disappointed, the certainty of a prophecy is only verified retrospectively, and all salvation is threatened by the possibility of a fall. Dante the prophet is reminding his readers that prophets too could have been mere 'could-have-beens'. No matter how supremely ordained, existence as represented in the *Commedia* is always played out on a plane of simultaneous possibilities. It is always, by its very essence, 'on the perennial verge of existence';[4] on the brink, as it were, of failure or success, of betrayal or promise, or—in terms closer to Dante's *Commedia*—of damnation or salvation.

---

[4] I am borrowing Ben Lerner's poignant expression from his novel *10:04* (London: Granta, 2014), p. 157.

2.1 The Affective Space: *Paradiso* VIII

Later in the chapter I will discuss the ways in which the *Commedia* finds a solution to the formal challenge of joining in the poem this binary theological view of human (after)life with a more nuanced existential take.[5] Suffice it to say, for now, that because the poem's theology requires readers to think of all life stories from their endpoint in the antithetical terms of the damned and the saved—with Dante as the one temporary exception to this rule—it does not follow that the poem is only interested in this binary point of view. On the contrary, the *Commedia* often promotes alternative perspectives through the souls' fantasies, regrets, and wishes that their life had been different. Their wishful thinking opens up a space that momentarily pauses the historical narrative it sparks from. Whenever such a fantastical space is opened, it is consecrated to affectivity. In the encounter with Brunetto, for instance, the prophecy contained in the old teacher's words quoted above ('*Se tu segui* tua stella, | non puoi fallire a glorïoso porto, | *se ben m'accorsi* ne la vita bella' ['[If you follow] your star | you cannot fail to reach a glorious port, | if I saw clearly in the happy life'], *Inf.* XV, 54–6, emphasis mine throughout) develops into an alternative storyline of mutual love ('e *s'io non fossi* sì per tempo morto, | veggendo il cielo a te così benigno, | *dato t'avrei* a l'opera conforto' ['Had I not died too soon, | seeing that Heaven so favors you, | I would have lent you comfort in your work'], 58–6), which the protagonist mirrors, when he replies, a few lines later, '*Se fosse* tutto pieno il mio dimando, | . . . *voi non sareste* ancora | de l'umana natura posto in bando' ['If all my prayers were answered, | . . . you would not yet | be banished from mankind'] (79–81). This desire for an alternative ending to their life story is not as exclusive to the damned as one may be led to expect. As high up as the heaven of the *spiriti amanti*, the blessed Carlo Martello expresses a similar wish as he imagines an alternative life of reciprocal affection: 'Assai m'amasti, e avesti ben onde; | che, *s'io fossi* giù stato, io ti mostrava | di mio

---

[5] Two scholars talk about the 'existential' perspective in Dante: Robert Pogue Harrison and Giuseppe Mazzotta. Harrison uses the expression 'Christian "existentiality"'—ironically, from the point of view of this study—to describe the *Vita nova*'s recapitulation of the present in the past, which I see as the teleological masterplot *in nuce* (*The Body of Beatrice* (Baltimore and London: Johns Hopkins University Press, 1988), p. 132 and ff.). Mazzotta uses the term 'existential' in relation to the experience of time of the *Purgatorio*, but I differ from his account, which ties the future-oriented perspective of the living to a return to the past: 'In *Purgatorio*, we are given an existential sense of time, which is understood as future-oriented, as a projection into some kind of future, and, at the same time, a return to the past' (*Reading Dante* (New Haven, CT: Yale University Press, 2014), p. 117).

90   DANTE'S MASTERPLOT AND ALTERNATIVE NARRATIVES

amor più oltre che le fronde' (*Paradiso* VIII, 55–7). That wish for a different life introduces in the poem a further layer to the binary distinction between the damned and the blessed, an affective dimension that takes on a life of its own.

The relation between these two narratives produces significant tensions in the poem. In *Paradiso* VIII, this personal, emotional, errant dimension outside the teleological timeline is so strong that in one instance it distorts the poem's syntax to the point of near ungrammaticality. Scholars have noticed the remarkable frequency of hypothetical clauses in this canto, which indeed displays the highest concentration of *se* ['if'] in the *Commedia*: thirteen over its 148 lines, compared to an average per canto of less than five (the other high-density canto is, interestingly, *Inferno* XV, with twelve occurrences, discussed below).[6] The hypotheticals play a structural role throughout the episode. The first of these is voiced by the prince Carlo Martello, as he answers Dante's question on his identity:

> Il mondo m'ebbe
> giù poco tempo; e se più fosse stato,
> molto sarà di mal, che non sarebbe.
>
> [The world kept me
> but a little while below, and, had that time been longer,
> much evil that shall be would not have been.]
>
> (*Par.* VIII, 49–51)

The meaning appears clear to all commentators: Carlo Martello died young; because of his death, many misfortunes will ensue, that would not have happened had he lived longer. But on a closer look, it becomes apparent that the syntax is not as plain as it seems and the paraphrase proposed, which coincides, give or take, with that offered by all commentators, is actually quite strained.[7] Two communicative intentions are interwoven in these lines.

---

[6] Among the scholars to have pointed out the hypotheticals: Carlo Muscetta, 'Canto VIII', in *Lectura Dantis Scaligera: III. 'Paradiso'* (Florence: Le Monnier, 1966), pp. 255–92 (p. 281); Michele Dell'Aquila, 'Gli spiriti amanti del cielo di Venere (*Par.* canti VIII e IX)', in *Al millesmo del vero: Letture dantesche* (Fasano: Schena, 1989), pp. 146–58 (p. 152); Eugenio Ragni, 'Il canto VIII del *Paradiso*', in *I primi undici canti del 'Paradiso'*, ed. Attilio Mellone (Rome: Bulzoni, 1992), pp. 157–75 (p. 164); Michelangelo Picone, 'Canto VIII', in *Lectura Dantis Turicensis: 'Paradiso'*, ed. Georges Güntert and Michelangelo Picone (Florence: Cesati, 2002), pp. 119–32 (p. 119); and commentators Giovanni Fallani, *ad Par.* VIII, 148; Giuseppe Giacalone, *ad Par.* VIII, 71 (DDP).

[7] The only two commentators to notice the 'distorted' and 'curious' construct are, respectively, C. H. Grangent and Charles S. Singleton, *ad Par.* VIII, 51, who, as non-native speakers, did

On the one hand, Carlo foresees, prophetically, that 'molto sarà di mal', much evil will ensue; on the other, he contemplates the alternative scenario in which 'se più fosse stato, | molto...mal...non sarebbe', if he had lived longer, much evil would not have happened. Thus unpacked, Carlo's thought seems perfectly intelligible, even though the extreme compression of Dante's poetry causes the sentence to test the limits of grammar. Syntactically, the prophecy 'molto sarà di mal' splits in two the hypothetical clause 'se più fosse stato' ['much evil...shall be'] from its rightful consequence 'molto...mal non sarebbe' ['much evil...would not have been'], bullying the latter into a relative clause. With that very violence, the reader is made to understand, death interrupted Carlo in the fulfilment of all his promise.

The sentence has a famous literary antecedent in the sixth book of Virgil's *Aeneid*:[8]

> si qua fata aspera rumpas,
> tu Marcellus eris.
> [if you could break the dire fates,
> you would be Marcellus.]
> (*Aeneid* VI, 882–3)

The untimely death of Marcus Claudius Marcellus—Augustus's beloved nephew and successor to the imperial throne (42–23 BC)—is the supreme example of wasted potential in the *Aeneid*. This episode is the basis of Dante's portrayal of Carlo Martello.[9] The poignancy of Virgil's counterfactual lies in the tension between the present subjunctive expressing the possibility ('rumpas': 'if you *could break* the dire fates...') and the future indicative of certitude ('eris': literally, 'you *will be* Marcellus'). Marcellus will be Marcellus regardless of his future; yet there is a sense in which he will never fully be Marcellus, inasmuch as he will never get to fulfil the promise of his potential, as he doubtless would have done—Virgil suggests—had he

---

not take this interesting syntax for granted. They both make reference to the construct of *Par.* VI, 146–8: 'e se 'l mondo sapesse il cor ch'elli ebbe | mendicando sua vita a frusto a frusto, | assai lo loda, e più lo loderebbe.' The manuscripts do not offer notable variants for this terzina, which suggests that it must have been generally intelligible to copyists.

[8] Virgil, *Eclogues. Georgics. Aeneid: Books 1–6*, trans. H. Rushton Fairclough, rev. G. P. Goold, Loeb Classical Library 63, new rev. edn (Cambridge, MA: Harvard University Press, 1999).

[9] Marcellus's precedent has been widely accepted by commentators: Carlo Grabher, *ad Par.* VIII, 142–8; Umberto Bosco-Giovanni Reggio, *ad Par.* VIII, 34–9; Anna Maria Chiavacci Leonardi, 'Introduzione' *ad Par.* VIII (DDP). Edward Peters, 'Human Diversity and Civil Society in *Paradiso* VIII', in *Dante Studies*, CIX (1991), 51–70 (62), compares Carlo Martello's untimely death to Manfredi's in *Purg.* III.

defeated the death lying in his destiny.[10] Yet the syntactical ambiguity also allows us to read the hypothetical clause in an even more pathetic way, as an optative subjunctive, which may be translated thus: 'Oh, if you could only break fate! | But you will only be Marcellus'. Bearing this reading of Virgil's lines in mind, it is possible to hear a voice of regret in Carlo Martello's words, which may be rendered with alternative punctuation than that proposed by the *Commedia*'s editor, Giorgio Petrocchi:

> e se più fosse stato!
> Molto sarà di mal, che non sarebbe.

Similarly to Marcellus's, the meaning of Carlo's life lies in the tension between 'what could have been and what has not been'.[11] The text tries to forestall melancholy interpretations of the young prince's story, carefully underlining, as many scholars are eager to point out, the growing 'allegrezza', the cheerfulness and joy of Carlo's soul as he relates it (*Par.* VIII, 46-9).[12] But the Virgilian allusion opens a space of disquietude, in that it betrays a trace of the regret for the individual destiny that has gone unfulfilled and a desire, within the text, for the alternative life story that would have realized that destiny. Behind Carlo Martello's allegedly 'impersonal', disinterested statement that his death 'would have avoided much of the evil that ensued' lies this affective dimension.[13]

It is important to clarify that I do not mean to suggest that Dante introduces here such intertextual ambiguity with the deliberate aim to undermine the *Commedia*'s view of the relationship between human beings and their ordained life story (as might more conceivably be argued, I think, in the case of Virgil's text); and I am not claiming, either, that we are witnessing here the author's slippage or an aporia in his text. I argue, rather, that lines 50-1 of *Paradiso* VIII, in their extreme compression, are the most

---

[10] I find similar comments in Ettore Paratore's edition of Virgil, *Eneide*, trans. Luca Canali (Milan: Mondadori, 1985), p. 641: 'solo nel caso in cui riuscisse a sconfiggere l'avverso destino che lo attende, il giovane potrebbe divenire un Marcello paragonabile al suo grande proavo,' the homonymous general from the second Punic War. The hypothetical '*si*' of line 882, writes Paratore, 'configura un'ipotesi irrealizzabile'.
[11] 'ciò che avrebbe potuto essere e ciò che non è stato' (Ragni, 'Il canto VIII del *Paradiso*', p. 164, trans. mine).
[12] Francesco Torraca, *ad Par.* VIII, 49–51 (DDP); Muscetta, 'Il canto VIII del *Paradiso*', p. 281; Nino Borsellino, *Il poeta giudice: Dante e il tribunale della 'Commedia'* (Turin: Aragno, 2011).
[13] 'avrebbe evitato molto di quel male' (Muscetta, 'Il canto VIII del *Paradiso*', p. 281, trans. mine). The claim of the text's 'impersonality' is Muscetta's own.

condensed expression of a desire for unresolved contradiction that sustains and animates the *Commedia*. The two voices that are distinct and yet harmonized in these lines—the teleological perspective underlying the prophetic mode and the existential perspective of infinite possibilities—express two seemingly incompatible narratives, in a poetic form that makes us perceive them as non-conflictual. The moment we choose to switch on the usual kind of thinking that is aware of contradiction, it is too late—the poem has already tricked us into thinking in its poetic mode, creating for us the experience of a universe where a paradoxical plurality of incompatible narratives is in fact possible.

Dante plays an analogous rhetorical trick with the musical simile of the two distinct and harmonized voices in this very canto, when he compares the dance of the *spiriti amanti* to sparks in a fire and voices in polyphony: 'E come in fiamma favilla si vede, | e come in voce voce si discerne, | quand'una è ferma e altra va e riede' ['And, as one sees a spark within a flame | or hears, within a song, a second voice, | holding its note while the other comes and goes'] (*Par.* VIII, 16–18). Thematically, the whole heaven of Venus is concerned with harmonizing heavenly influences and human freedom, showing that 'the fact of their diversity makes possible a "concord" or "harmony",[14] which in turn 'stems from the strong opposition of different notes and would be inconceivable if it were deprived of it'.[15] But it is on the formal level that Dante is able to pull off poetically what the poem is concerned with thematically. With the antanaclasis of *voce*, the repeated word expresses two different meanings at the same time: first the choir that sustains one note collectively, and then the single voice that soloes over it: although *voce* means here two opposite things, we do not experience it as contradiction.

One may bear this in mind when reading the counterfactuals in the episode of Carlo Martello (*Par.* VIII, 55–140).[16] The same rhetorical tool is

---

[14] Patrick Boyde, *Perception and Passion in Dante's 'Comedy'* (Cambridge: Cambridge University Press, 1993), p. 283. See also *Par.* VI, 124–6.

[15] '[O]rigina dalla ferma opposizione di note diverse ed è inconcepibile se ne viene privata' (Giuseppe Mazzotta, 'Musica e storia nel *Paradiso* 15–17', *Critica del testo*, 14.2 (2011), 333–48 (338), trans. mine).

[16] In the ninety-eight lines from its first appearance, the hypothetical conjunction *se* appears thirteen times—on average once every two and a half terzinas. The one category of virtual hypotheticals are: 'e se più fosse stato, | molto sarà di mal, che non sarebbe' (50–1); 's'io fossi giù stato, io ti mostrava' (57); 'attesi avrebbe i suoi regi ancora |...| se mala segnoria...|...non avesse | mosso' (71–5); 'E se mio frate questo antivedesse |...| già fuggeria' (76–8). The other category of syllogistic hypotheticals are: 'S'io posso | mostrarti un vero,...| terrai lo viso' (94–6); 'Se ciò non fosse, il ciel che tu cammine | producerebbe' (106–7); 'ciò esser non può, se li

used to express two opposite modes of storytelling. On the one hand, the four hypotheticals in the first half of this section (lines 55–93) refer to the universe of unexpressed potential of Carlo's affective 'virtual history' and on its consequences for the future;[17] in the second half, on the other hand (lines 94–140), the counterfactuals become the means of an argumentative logic aimed at demonstrating syllogistically scientific-theological truths on heavenly influence. Dante and Carlo themselves draw attention to the logical nature of the second half of the canto as they make use of the technical terms *deducendo* [literally, 'deducing'] (121), *conchiuse* ['concluded'] (122), and *corollario* ['corollary'] (138); indeed, the preferred rhetorical strategy of this part, in six out of nine cases, is the *reductio ad absurdum*, which was commonly employed in scholastic diatribes to support one's claims by demonstrating the absurdity of the alternative hypothesis.[18] This mechanism, especially, shows the radical difference between the two very different goals to which hypothetical thinking is bent in this canto: on the one hand, the scientific reasoning aims at eliminating alternative possibilities in order to enforce an exact truth; on the other hand, Carlo's virtual life story aims at exploring alternatives affectively, defending their 'thinkability'. This kind of narrative thinking precedes, in the reader's experience of the poem, our usual rational understanding. By giving free rein to alternative futures, the prince's speech expresses a model of causality that is fluid, open, and free; but it does this with the same rhetorical tools that he employs to express the exact and univocal truths of theological knowledge. This is the natural development of the paradox compressed in Carlo Martello's pithy one-liner, which gave us a chance to glimpse another side of the intrinsically paradoxical nature of the *Commedia*. Without sacrificing a human desire to a theological truth but emphasizing continuity between the two by the same formal means (the hypothetical period), Dante narrates a history that never happened through the hopes and regrets of a young prince who was never king, even as he writes about the grand march of what happened by providence. The fact that these contradictions are not perceived as such

'ntelletti |…non son manchi' (109–10); 'sarebbe il peggio | per l'omo in terra, se non fosse cive?' (115–16); 'E puot' elli esser, se giù non si vive' (118); 'Non, se 'l maestro vostro ben vi scrive' (120); 'Natura generata il suo cammino | simil farebbe…| se non vincesse il proveder divino' (133–5); 'Sempre natura, se fortuna trova | discorde a sé…|…fa mala prova' (139–41); 'E se 'l mondo la giù ponesse mente |…|…avria buona la gente' (142–4).

[17] I am borrowing the expression 'storia virtuale' from Picone, 'Canto VIII', p. 119.
[18] As noted by Umberto Bosco and Giovanni Reggio, *ad Par*. VIII, 106–11, and Anna Maria Chiavacci Leonardi, *ad Par*. VIII, 109–11 (DDP).

is one of the greatest testaments to the triumph of the *Commedia*'s narrative pluralism.

The emphasis on possible storylines is an essential part of the poem's universe. Generally, affective possibilities and the grand teleological narrative are not mutually exclusive but in productive tension and equally truthful. There are, however, rare moments in the poem when an affective storyline appears to push the poem's theological system a little further. This occurs in *Purgatorio* XXI, when the soul of the poet Statius meets his poetic hero and saviour, Virgil. Statius, who has just completed his purgatorial journey and is free to take his seat in heaven, expresses the following wish:

> E per esser vivuto di là quando
> visse Virgilio, assentirei un sole
> più che non deggio al mio uscir di bando.
>
> [To have lived on earth when Virgil lived
> I would have stayed one year's sun longer than I owed
> before I came forth from my exile.]
>
> (*Purg.* XXI, 100–2)

Voiced by a soul that is presented as emblematic in its freedom to fulfil the greatest desire of all, Statius's paradoxical wish to delay eternal bliss for the sake of his admiration for a pagan poet is striking, 'utterly implausible',[19] 'a little unorthodox',[20] and even 'impious'.[21] This centrifugal desire is voiced in the language of possibility. As was the case with Dante's Edenic encounter with Beatrice, the imaginative alternative opened up by the conditional 'assentirei' [literally, 'I would agree'] (101) is contrasted with the normative language of the afterlife ('deggio' ['I owed'], 102), the linear trajectory leading to heaven suspended for a moment of contemplation of a world where human affectivity could have had its way. Statius's wish remains just that—a wish. But such wishes, in this newly blessed soul, and in the other 'could-have-beens' of the *Commedia*, leave poetic trace of the paradoxical nature of memory, affectivity, and desire that occasionally branch off from the sublimations of the teleological narrative.

---

[19] Winthrop Wetherbee, *The Ancient Flame: Dante and the Poets* (Notre Dame, IN: University of Notre Dame Press, 2008), p. 197.
[20] Sapegno, *ad Purg.* XXI, 92–4 (DDP), trans. mine.
[21] Chiavacci Leonardi, *ad Purg.* XXI, 101 (DDP), trans. mine.

2.2 The 'Disnarrated' and Free Will in the *Commedia*: a Comparison with Two Twentieth-century Poems and the *Convivio*

It is my contention that this attention to the alternative lives that could have been, as opposed to the predetermined storylines of what was and what should have been, is a trademark of the *Commedia*. This formal technique reflects the poem's theological concerns and is of structural importance. Alternative endings, as I suggested above, are the formal expression of the theological doctrine of free will: they inhabit the space between the given narratives of a person's past actions and their moral value in the normative framework of the poem; at the same time, and more significantly, they are a reminder to the reader that the life that eventually unfolded was originally played out on the stage of freedom, where historical actions and their moral value are yet to be revealed. This use of alternative narratives is structural to the *Commedia*'s theological framework, where freedom and the grand teleological narrative are not in contradiction but are instead simultaneous and equally true. The formal technique itself, of course, is not original; but the structural role it plays in the poem's theology is not only unique to Dante but, more specifically, to the narrative poetry of the *Commedia* (as opposed to the argumentative prose of Dante's treatises), as I will now argue.

In his studies on the French novel, Gerald Prince formalized what I have so far called alternative or hypothetical lives as the narrative category of the 'disnarrated'. The disnarrated, according to Prince's definition, 'covers all the events that *do not* happen though they could have and are nonetheless referred to (in a negative or hypothetical mode) by the narrative text'.[22] Unlike virtual storylines, which take place in an imaginary world of possibility without ever having to intersect with actuality, the disnarrated is 'only relative to a given diegesis, and only if it designates in that diegesis a possibility that remains unrealized'.[23] We appreciate its value best when it brings out the fact that the main story 'could have been otherwise,... *it* usually is otherwise,... *it* was *not* otherwise.'[24] The *Commedia* employs the disnarrated to highlight this intersection between the choices always open to free will in the present and the retrospective determinism of a teleological narrative.

---

[22] Gerald Prince, *Narrative as Theme: Studies in French Fiction* (Lincoln: University of Nebraska Press, 1992), p. 30.
[23] Ibid., p. 30.   [24] Ibid., p. 36.

The paradoxical simultaneity of these two perspectives is a particular concern of the *Commedia*, as will appear clearer if we compare it to two twentieth-century poems also concerned with 'what might have been'. Robert Frost's famous poem *The Road Not Taken* bears the disnarrated on its sleeve.[25] The narrator looks back on a time when he found two roads diverging on his path and cannot help but wonder what might have been. The poem ends on the conclusion that the choice between the two roads, although ultimately arbitrary, 'has made all the difference' (line 20). One can easily recognize the symbolic implications of the narrator's dilemma, where the stress is placed on the intrinsic impossibility for a single life to follow more than one of the divergent futures opened up by different choices. The impossibility lies in what is conceived as the linear temporality of existence; it is arguably ontological: 'I could not travel both | And be one traveler' (2–3). It is not by chance, then, that the alternative future of the road not taken remains opaque to the narrator as the roads appear identical ('the other, as just as fair', 6; 'both... equally lay', 11): he can only sense that there was some 'difference', and is forever unable to know its specific quality or visualize it with any guarantee of certainty.[26] This perspective remains active in Dante's *Commedia* despite the retrospective clairvoyance claimed by the narrator after his otherworldly journey. Indeed, the alternative perspective's function is to remind readers of its pertinence right when the teleological narrative that Dante is so committed to sell us could induce us to overlook it.

But is this 'what might have been' just 'an abstraction | Remaining a perpetual possibility | Only in a world of speculation'? T. S. Eliot claimed as much in the first of his *Four Quartets* (lines 6–15):[27]

> What might have been is an abstraction
> Remaining a perpetual possibility
> Only in a world of speculation.
> What might have been and what has been
> Point to one end, which is always present.
> Footfalls echo in the memory
> Down the passage which we did not take

---

[25] Robert Frost, *The Road Not Taken*, in *The Mountain Interval* (New York: Quinn & Boden Co., 1916).
[26] See Frank Lentricchia, *Modernist Quartet* (Cambridge: Cambridge University Press) pp. 73–6.
[27] T. S. Eliot, *Four Quartets* (New York: Harcourt, Brace & Co., 1943).

> Towards the door we never opened
> Into the rose-garden. My words echo
> Thus, in your mind.

Artfully leading his reader into a disnarrative universe ('Down the passage which *we did not take* | Towards the door *we never opened* | Into the rose-garden'), Eliot eventually reflects, 'But to what purpose | Disturbing the dust on a bowl of rose-leaves | I do not know.' Eliot's speculative journey into the rose garden does not seem to have any obvious purpose. It is a virtuoso trick that manifests by contrast the extent to which Dante's own exploration of the disnarrated is of such structural importance to the *Commedia*'s innermost purpose. Just when the protagonist of Dante's poem finds himself at the end of time and can see clearly the main narrative thread, this is also interwoven with the existential perspective of free, open, undivinable choices. Similarly to the postmodern narrator of Ben Lerner's novel *10:04*, Dante 'resolve[s] to dilate [his] story' not in the reassuring direction of the retrospective teleological narrative but from the viewpoint of the living, branching out 'into an actual present alive with multiple futures'.[28] The *Commedia*, thus, finds formal solution to the ontological problem of time's linearity, while making that formal solution essential to the experience of existence that the poem is striving to represent. Thus in the *Commedia*'s narrative pluralism, the alternative and disnarrated storylines of the poem slice through its retrospective necessities, expressing 'the narrow cleft of earthly human history, the span of man's life on earth, in which the great and dramatic decision must fall'. This cleft, as Erich Auerbach awesomely wrote, is 'the magnificent and terrible gift of potential freedom which creates the urgent, restless, human, and Christian-European atmosphere of the irretrievable, fleeting moment that must be taken advantage of'.[29] As James I. Porter comments, '[i]t is the experience of these possibilities, not their realization *per se*' that Auerbach recognized in Dante.[30]

This existential dimension of potential freedom animates the *Commedia*'s poetic form and distinguishes it markedly from Dante's prose in the

---

[28] Lerner, *10:04*, p. 194.
[29] Erich Auerbach, *Dante: Poet of the Secular World*, trans. Ralph Manheim (Chicago: University of Chicago Press, 1961), p. 132.
[30] James I. Porter, 'Introduction' to *Time, History and Literature: Selected Essays of Erich Auerbach*, ed. James I. Porter, trans. Jane O. Newman (Princeton, NJ: Princeton University Press, 2014), p. xiv.

Convivio. The treatment of Guido da Montefeltro in the two works offers an insight into what the *Commedia*'s poetic form brings to its theological content. The most evident difference between the treatment of Guido in the two works, as most commentators point out, is that the fraudulent counsel to Boniface VIII that determines Guido's damnation in *Inferno* XXVII does not in fact appear in the *Convivio*, where Dante speaks, rather, in praise of the man's conversion in no uncertain terms, calling him 'lo nobilissimo nostro latino Guido montefeltrano' ['the most noble of our Italians, Guido of Montefeltro'] (*Conv.* IV, xxviii, 8).[31] This discrepancy between the two works has led to some speculation as to whether access to new information may have induced Dante to change his mind on Guido da Montefeltro. A scholarly hunt for possible historical sources is ongoing.[32] In a recent article, Mirko Tavoni meticulously reviews these sources and dismisses them on the grounds of their late chronology, as he reclaims Dante's 'total freedom, with his powerful and supreme fantasy, to create his own paths of meaning'.[33] And indeed there is a sense in which that freedom to create personal paths of meaning is deeply embedded into *Inferno* XXVII, possibly more so than Tavoni himself suggests, constituting what is formally the most significant change from the Montefeltro chapter in the *Convivio*. There Dante commented on the line 'Poi ne la quarta parte de la vita' ['And then in the fourth phase of life'] of the related canzone 'Le dolci rime d'amor ch'i' solia' (136) with a discussion of the kinds of affect appropriate to old age:

> E sì come a colui che viene di lungo cammino, anzi ch'entri nella porta della sua cittade, se li fanno incontro li cittadini di quella, così alla nobile anima si fanno incontro, e *deono* fare, quelli cittadini della etterna vita; e così fanno per le sue buone operazioni e contemplazioni: ché, già essendo a Dio renduta e astrattasi dalle mondane cose e cogitazioni, vedere le pare coloro che apresso di Dio crede che siano.... Rendesi dunque a Dio la nobile anima in questa etade, e attende lo fine di questa vita con molto desiderio e uscire le pare dell'albergo e ritornare nella propia mansione, uscire le pare di cammino e tornar in cittade, uscire le pare di mare e tornare a porto. O miseri e vili che colle vele alte corrette a questo porto,

---

[31] Mirko Tavoni, 'Guido da Montefeltro dal *Convivio* all'*Inferno*', *Nuova Rivista di Letteratura Italiana*, 13 (2010), 167–98 (171), reads this as a relative superlative: 'the noblest of all Italians'.
[32] See Tavoni's recent review thereof, in 'Guido da Montefeltro'.
[33] 'totale libertà, potentemente e sovranamente fantastica, nel creare i suoi propri percorsi di senso' (Tavoni, 'Guido da Montefeltro', p. 174, trans. mine).

e là ove *dovereste* riposare, per lo impeto del vento rompete, e perdete voi medesimi là dove tanto camminato avete!

[And just as a man returning from a long journey is met by the citizens of his city as he enters its gates, so the noble soul is met, as it *should* be, by the citizens of the eternal life. This they do by means of their good works and thoughts: for having already surrendered itself to God and disengaged itself from worldly matters and preoccupations, the soul seems to see those whom it believes to be with God.... The noble soul, then, surrenders itself to God in this age of life and awaits the end of this life with great desire, and seems to be leaving an inn and returning to its proper dwelling, seems to be coming back from a journey and returning to the city, seems to be coming in from the sea and returning to port. O you miserable and debased beings who speed into this port with sails raised high! Where you *should* take your rest, you shipwreck yourselves against the force of the wind and perish at the very place to which you have so long been journeying!]   (*Conv.* IV, xxviii, 5 and 7, italics mine)

Upon reading the passage closely alongside the *Commedia*, it is apparent that the treatise's moral language is unequivocally normative: 'noi *dovemo* calare le vele' ['*we must* lower the sails'] (3, *emphases* mine throughout); 'così a la nobile anima si fanno incontro, e *deono* fare, quelli cittadini de la etterna vita' ['so the noble soul is met, *as it should* be, by the citizens of the eternal life'] (5); 'O miseri e vili...! [D]*overeste* riposare, per lo impeto del vento rompete' ['O you miserable and debased beings!... [Y]*ou should* take your rest'] (7). The prose work relies on clear-cut value judgements: through its use of adjectives, it creates binaries between the positive 'buono marinaio' ['good sailor'] (3), 'buono mercatante' ['good merchant'] (9), 'nobile anima' ['noble soul'] (5, 7, and 11) on the one hand, and the negative 'miseri e vili' ['miserable and debased'] (7), 'sventurati e male nati' ['unhappy and misbegotten beings'] (19) on the other; praising the former ('*Bene* questi nobili calaro le vele de le mondane operazioni' ['These noble men did [*well* in] lowering the sails'], 8; '*bene* li può benedicere' ['*well* may it bless them'], 11), while inveighing against the latter in the vocative (7). The two similes of the sailor and the pilgrim certainly make the passage poetic, but they are meant as normative *exempla*: they are the moral paradigm that we readers must follow.

Inferno XXVII, on the other hand, makes use of analogous normative language, yet turns it to a radically different use. The following terzinas contain Dante's most notable self-quotation of the passage from *Convivio*:

Quando mi vidi giunto in quella parte
di mia etade ove ciascun dovrebbe
calar le vele e raccoglier le sarte,
   ciò che pria mi piacëa, allor m'increbbe,
e pentuto e confesso mi rendei;
ahi miser lasso! e giovato sarebbe.

[When I saw I had reached that stage of life
when all men ought to think
of lowering sail and coiling up the ropes,
   I grew displeased with what had pleased me once.
Repentant and shriven, I became a friar.
And woe is me! it would have served.]

(*Inf.* XXVII, 79–84)

In Guido's words, the textual parallel 'ciascun dovrebbe | calar le vele' ['all men ought to think | of lowering sail'] (80–1) turns the original 'noi dovemo calare le vele' ['we must lower sails'] (*Conv.* IV, xxviii, 5) to a more prudent conditional mood, and keeps the verb impersonal ('ciascun dovrebbe' ['all men ought']), where the *Convivio*'s more overt didacticism seeks to involve its audience in the first-person plural ('noi dovemo' ['we must']). Instead of entrusting moral normativity to the verb 'doverebbe', the poem entrusts it to its rhyme-word 'giovato sarebbe' ['it would have served'] (84). The conditional briefly imagines an alternative life for Guido, in which he withheld the fatal advice instead of giving it—a rhetorical trick also pulled in a previous conditional ('credendomi, sì cinto, fare ammenda; | e certo il creder mio venìa intero' ['thinking, cinctured so, to make amends. | And surely would my thought have come to pass'], 68–9). The value judgement implicit in the verb *giovare* can do without a personal pronoun here because the past tense makes it clear that 'it would have served' not in the absolute, of course, but in Guido's personal case. The pathetic poignancy of this man's destiny is expressed in the exclamation 'ahi miser lasso!' ['woe is me!'] (84). The *miser* here is not some generic target of invective, as in the *Convivio* ('miseri e vili' ['miserable and debased'] 7) but the damned Guido da Montefeltro himself. The alternative story points to the juncture between two potential destinies, one of which was discarded at the time, and now takes on a life of its own in the affective realm of Guido's anger and regret.

In this episode, then, the *Commedia* weaves together the three narrative modes of moral duty, historical storytelling, and affective storylines into one organic whole in a manner that radically distinguishes its narrative pluralism from the moral didacticism of the prose of the *Convivio*. Indeed, the narrative poem's urge to accommodate in its form the tensions between the personal and the universal, the existential and the moral, the affective and the historical, without compartmentalizing them into the *Convivio*'s incompatible binaries, plays a structural role in the theological and existential truths that the *Commedia* is concerned with at the level of its content.

2.3 'La tecnica dell'episodio parallelo': Parallel Lives as Narrative Correlative of Alternative Endings

It is not by chance that the disnarrated narrative discussed above is employed in the context of the most artistically self-conscious parallel lives in the poem: Guido da Montefeltro's damnation in *Inferno* XXVII and his son Buonconte's complementary salvation in *Purgatorio* V. Indeed, the narrative 'technique of parallel episodes', as Amilcare Iannucci named it in an important essay, may be interpreted as the narrative counterpart of the poetic practice of alternative endings.[34] What Dante achieves over the course of a few lines in a character's fantasies of the life they could have lived, he also replicates over the long-range across different canticas. Scholars have pointed out long-range parallels such as that of the two Montefeltros, but the significant correlation between the two techniques has gone undetected. The potential openness of Guido da Montefeltro's life, for instance, is already embedded in the text of *Inferno* XXVII independently of its purgatorial parallel, beginning with the original teleological transformation from 'uom d'arme' ['warrior'] to 'cordigliero' ['corded friar'] (*Inf.* XXVII, 67). Faithful to its etymology, Guido's initial conversion overturns with ease the value of the two terms. 'Ciò che pria mi piacëa, allor m'increbbe' (82), he says: these lifestyles are to him only relative and easily interchangeable. It makes sense that Dante applies this interchangeability also over different canticas. Iannucci picks up on this, as he asks, rhetorically, 'Who would have ever thought to find Buonconte among those that are saved and his father among the damned? One would have expected the exact opposite.'[35] Indeed, the

---

[34] Amilcare Iannucci, 'Autoesegesi dantesca: La tecnica dell'episodio parallelo (*Inferno* XV–*Purgatorio* XI)', in *Forma ed evento nella 'Divina Commedia'* (Rome: Bulzoni, 1984), pp. 83–114.
[35] 'Chi avrebbe mai pensato di trovare Buonconte tra coloro che si salvano e il padre tra i dannati? Ci si sarebbe aspettato esattamente l'opposto' (Iannucci, 'Autoesegesi dantesca', p. 95, trans. mine).

parallel episodes pivot on 'that "punto" in which a life is decided, and which is typical of all of Dante's greatest tales',[36] Auerbach's 'narrow cleft... in which the great and dramatic decision must fall.'[37] That moment is decisive but also so elusive as to confound even a saint and a devil in the moments of the two men's deaths in *Inferno* XXVII and *Purgatorio* V.[38] Commentators refer to relevant disputes between angels and devils in the legendary lives of saints or in contemporary religious theatre, but arguably the point of Dante's use of the trope is to stage the interpretative failure even of those who are supposed to be experts on the matter, or at least have the benefit of judging a concluded life in retrospect. The scene's reversal in the parallel episode stresses the decisive, yet elusive, moment when, for the Montefeltros, as for any living person in their place, it could have gone either way. In contrast with Robert Frost's poem, Dante's speculative, creative interest lies with the anatomy of the moment that 'made all the difference', not with what that difference turned out to be retrospectively: in the fiction of his otherworldly journey, he does, after all, already know this.

In the vast universe of the *Commedia* parallel episodes are numberless, if only for the obvious fact that 'any work of a certain size becomes self-commentary simply by virtue of creating the possibility of viewing it in retrospect'.[39] Iannucci's article is interested in parallel lives proper (such as the Montefeltros; Pier de le Vigne/Romeo di Villanova; Brunetto Latini/ Oderisi da Gubbio), but his definition of 'parallel episode' also includes whole cantos sharing larger themes such as *Inferno* I (which he correlates with cantos as diverse as *Purgatorio* I, XXX, XXXI, and *Paradiso* VII), and Ulysses's 'special case' seen as the key to the whole poem.[40] By way of comparison, another critic, Ernest H. Wilkins, comprises in his definition of 'pendant passages' only three episodes: the Montefeltros' parallel lives, naturally, but also analogous scenes such as 'the account of the passage of Acheron in the third canto of the *Inferno* and the account of the passage from Tiber to Purgatory in the second canto of the *Purgatorio*', and the protagonist's encounters with the two Donati siblings Forese and Piccarda in

---

[36] '[Q]uel 'punto' in cui si decide una vita, e che è tipico di tutti i grandi racconti danteschi' (Chiavacci Leonardi, 'Introduction' to *Inferno* XXVII (DDP), trans. mine).
[37] Auerbach, *Dante: Poet of the Secular World*, p. 132.
[38] See Iannucci, 'Autoesegesi dantesca', p. 95, and Robert Hollander, *ad Inf.* XXVII, 112–14, on the deception (DDP).
[39] 'qualsiasi opera di una certa grandezza si autocommenta semplicemente creando la possibilità di una visione retrospettiva' (Iannucci, 'Autoesegesi dantesca', p. 93, trans. mine).
[40] Ibid., p. 97.

Purgatorio XXIII and *Paradiso* III.[41] A more precise definition of what we are looking for seems desirable. In line with this chapter's interest in alternative lives, I limit my definition here to the self-contained episodes in different canticas that show significant correlation at the level of their rhetorical form and/or of the fiction of the poem *in their representation of two characters' life stories*. Thus, although the word *folle* does indeed create many meaningful connections between Ulysses and Dante throughout the poem, I do not consider this a parallel life proper because it is not self-contained; conversely, all self-contained episodes that are intratextually linked by a theme but not by a life story lie outside the scope of this chapter. The best example of parallel lives, as both Iannucci and Wilkins point out, is that of Guido and Buonconte da Montefeltro, but the parallel lives of Francesco and Domenico in the twin cantos *Paradiso* XI and XII are no less deliberate in their symmetry;[42] the episode of Francesca (*Inf.* V) has many analogues throughout the text, yet her collocation among the lustful in the fiction of the poem arguably makes her life a closer parallel to that of the *spirito amante* Cunizza da Romano (*Par.* IX); as a victim of envy and injustice, Pier de le Vigne (*Inf.* XIII) suffers a similar fate as Romeo di Villanova (not to mention Dante himself) (*Par.* VI), but his suicide also invites comparison with Cato (*Purg.* I–II); Brunetto Latini (*Inf.* XV) can be likened to Oderisi da Gubbio if one thinks of his story from the point of view of earthly fame, as does Iannucci (*Purg.* IX); Virgil's fate as a damned pagan poet bears relation to that of the saved pagan poet Statius (*Purg.* XXII); more examples can certainly be put forward.

If we look at these instances we may notice that many doubles and self-divisions appear within the confines of each of these episodes: although not as explicit as the alternative storylines of *Inferno* XXVII, they serve the same purpose by pointing towards the many possibilities beyond the apparent narrative unity of a character's life. It is true, for instance, that with the 'episode of Romeo di Villanova (*Par.* VI, 127–42)... Dante carefully constructs a situation parallel to that of the episode of Pier della Vigna: an envious court, an ingrate prince, a just man', as Iannucci observes, yet it is also worth taking

---

[41] Ernest H. Wilkins, 'Reminiscence and Anticipation in the *Divine Comedy*', *Dante Studies*, 118 (2000), 95–107 (104–5).
[42] For a close reading of the two passages in parallel see Barolini, *Undivine 'Comedy'*, pp. 218–56, pointing out that 'The two narratives are, moreover, essentially the verbal equivalent of the double rainbow invoked to describe the two circles of souls' (p. 198). Barolini also remarks on the 'parallel syntax' in *Par.* X, 1–6, noticed by John Freccero, 'The Dance of the Stars: *Paradiso* X', in *Dante: The Poetics of Conversion*, pp. 221–44 (pp. 242–3).

a closer look at the 'crucial terzina' describing the latter's suicide that seals his fate and marks the moment when the two parallel lives diverge:[43]

> L'animo mio, per disdegnoso gusto,
> credendo col morir fuggir disdegno,
> ingiusto fece me contra me giusto.
>
> [My mind, in scornful temper,
> hoping by dying to escape from scorn,
> made me, though just, against myself unjust.]
>
> (*Inf.* XIII, 70–2)

Here 'Dante distinguishes between two Pier della Vigna: one, just (the man who did not betray the trust of his lord); the other, unjust (the man who, despite his innocence, committed suicide'.[44] The rhyme-word *giusto* (72), on which this self-division with *ingiusto* revolves, also serves as the link to the parallel life of Romeo, referred to simply as 'questo giusto' (*Par.* VI, 137), whose voluntary exile can thus easily be read as Pier delle Vigne's own road not taken.

Inferno XV sets up a binary comparable to that of *Inferno* XIII, when Brunetto Latini is famously compared to 'quelli che vince, non colui che perde' ['more the winner | than the one who trails the field'] (*Inf.* XV, 124) among the competitors who ran a country race in Verona for the prize of a green banner: here the positive *vince* [literally, 'wins'] struggles to counter the negative *perde* [literally, 'loses'], which it cannot help but conjure up, in much the same way as 'la cara e buona imagine paterna' ['the cherished, kind, paternal image'] (83) has to contend with the 'cotto aspetto' ['scorched face'] (26) and 'viso abbrusciato' ['charred disfigurement'] (27), leaving scholars free rein in their arguments as to which side is the more significant.[45] But in *Purgatorio* XI the terms of the antithesis are exposed in their

---

[43] '[E]pisodio di Romeo di Villanova (*Par.* VI, 127–42) ... Dante costruisce attentamente una situazione parallela a quella dell'episodio di Pier della Vigna: una corte invidiosa, un principe ingrato, un uomo giusto' (Iannucci, 'Autoesegesi dantesca', p. 96, trans. mine).
[44] 'Dante distingue due Pier della Vigna: uno, giusto (l'uomo che non tradì la fiducia del suo signore); l'altro, ingiusto (l'uomo che, nonostante la sua innocenza, si suicidò)' (ibid.).
[45] Among the scholars who reflect on the affective life conjured up by Brunetto, Hollander, *ad Inf.* XV, 121–4 (DDP): 'The canto concludes with a simile that perfectly expresses Dante's ambivalent feelings about Brunetto. He looks every bit the winner – but he is in last place.... The case can be made that Dante treats Brunetto in exactly both these ways'; and Chiavacci Leonardi, *ad Inf.* XV, 124 (DDP): 'la *cara e buona imagine paterna* ha sopraffatto per sempre il *viso abbrusciato* di Brunetto? In realtà questo discorso non è fattibile, perché tutta la forza e bellezza di quella immagine, tutta la dolcezza e il dolore della grande scena infernale stanno

interchangeability: doubles seem to spawn each other into infinity when Oderisi da Gubbio is overshadowed by Franco Bolognese, Cimabue by Giotto, and one Guido is replaced by his Doppelgänger, soon to give way in turn to someone who looks suspiciously like Dante Alighieri himself, in an endless series of duplicates where everyone who won also lost.[46] Similarly, the colour of the *drappo* ['cloth'] that Brunetto seemed to have won turns out to be green ('verde', *Inf.* XV, 122): the 'verde...color d'erba' ['green... colour of grass'] (*Purg.* XI, 92 and 115) is the ephemeral colour that in Oderisi's speech 'poco...dura' ['briefly lasts'] and 'viene e va' ['comes | and goes'] (92, 116). *Inferno* XV is, after all, the canto with the second-highest density of counterfactuals in the *Commedia* (12 over 124 lines) and at least two of these express the wish for an alternative life that death brought to a full stop: Brunetto's words to Dante, discussed above in this chapter, 's'io non fossi sì per tempo morto...dato t'avrei all'opera conforto' (*Inf.* XV, 58–60) and the protagonist's specular reply, '"Se fosse tutto pieno il mio dimando", | rispuos'io lui, "voi non sareste ancora | de l'umana natura posto in bando"'] (79–81). But whereas the desire for an alternative storyline expressed here leaps over the ruling narrative of Brunetto's death with the power of imagination, the hypothetical periods in Oderisi's speech use conditionals to leap imaginatively into his potential death:

> Ben *non sare' io stato* sì cortese
> mentre ch'io vissi, per lo gran disio
> de l'eccellenza ove mio core intese.
> Di tal superbia qui si paga il fio;
> e ancor *non sarei qui, se non fosse*
> che, possendo peccar, mi volsi a Dio.
>
> [Indeed, *I hardly would have been* so courteous
> while I still lived—an overwhelming need
> to excel at any cost held fast my heart.
> For such pride here we pay our debt;
> *I would not be here* yet, *except*, while living,
> and with the means to sin, I turned to God.]
>
> (*Purg.* XI, 85–90, italics mine)

---

proprio nel drammatico rapporto tra le due realtà, tra la dignità e grandezza umana di Brunetto e la sua rovina eterna.'

[46] On this perversely infinite succession of winners and losers, see Nicolò Crisafi, 'Problemi narrativi nella cornice dei superbi (*Purgatorio* X–XII): Teleologia, cattiva infinità, e possibilità', *Chroniques Italiennes*, 39.2 (2020), 242–60 (271–7).

Through the repeated use of negative counterfactuals, Oderisi's life is represented here as the negation of a possible storyline made of unkindness and excessive desire for excellence. It is the fatal determinism of this hubristic road that Oderisi chose not to take the moment he turned to God, though free to fall. As the negation of the ruling storyline, it is the converted, righteous life, not the straying one, that is presented here as the alternative narrative.[47]

The key expression is *possendo peccar*, still able to sin (90). Once again, the *Commedia* reminds readers that the narrative it represents as so inevitable and teleologically driven is given greater significance by the fact that it came so close to never happening. Again, the message is the plane of potential freedom on which every human action is being played out even when it will eventually be revealed to have a retrospective meaning. The narrative form this insight takes is that of alternative endings and parallel lives. These restore the existential perspective of potentials that the teleology of the *Commedia* risks ending and expropriating: 'Se prima fu *la possa* in te finita | di peccar più, che sovvenisse l'ora | del buon dolor ch'a Dio ne rimarita, | come se' tu qua sù venuto ancora?' ['If your *power to keep on sinning* ended | just before the hour of blessed sorrow | that marries us once more to God, | how did you come so far so fast?'] (*Purg.* XXIII, 79–82, emphases mine); the afterlife is indeed described as the place where possibility is taken away, 'dove *poter peccar* non è più nostro' ['where we no longer have the *power to sin*'] (*Purg.* XXVI, 132, emphasis mine). Through alternative endings and parallel lives, the *Commedia* seeks to create this potential perspective anew.

2.4 Interpreting Alternative Endings and Parallel Lives: *Paradiso* XIII

The potential perspective represented in the *Commedia* through alternative endings and parallel lives offers a useful alternative to the hermeneutics of teleology. A teleological prejudice is evident in many studies on the structure of the poem. When Amilcare Iannucci, for instance, writes that '[t]he ascending structure of the *Commedia* denies the perverse brunettian notion of what immortality consists in, but, above all else, it is the technique of the

---

[47] This can be compared to Beatrice's speech in *Purg.* XXX, discussed at the start of the chapter, where Dante's virtual life of marvellous exploits is presented as a possible alternative that Dante, however, failed to realize.

parallel episode that destroys his reasoning', the underlying assumption is that the relation between the two episodes is teleological, that the old life is *denied* or *destroyed* by the new one.[48] Notwithstanding the general argument that the parallel-episode technique is a hierarchical strategy of self-commentary embedded in the text of the *Commedia*—whereby one episode 'reveals and overturns' the other, 'completing and clarifying' it,[49] or provides 'critical parameters', 'hermeneutic keys', or 'refers us to the context and illuminates intentions', or 'brings the language in focus'[50]—the language of Iannucci's article seems to sense a more dynamic and reciprocal relation between the two parallel episodes: the scholar writes, in fact, of '*mutual* clarification'; the two episodes, in his words, 'illuminate *each other*'.[51] To borrow from Erich Auerbach's seminal article on figural interpretation, the two phases 'point to one another'.[52] Before one episode can be said to deny, destroy, or sublimate its parallel according to the logic of teleology—which remains a fundamental mode of creating meaning in the *Commedia*—it is important to first call attention to the fact that both events point to one another as two fulfilments of the same potential. From an existential perspective, it is not a case of the one fulfilling the other teleologically but of both actualizing in a different narrative the same potential openness of life. Auerbach's study seems to be aware of the teleological as well as the existential side of the issue, as his text often interweaves the two aspects. With perfect teleological logic, the Romance philologist writes that 'The first event points to the second, the second fulfils the first'. But he immediately adds: 'To be sure, both remain concrete events that have taken place within history. Yet, when seen from this perspective, both also have something provisional and incomplete about them.'[53] The sense of this 'provisional and incomplete' quality, I wish to suggest, is the sense of the present alive with multiple futures that alternative narratives and parallel episodes try to convey as they point to one another. Holding together the two perspectives, Auerbach writes, 'They point to one another *and* both point to something

---

[48] 'La struttura ascensionale della *Commedia* nega la perversa nozione brunettiana di cosa costituisca l'immortalità, ma è soprattutto l'episodio parallelo che distrugge il suo ragionamento' (Iannucci, 'Autoesegesi dantesca', p. 109, trans. mine).
[49] 'rivela e capovolge', 'completandolo e chiarendolo' (ibid., p. 94, trans. mine).
[50] 'parametri critici' and 'chiavi interpretative', or 'ci riporta al contesto e illumina le intenzioni', or 'mette a fuoco il linguaggio' (ibid., p. 105, trans. mine).
[51] '*mutuo* chiarimento' and 's'illuminano *a vicenda*' (ibid., emphases mine).
[52] Erich Auerbach, 'Figura' [1938], in *Time, History, and Literature: Selected Essays of Erich Auerbach*, ed. James I. Porter, trans. Jane O. Newman (Princeton, NJ: Princeton University Press, 2014), pp. 65–113, p. 100.
[53] Ibid., p. 100.

in the future that is still to come. This will be the actual, complete, real, and final event.'[54] 'Both' is here the keyword, one which abolishes teleology and the primacy of 'the actual, complete, real, and final event': 'there is no either/or here, no choice to be made' between the two episodes in the poem; 'It is both at once'.[55] This two-fold perspective of the *Commedia*, at once retrospective and existential, is what Charles Singleton most memorably grasps as the underlying paradox at the heart of 'the understanding of the *Commedia*':

> For the understanding of the *Commedia* does, in the end, attain to a vista in retrospect of a total unity and harmony, which is itself one of the great experiences the Poem holds for us. But it is one experience among others and does not (as if it were some beatific vision) *cancel out the many other experiences* that are had along the way to the end.[56]

In this dazzling refusal to cancel out the alternative endings and parallel lives, the *Commedia* is closer to the novel than the teleological narrative it is more often identified with.[57] In fact, this chapter's impassioned apology for the autonomy of each parallel episode from the teleological narrative, which, in Singleton's terms, seeks 'to cancel out the many other experiences that are had along the way' in the name of 'a total unity and harmony', would probably not have to be as argumentative if it concerned the genre that makes it its point to welcome the superfluous, the manifold, the contingent, the errant, the centrifugal.[58] Indeed, a novelist who could be said to be at once radically existential and radically teleological, such as Marcel Proust, depicts the narrative ploy of parallel characters as a trite convention when he relates a notable dream of Charles Swann in *Un amour de Swann*. After Swann wakes up from a dream of a mysterious man wearing a fez, the narrator comments that Swann and the man were two sides of the same person:

> Ainsi Swann se parlait-il à lui-même, car le jeune homme qu'il n'avait pu identifier d'abord était aussi lui; comme certains romanciers, il avait

---

[54] Ibid., p. 100.   [55] Ibid., p. 107.
[56] Charles S. Singleton, 'The Vistas in Retrospect', *MLN*, 81.1 (1966), 55–80 (63), my italics.
[57] Roberto Mercuri argues that the *Commedia* anticipates the modern novel in 'Il metodo intertestuale nella lettura della *Commedia*', *Critica del testo*, 14.1 (2011), 111–51. It was an argument also made by György Lukács, *The Theory of the Novel: A Historico-Philosophical Essay on the Forms of Great Epic Literature*, trans. Anna Bostock (London: Merlin Press, 1971).
[58] Singleton, 'The Vistas in Retrospect', p. 63.

distribué sa personnalité à deux personnages, celui qui faisait le rêve, et un qu'il voyait devant lui coiffé d'un fez.

[So Swann reasoned with himself, for the young man whom he had failed at first to identify was himself too; like certain novelists, he had distributed his own personality between two characters, the one who was dreaming the dream, and another whom he saw in front of him sporting a fez.][59]

The impression that parallel lives are somehow more at home in the novel than in the *Commedia* says more about the teleological prejudice that holds sway over its readers than about the nature of this extraordinary narrative poem. Indeed, my goal in this chapter has been precisely to show how the ruling teleological narrative is counterpointed within the poem by an attention to alternative storylines, centrifugal narratives, affective spaces that work as in the novel. This is not to say that the *Commedia* is a novel, though it may be very helpful to think of it in terms of the narrative techniques active in it that one generally regards as novelistic.[60] The passage by Proust gives the measure of the specific distance between a novel like the *Recherche* and the narrative poem *Commedia*. Proust's 'certain novelists' are more concerned with the 'personality' of the characters; parallel episodes are arguably for them a way of exploring human psychology analytically by 'distributing' it over two characters. Although Dante doubtless shares a comparable interest in characterization, the focus of his parallel lives is not on personality per se as much as on its relation to the moment of salvation or damnation. The fact that this relation is not arbitrary, but structural, is characteristic of the *Commedia*. Nothing intrinsic beyond character psychology keeps together Swann and the man with the fez in the dream. The point of Dante's alternative endings and parallel lives, on the other hand, is that each character could have had the other's fate. The *Commedia* is the dramatic tale of how they could have had it, even when, in the end, they did not.

The most explicit, almost theoretical, statement about parallel lives appears in *Paradiso* XIII, as Iannucci recognized: 'As the purpose of the episode of Guido is to comment on *Convivio* IV, xxviii, 8, similarly the purpose of Buonconte's episode is to comment on that of Guido. Dante's critical

---

[59] Marcel Proust, *Un amour de Swann*, in *Du côté de chez Swann* (Paris: Grasset, 1913), p. 379; English trans.: Marcel Proust, *In Search of Lost Time. Volume I: Swann's Way*, trans. C. K. Scott Moncrieff and Terence Kilmartin, rev. R. J. Enright (New York: Modern Library, 1992), p. 518, emphases mine.
[60] On the *Commedia* as a proto-novel, see the classic study by Lukàcs, *The Theory of the Novel*.

reflections on Guido are complete or nearly so: the words of Thomas regarding the limits of human judgement in *Paradiso* XIII, 109–142 explicitly address a theme that Dante has represented in dramatized form in *Inferno* XXVII and *Purgatorio* V.[61] Iannucci's distinction between explicit treatment and dramatic representation is helpful when referred to the original aspects of the poetic thinking of the *Commedia* as opposed to the theoretical prose of the *Convivio*, discussed above; but, more interestingly, the distinction also captures the internal dynamic of *Paradiso* XIII, which in turn gives an insight into how the *Commedia* asks to be read. The target of Thomas's admonition, in fact, is initially errors of reading, starting with Dante's own doubt regarding Thomas's earlier biblical allusion to 3 Kings 3:12 (*Par.* X, 114).[62] The theologian then warns the protagonist against rash judgement when it comes to '[i]l sì e [i]l no che tu non vedi' ['yes or no [which] you [do not] see...clearly'] (*Par.* XIII, 114) and reproaches any person 'che sanza distinzion afferma e nega' ['who, without making clear distinctions, affirms or denies'] (116) and 'chi pesca per lo vero e non ha l'arte' ['who casts off from shore to fish for truth'] (123). In line with the overarching theme of the heaven of the sun, home to the *spiriti sapienti*, Thomas attacks the speculative thinkers—first the pagan philosophers who used fallacious syllogisms, then the early heretical theologians who misinterpreted the Scriptures—in the binary technical language of logic ('distinzion' ['distinction'] 109, 116; 'al sì e al no' ['yes or no'], 114; 'afferma e nega' ['affirms or denies'], 116; 'aperte prove' ['clear proofs'], 124). Yet at this point Thomas moves the discussion to another plane. As recent commentators notice, the *ancor* introduces 'a shift in the object of Thomas's measured scorn, from the schooled (philosophers and theologians) to the unschooled, ordinary folk ('donna Berta e ser Martino', i.e., Tom, Dick or Harry), as well as in the subject in which their misprision functions, from thoughts about the nature of things to the afterlife of one's neighbors'.[63] Thomas's admonition against rash judgement remains the same, but 'from philosophical judgement (on what is true or

---

[61] 'Come l'episodio di Guido serve a commentare il *Convivio* IV, xxviii, 8, così quello di Buonconte commenta quello di Guido. Le riflessioni critiche di Dante su Guido sono complete o quasi: le parole di S. Tommaso riguardanti i limiti del giudizio umano nel *Paradiso* XIII, 109–42 trattano esplicitamente un tema che Dante ha rappresentato drammaticamente in *Inferno* XXVII e *Purgatorio* V' (Iannucci, 'Autoesegesi dantesca', p. 96, trans. mine). See also John S. Carroll, *ad Par.* XIII, 129–42; Ernesto Trucchi, *ad* ll. 139–42; Umberto Bosco and Giovanni Reggio, *ad* ll. 112–42; Anna Maria Chiavacci Leonardi, *ad* ll. 136–8; Robert Hollander, *ad* ll. 133–8 (DDP).

[62] The biblical passage Dante refers to is: 'there was none like thee [Solomon] before thee, neither after thee shall any arise like unto thee' (3 Kings 3:12, King James Version).

[63] Robert Hollander, *ad Par.* XIII, 130–2 (DDP).

false) there's a shift to ethical judgement, on the behaviour of people (and thus on their eternal destiny, of salvation or perdition)':[64]

> Non sien le genti, ancor, troppo sicure
> a giudicar, sì come quei che stima
> le biade in campo pria che sien mature;
> ch'i' ho veduto tutto 'l verno prima
> lo prun mostrarsi rigido e feroce;
> poscia portar la rosa in su la cima;
> e legno vidi già dritto e veloce
> correr lo mar per tutto suo cammino,
> perire al fine a l'intrar de la foce.
> Non creda donna Berta e ser Martino,
> per vedere un furare, altro offerere,
> vederli dentro al consiglio divino;
> ché quel può surgere, e quel può cadere.
>
> [Let the people, then, not be too certain
> in their judgments, like those that harvest in their minds
> corn still in the field before it ripens.
> For I have seen the briar first look dry and thorny
> right through all the winter's cold,
> then later wear the bloom of roses at its tip,
> and once I saw a ship, which had sailed straight
> and swift upon the sea through all its voyage,
> sinking at the end as it made its way to port.
> Let not Dame Bertha and Master Martin,
> when they see one steal and another offer alms,
> think that they behold them with God's wisdom,
> for the first may still rise up, the other fall.]
> (*Par.* XIII, 130–42)

Here the binary *sì* and *no* are translated into metaphorical allusions to salvation and damnation, where the distinction becomes the temporal one between *before* ('pria', 130; 'prima', 133; 'già', 136) and *after* ('poscia', 135;

---

[64] '[D]al giudizio filosofico (su ciò che è vero o falso) si passa a quello etico, sul comportamento degli uomini (e quindi sul loro destino eterno, di salvezza o perdizione)' (Anna Maria Chiavacci Leonardi, *ad Par.* XIII, 130 (DDP)). See also Umberto Bosco and Giuseppe Reggio, *ad Par.* XIII, 130–2; Nicola Fosca, *ad* 130–2 (DDP).

'al fine', 138) a determining event: the two images of the thorn-bush budding at last into a rose and the ship sinking as it reached the shore are examples of the constant openness of possibilities in the human world of time; the same possibilities that were explored with Guido da Montefeltro's relapse into sin and Buonconte's last-minute conversion. The seeming antitheses between *furare* and *offerere* ['steal' and 'offer alms'] (140) and between the rhyming-line *surgere* and *cadere* ['rise up' and 'fall'] (142) are overturned. The pivoting point of this decisive overturning falls on the unassuming but all-important keyword of the passage, *può* ['may']: the reason why we must not judge rashly is 'ché quel *può* surgere, e quel *può* cadere' ['for the first *may* still rise up, the other [*may*] fall'] (142). The present in the *Commedia* is on the perennial verge of existence and always alive with multiple futures: the thief's and the benefactor's lives are interchangeable for as long as this world of potential remains open. And this perspective on existence is not limited to the living alone. On the contrary, it is so deeply engrained in the theological poetry of the *Commedia* that it is at home in heaven among the blessed ('E voi, mortali, tenetevi stretti | a giudicar: ché noi, che Dio vedemo, | non conosciamo ancor tutti li eletti' ['And you mortals, find some restraint | in making judgments, for we, who gaze on God, | have yet to know all those who are elect'], *Par.* XX, 133–5). Even there, potential remains radically open.

2.5 Secret as Narrative Freedom

I conclude this chapter by observing that once we begin to see the existential dimension of the present alive with multiple futures beneath the surface of the grand teleological narrative and we appreciate how deeply embedded it is within the form of the *Commedia* in the techniques of alternative endings and parallel lives, a recurrent theme comes into view, which has significant implications: in all the parallel lives I have identified, Dante relates events that were known only to the characters that tell the story. There is, in other words, no historical record of the various stories that Dante tells other than the testimony provided in the fiction of the *Commedia*. This fact, so obvious as to often pass without remark, is often self-consciously brought up by the characters themselves.[65] Enticed by Virgil's offer to have Dante

---

[65] Cf. Albert Russell Ascoli, *Dante and the Making of a Modern Author* (Cambridge: Cambridge University Press, 2008), p. 326: 'throughout the *Commedia* Dante makes frequent

refresh his *fama* ['fame'] (*Inf.* XIII, 53), Pier de le Vigne—himself a proud keeper of his lord's *secreto* [literally, 'secret'] (61)—is induced to give a posthumous account of his innocence, which he rounds off by asking the protagonist to publish it in *Inferno* XIII; similarly, in *Purgatorio* V, Buonconte da Montefeltro claims that he will finally tell the truth so that Dante may relate it to the living, whereas Guido da Montefeltro in *Inferno* XXVII, conversely, only agrees to break his peace when he is persuaded, mistakenly, that his story will never be divulged on earth. Surprise plays an important part in the reception of the stories the characters of the *Commedia* tell. Although in *Inferno* XV Brunetto does not expressly dwell on the circumstances of his sin, his presence in the seventh circle seems to come as a surprise to the pilgrim; analogously, Statius's conversion and salvation baffles Virgil, until the Silver Age poet in the fiction explains that he only lived as a closeted Christian ('chiuso cristiano' ['a secret Christian'], *Purg.* XXII, 90) out of fear, pretending for a long time to be a pagan ('lungamente mostrando paganesmo' ['long pretending I was still a pagan'], 91), and that he is now safe to reveal his secret. Secrets allow the characters to dwell on the affective dimension that would have been otherwise forgotten. In *Paradiso* VI, Justinian gestures towards Romeo di Villanova's private emotions as an exile as he mentions the praise that would rain on him if only the world knew them; and in *Inferno* V, Francesca's narration gives the protagonist exclusive knowledge of the decisive, but until then private, moment when the two lovers fell in love. This is not to mention the numerous instances, beyond our limited set of parallel episodes, when the protagonist is acquainted with a secret, intimate, or affective narration of the events that he would otherwise have had no access to—one may only consider the celebrated stories of Ulysses or Ugolino.

In the light of this chapter it will be evident that secret narratives are another way in which the *Commedia* carves out for itself a creative poetic space beyond the factual exigencies of a fictional narrative that aspires to present itself as historical. On the one hand, the topos of the tale that was

---

use of shockingly unexpected appearances (Guido da Montefeltro in Hell [canto 27]; his son in Purgatory [canto 5]; Cato, a suicide, in Purgatory [cantos 1–2]; Ripheus in the Heaven of Jupiter [canto 20]; and so on) to reinforce the rhetorical effect that his voyages in the world outside of history give him special access to hidden truths'; Manlio Pastore Stocchi, 'Dante Giudice Pentito', *Rivista di Studi Danteschi*, 15.1 (2015), 28–65 (29–30): 'di colpe ignote alle cronache, di virtù sconosciute, di segreti delle coscienze che solo allo sugardo onnisciente di Dio sarebbe dato penetrare...Dante si arroga la rivelazione quando giudica dannando o assolvendo, diciamo a mo' di esempio, Brunetto Latini, Guido e Buonconte da Montefeltro, o Stazio e Romeo di Villanova'.

secret up until its exclusive revelation is yet another trick of Dante's realism—the rhetorical strategy of presenting his journey as real so as to make it the foundation of its own truthfulness; on the other hand, however, the secret opens up for the author a creative space for poetic invention. Mirko Tavoni puts his finger on it in his discussion of 'the theme of defamation' in the episodes of Guido da Montefeltro and Ugolino della Gherardesca. The fact that both characters draw attention to their 'divulging on earth [their] defaming *segreto*' (Guido at *Inf.* XXVII, 61–66 and Ugolino at *Inf.* XXXIII, 4–9) 'makes it a sign of Dante's invention—or rather, an invention-revelation, conferred on the reader *sub specie aeternitatis*'.[66] Insisting on Dante's creative freedom and his autonomy from the narrative exigencies of historical accuracy, Tavoni comes full circle in the passage already quoted in part above, as he reminds us that 'Dante is not Minos's deputy, conscientious in undertaking his office on the basis of the information available to him. He is a poet of boundless audacity who, in treating characters and episodes from history and contemporary news, pretending to tell them truthfully *sub specie aeternitatis*...reserves the right to have total freedom, with his powerful and supreme fantasy, to create his own paths of meaning.'[67] Guido da Montefeltro's secret narrative, with its ventures into alternative endings and its reversal into a parallel life that confounds a devil and a saint, is a testament to the imaginative, creative, and affective space that the *Commedia* carves out for itself between the theological and historical necessities so unwaveringly guarded, with great wrath, by the infernal judge Minos.

[66] 'propalazione in terra di un segreto infamante...ne fa un segnale di invenzione dantesca— ma invenzione-rivelazione, imposta al lettore *sub specie aeternitatis*' (Tavoni, 'Guido da Montefeltro', p. 184).
[67] 'Dante non è il vice di Minosse, che adempia al suo ufficio coscienziosamente sulla base delle informazioni in suo possesso. È un poeta di audacia smisurata che, nel trattare personaggi ed episodi di storia e di cronaca, pretendendo di dirne la verità *sub specie aeternitatis*..., si riserva com'è ovvio una totale libertà, potentemente e sovranamente fantastica, nel creare i suoi propri percorsi di senso' (ibid., p. 174).

3
The Future In/Out of the *Commedia*

In the previous chapter I explored the role played by the *Commedia*'s alternative endings and parallel lives in the representation of the existential perspective of the living, who are 'on the perennial verge of existence', as opposed to the retrospective perspective of the dead, who are able to understand life from its endpoint. The philosopher Søren Kierkegaard expresses the difference between the two perspectives clearly in his journal:

> It is quite true...that life must be understood backwards. But then one forgets the other principle: that it must be lived forwards. Which principle, the more one thinks it through, ends exactly with the thought that temporal life can never properly be understood precisely because I can at no instant find complete rest in which to adopt a position: backwards.[1]

The *Commedia* is based precisely on the fiction that the 'position backwards' is ultimately possible; the poem can be read as the extended fantasy of an absolute endpoint from which this mess that is life can be finally 'understood backwards'.[2] At the same time, however, Dante also interweaves in the *Commedia* the experience of 'living forwards', and, as I have argued in Chapter 2, he employs this existential perspective to counterpoint the impressions of determinism arising from the main retrospective narrative. The interweaving of the two perspectives of perfect past and open present is an important pattern in the fabric of the *Commedia*, right from its famous first lines:

---

[1] Søren Kierkegaard, *Journals and Papers*, ed. Howard V. Hong and Edna H. Hong (Charlottesville, VA: InterLex Corp., 1995), IV A 164 [1843].
[2] Cf. Prue Shaw's dictum: 'We live forward, but we understand backwards' (*Reading Dante: From Here to Eternity* (New York: Liveright, 2014), p. 134). See also John Freccero on the poem's motion, which like the *terza rima*, 'proceed[s] by a forward motion that is at the same time recapitulatory' ('The Significance of *Terza Rima*', in *Dante: The Poetics of Conversion*, ed. Rachel Jacoff (Cambridge, MA: Harvard University Press, 1986), pp. 258–71 (p. 263)).

Nel mezzo del cammin di nostra vita
mi ritrovai per una selva oscura
ché la diritta via *era smarrita.*
Ahi quanto a dir qual *era* è cosa dura
esta selva selvaggia e aspra e forte
che nel pensier rinova la paura!
Tant'è amara che poco è più morte;
ma per trattar del ben ch'i' vi *trovai,*
dirò de l'altre cose ch'i' v'*ho scorte.*

[Midway in the journey of our life
I *came* to myself in a dark wood,
for the straight way *was lost.*
Ah, how hard it is to tell
the nature of that wood, savage, dense and harsh—
the very thought of it renews my fear!
It is so bitter death is hardly more so.
But to set forth the good I *found*
I **will recount** the other things I *saw.*]

(*Inf.* I, 1–9, emphases mine)

The incipit of *Inferno* I is emblematic of what Maria Grazia Riccobono, inserting herself in a long hermeneutic tradition, calls 'the poem's double temporality: the present of writing and the closed, complete past of the journey'.[3] The verb tenses of *Inferno* I establish a precise fictional time frame: the diegetic level of the voyage is evoked by the past tense ('mi ritrovai', 'era smarrita', 'qual era', 'trovai', 'ho scorte', italicized), while the extradiegetic level of its narration is entrusted to the present tense ('è cosa dura', 'rinova la paura', underlined). This dual temporality has been variously interpreted by scholars who generally conceptualize it as a distinction between Dante *personaggio* (the character that journeys through the afterlife) and Dante *poeta* (the narrator's persona that tells the story of that journey).[4] Of course, there is some degree of continuity between the two

---

[3] '[L]a struttura a due tempi del poema: il presente della scrittura e il passato chiuso e compiuto del viaggio' (Maria Grazia Riccobono, *Dante Poeta-Profeta, Pellegrino, Autore: Strutturazione Espressiva della Commedia e Visione Escatologica Dantesca* (Rome: Aracne, 2012), p. 12, trans. mine).

[4] Some scholars have drawn a further distinction between Dante *poeta* and Dante *autore*, the historical man writing the poem that contains the fictional character and narrator by the same name. I am adopting the tripartite terminology of Robert Wilson, *Prophecies and Prophecy in Dante's 'Commedia'* (Florence: Olschki, 2008). Wilson objects to the categorizations offered by

Dantes, as Gianfranco Contini highlights in his seminal essay 'Dante come personaggio-poeta'. This continuity is specifically temporal: in the story's time frame, *personaggio* and *poeta* are the same character at two successive points in history, the one moving forward, the other looking back along the same timeline.[5] And indeed, their 'historical' aspect is what sets these verbs apart from the other present tenses in the passage. The line 'Tant' amara che poco è più morte' ['It is so bitter death is hardly more so'] (7), for instance, expresses a kind of present that is not, strictly speaking, historical; its truth value is universal in that it does not depend on a specific moment in time. In the first half of the line, the full weight of the adjective *amara* ['bitter'] would be lost on us if we took it only literally and did not know beforehand the significance of the *selva* as a symbol of spiritual perdition for the pilgrim and, more universally, for humanity's eternal destiny; the adjective *amara*, in other words, only makes full sense once we interpret it from this eschatological perspective. Similarly, the second half of the line 'poco è più morte' is making the claim that death is *always* bitter, regardless of historical contingencies. The present is used here in its so-called gnomic aspect, to express a universal truth. Something comparable is occurring in the first line 'Nel mezzo del cammin di nostra vita' ['Midway in the journey of our life'], where the phrase indicates a very precise historical time (the year AD 1300, when the 35-year-old narrator got lost in a dark wood) but does so by reference to a then universally accepted truth: that 'our' human life *always* lasts on average seventy years.[6] In its interplay of tenses, then, the first canto of *Inferno* already establishes the poem's meticulous time frame that will become familiar to readers of the poem: hinging on two moments in a continuous timeline—the *personaggio*'s diegetic past and the *poeta*'s

---

Robin Kirkpatrick (*Dante's 'Inferno': Difficulty and Dead Poetry* (Cambridge: Cambridge University Press, 1987), p. xii), Chandler B. Beall ('Dante and his Reader', *Forum Italicum*, 13 (1979), 299–343 (309)), and Tibor Wlassics (*Dante narratore: saggi sullo stile della 'Commedia'* (Florence: Olschki, 1975), p. 113) for failing to observe the distinction between fact and fiction.

[5] See Gianfranco Contini, 'Dante come personaggio-poeta della Commedia', in *Un'idea di Dante: Studi danteschi* (Turin: Einaudi, 1970), pp. 33–62 (p. 34), drawing a comparison with Proust. Julia Hartley critiques the assumptions behind Contini's 'now outdated *Bildungsroman* interpretation of the *Recherche*' as follows: 'while Contini does connect protagonist and narrator, he preserves their separation by expressing their relationship teleologically in terms of a linear evolution from the status of protagonist to the status of narrator, which is achieved through the expurgation of the protagonist's poetic past' (Julia Caterina Hartley, *Reading Dante and Proust by Analogy* (Cambridge: Legenda, 2019), p. 11). For further bibliographical references on the *personaggio-poeta*, see above, Introduction, n. 51.

[6] For the distinction between individual and universal (or type), see the Introduction, Section I.4, above.

extradiegetic present—it takes place on two planes—history and a universal or eschatological timelessness.[7]

But then something different happens with the occurrence of the verb *dirò* at line 9: 'dirò de l'altre cose ch'i' v'ho scorte' ['I will recount the other things I saw']. On the one hand, the first future tense of the *Commedia* finds its place in the network of verbs that constitute the poem's historical time frame: the time when Dante will write down his story for us is on a continuum with the time of the (fictional) journey itself, in the early fourteenth century. On the other hand, however, the verb *dirò* does something subtle but unexpected: it upsets the accepted division of labour between the character who lives forward and the narrator who understands backwards. This division of labour is assumed already by the early commentators' use of the terms *agens* and *auctor* to connote the two Dantes, the one partaking in the poem's action, the other in its narration, perfectly compartmentalized. And yet in promising a future action right from the start of the poem, the *Commedia* casts the *auctor* in the role of an agent projected forward. The verb unseats him from his safe position as the retrospective assessor of the past, and throws him in the arena with those who live forward. The narrator here is no longer simply connoting his storytelling as retrospective ('quanto a dir', *now*, 'è cosa dura' ['Ah, how hard it is to tell' *now*], 4) but projecting the act of narration into the future (*dirò*), a time over which Dante cannot display the same mastery that he claims over narratives in the past tense. The future *dirò*, in other words, plants the first of a series of clues that the story of Dante—*poeta* and *personaggio*—is as open-ended at the time of writing as it was during the journey.

3.1 *Poeta* Writing into the Future

As the proemial position of the verb *dirò* suggests, future tenses play an important role throughout the *Commedia*. Dante's exposure to an open-ended future is confirmed in many passages where the distinction between *personaggio* and *poeta* not only appears to be otherwise unproblematic but is often taken as an important criterion in the interpretation of the poem. A typical example is *Inferno* XXVI. Here Dante famously meets the Greek hero Ulysses, with whom he shares a talent for rhetoric and desire for

---

[7] On this idea, see Auerbach, 'Figura', pp. 106–13.

daring voyages but whose tragic shipwreck looms large over Dante's otherworldly journey. The interpretation of the canto has generally revolved around the question of the relationship between Dante's past and present 'I': given their affinities, should we consider Ulysses an alter ego of Dante's younger and more naïve self? As the canto begins, and Dante is about to retell the tale of his encounter, the narrator exclaims the following:

> Allor mi dolsi, e ora mi ridoglio
> quando drizzo la mente a ciò ch'io vidi,
> e più lo 'ngegno affreno ch'i' non soglio,
>   perché non corra che virtù nol guidi;
> sì che, se stella bona o miglior cosa
> m'ha dato 'l ben, ch'io stessi nol m'invidi.
>
> [I grieved then and now I grieve again
> as my thoughts turn to what I saw,
> and more than is my way, I curb my powers
>   lest they run on where virtue fail to guide them,
> so that, if friendly star or something better still
> has granted me its boon, I don't misuse the gift].
>
> (*Inf.* XXVI, 19–24)

The sharp one-liner 'Allor mi dolsi, e ora mi ridoglio' ['I grieved then and now I grieve again'] (19) seems to confirm the distinction between the *personaggio*'s journey in the past and the *poeta*'s reflection: here the same verb (*dolersi* [literally, 'to be pained']) is conjugated first in the *personaggio*'s past tense ('mi dolsi'), then in the *poeta*'s present ('mi ridoglio'); on the one hand, we have the diegetic past (*Allor*), and on the other, the extradiegetic present (*ora*). When it comes to the line 'Allor mi dolsi, e ora mi ridoglio', on the one hand we have scholars who, like Robert Hollander, argue that 'Dante, in this passage, is fully conscious of his *previous* "Ulyssean" efforts, undertaken by his venturesome and prideful intellect, and *now* hopes to keep them under control'.[8] On the other hand, we have Lino Pertile's critique of this position and counterargument that 'those who propose a negative view of Ulysses fail to acknowledge the importance of these verses, which reveal the poet's

---

[8] Robert Hollander, ad *Inf.* XXVI, 19 (DDP), italics mine. Cf. Robert Hollander, *Allegory in Dante's 'Commedia'* (Princeton, NJ: Princeton University Press, 1969), pp. 115–6. For this 'palinodic moment', see also John Freccero, 'Dante's Ulysses: From Epic to Novel', in *Dante: The Poetics of Conversion*, ed. Rachel Jacoff (Cambridge, MA: Harvard University Press, 1986), pp. 136–51.

sympathy for the Greek hero *even now* as he writes of him'.⁹ Both Hollander's and Pertile's interpretations are rooted in the distinction between a 'previous' Dante and Dante 'now'; both scholars work under the assumption that the present of writing has the last word on the episode; but the teleological model implicit in this *modus legendi* appears to go unquestioned. What would happen to these interpretations if the narrator's present were not as definitive an endpoint as they make it out to be?

This is a necessary question once we consider the fact that, just like the poem's incipit, the context of the first part of *Inferno* XXVI does precisely this: it problematizes the very possibility of a conclusive 'position backwards' on which these and similar interpretations are predicated. This occurs twice in the space of a few terzinas before and after line 19. The first instance is when the terzinas following the line 'Allor mi dolsi, e ora mi ridoglio' place the stress not so much on the certainty of Dante's illustrious destiny but on its contingency and openness to failure, as I discussed in the previous chapter: the positive influence of the heavens ('bona stella o miglior cosa' ['friendly star or something better still'], 23) is surrounded by the uncertainty of hypotheticals (*se* ['if']), as the narrator, who in theory is safe and out of danger, is represented as still at risk of losing 'l ben' that his journey has earned him. But even before that, the canto uses the narrator's prophecy of Florence's ills to remind readers of Dante's continuing involvement in the future:

> Ma se presso al mattin del ver si sogna,
> tu sentirai di qua da picciol tempo
> di quel che Prato, non ch'altri, t'agogna.
> E se già fosse, non saria per tempo.
> Così foss'ei, da che pur esser dee!
> ché più mi graverà, com'più m'attempo.
>
> [But if as morning nears we dream the truth,
> it won't be long before you feel the pain
> that Prato, to name but one, desires for you.
> Were it already come, it would not be too soon.
> But let it come, since come indeed it must,
> and it will weigh the more on me the more I age.]
>
> (*Inf.* XXVI, 7–12)

---

⁹ Robert Hollander, *ad Inf.* XXVI, 19 (DDP), italics mine, referring, with fair play, to Lino Pertile, 'Dante e l'ingegno di Ulisse,' *Stanford Italian Review*, 1 (1979), 35–65.

As Robert Wilson observes in his study of prophecies in the *Commedia*, 'this prophecy stands apart from the others as it is delivered by Dante *poeta*, and may be described as extra-diegetic', which contrasts with the way prophecies are usually delivered to Dante *personaggio* by other characters in his fictional journey.[10] The prophetic pose expressed by the apostrophe in the future tense ('tu sentirai' [literally, 'you will experience'], 8) and by the imperative ('esser dee' ['come indeed it must'], 11) is immediately complicated by a whole host of counterfactuals, imperfect subjunctives, and conditionals (*se* ['if'], twice; *saria* ['it would...be']; *foss'ei* ['were it already come'], 10–11)—the formal means through which Dante explores alternative endings, discussed in the previous chapter. The subjunctives make it clear 'that what [Dante] has dreamt has not yet happened, whilst...also stat[ing] unequivocally that it must occur (11)'.[11] The tension between the certainty that the events prophesied must unfold ('pur esser dee' ['come indeed it must'], 11) and the uncertainty of when exactly this might happen ('non saria per tempo' ['it would not be too soon'], 10) is at the heart of these lines. This prophecy, voiced by the narrator, hangs on his conflicted wish to accelerate his city's demise as a means to soothe his anxiety in the anticipation.[12] The future tense that follows ('ché più mi graverà, com' più m'attempo' ['it will weigh the more on me the more I age'], 12) expresses this anxiety: the narrator is here not the direct object of the prophecy but, as it were, its collateral damage. The sentence, in fact, is not an act of prophecy as much as of poetic imagination. The specific way in which the narrator will eventually inhabit that future is available to him only imaginatively. The future remains open. Read in this light, the scholarly debate among early and modern commentators over whether Dante is saying here that he will be weighed down more by Florence's downfall or by the thought that it may not happen is particularly telling, since, whatever answer is proposed, the debate is a reflection of the anxiety at the heart of the passage: Dante *poeta*'s own uncertainty when it comes to what awaits him living forwards.[13]

These two passages are emblematic of how the critical practice of distinguishing between Dante *personaggio* and Dante *poeta* has the unintended side effect of characterizing their relationship as exclusively self-reflexive, inclining us to imagine the two Dantes as forever moving toward each

---

[10] Wilson, *Prophecies and Prophecy*, p. 61. It should be noted that Wilson does not consider *Paradiso* XXV, 1–9, a prophecy *stricto sensu* (see n. 99 below).
[11] Wilson, *Prophecies and Prophecy*, p. 61.
[12] See *Paradiso* XVII, 22–7, for a comparable wish.
[13] Nicola Fosca, *ad Inf.* XXVI, 12 (DDP).

other—the one living forwards, the other narrating backwards. Actually, the *Commedia* resists this clear-cut distinction by involving the *poeta*, time and time again, in the living forwards that is traditionally conceived as the province of the *personaggio*. Dante, in the *Commedia*, is not only the *personaggio-poeta* who was pained *then* and is pained *now* by Ulysses's fate ('Allor mi dolsi, e ora mi ridoglio', *Inf.* XXVI, 19) but also the narrator who is shivering *now* at the thought of the icy lakes of Hell and claims that he *will always shiver* ('Onde mi vien riprezzo, | e verrà sempre, de' gelati guazzi', *Inf.* XXXII, 71–2). He is not just the narrator who says, in the past tense, that ever since his return he *has never stopped* wishing he could hear again the celestial 'Hosanna' ('sì, che unque poi | di riudir non fui sanza disiro', *Par.* VIII, 29–30); or, in the present tense, that Beatrice's name *is always* on his mind ('il nome | che ne la mente sempre mi rampolla', *Purg.* XXVII, 41–2); but he is also the one who claims, in the future tense, that aristocratic pride *will never surprise* him, even after his otherworldly pilgrimage ('mirabil cosa non mi sarà mai' *Par.* XVI, 4).[14] The narrator, in other words, inhabits all three moments of time—past, present, and future—and he too lives forward. And why should this surprise us? If the other characters in the *Commedia* imaginatively inhabit alternative endings, as I have shown in the previous chapter, there is no reason to exclude the narrator from imagining different futures, especially considering that he is not dead yet and therefore makes an even better candidate for the position 'living forwards'. Quite the contrary, Dante systematically unseats the narrator from his safe judging position and fully involves him and his poem in the fearsome and changing world of time and circumstance.

3.2 The Proems of the Poem

Once we begin paying attention to the future tenses in the *Commedia*, interesting patterns begin to emerge. The narrator's future occupies a strategic

---

[14] Further examples of the narrator's continuing affective participation also include fear ('de lo spavento | la mente di sudore ancor mi bagna', *Inf.* III, 131–2); praise ('quello strazio |…che Dio ancor ne lodo e ne ringrazio', *Inf.* VIII, 58–60); horror ('un picciol fiumicello, | lo cui rossore ancor mi raccapriccia', *Inf.* XIV, 77–8; 'e anco il cor me n'accapriccia', *Inf.* XXII, 31; see also 'la memoria ancor mi scipa', *Inf.* XXIV, 82–4); pain ('Ancor men duol pur ch' me ne rimembri', *Inf.* XVI, 12); shame ('con tal vergogna, | ch'ancor per la memoria mi si gira', *Inf.* XXX, 133–5); and sweetness ("Amor che ne la mente mi ragiona" | cominciò elli allor sì dolcemente, | che la dolcezza ancor dentro mi suona', *Purg.* II, 112–14). On this recurring trope, see also Lina Bolzoni, 'Memory', in *The Oxford Handbook of Dante*, ed. Manuele Gragnolati, Elena Lombardi, and Francesca Southerden (Oxford: Oxford University Press, 2021), pp. 17–33 (p. 28).

place in each proemial canto of the *Commedia* where it is closely bound with writing and its creative metaphors: speaking, painting, and singing. The use of the future tense says something fundamental about the processual nature of writing. We have already seen the future tense *dirò* in the general proem of *Inferno* I (9). *Inferno* II follows suit:

> e io sol uno
> m'apparecchiava a sostener la guerra
> sì del cammino e sì de la pietate,
> che *ritrarrà* la mente che non erra.
> O muse, o alto ingegno, or m'aiutate;
> o mente che scrivesti ciò ch'io vidi,
> qui si parrà la tua nobilitate.
>
> [and I, alone,
> prepared to face the struggle—
> of the way and of the pity of it—
> which memory, unerring, *shall retrace*.
> O Muses, O lofty genius, aid me now!
> O memory, that set down what I saw,
> here *shall* your worth *be shown*.]
>
> (*Inf.* II, 3–9, italics mine)

The dialectic at work here is the familiar one between the time of the action (diegesis) and the time of writing (extradiegesis). The latter, however, is not expressed in the present tense, as one might expect from the *personaggio-poeta* division of labour, but in the future: the future tenses 'ritrarrà' ['shall retrace'] (6) and 'si parrà' ['shall…be shown'] (9) indicate writing as the activity that will happen from now on. The narrator does use the present when he asks for help with his writing ('or m'aiutate' ['aid me now'], 7),[15] but for the act of writing itself he employs the future tense. This choice is another important piece in the puzzle that shows the narrator's involvement in the future. It expresses what I imagine is no more than common sense for many writers. Writing is a progressive activity that takes place gradually and patiently over time; therefore it must, by its very nature, partake in the future. The duration of the activity and its partaking in the future are two

---

[15] Robert Hollander, 'The "Canto of the Word" (*Inferno* 2)', *Lectura Dantis Newberryana*, ed. Paolo Cherchi and Antonio C. Mastrobuono, 2 vols (Evanston, IL: Northwestern University Press, 1990), II, pp. 98–100.

sides of the same coin. Saying that something has a duration is tantamount to saying that it requires extension into the future. Language offers a clue into this aspect: the English noun *writing* derives from a gerund (suffix '*-ing*') which stresses the aspect of duration; the Italian *scrittura*, analogously, derives from a Latin future participle (suffix '*-ura*') and emphasizes the future-bound aspect of the activity. The time of writ*ing* involves indeed the future.

It is no surprise, then, if the character of the narrator is deeply implicated into the future, especially when his writing comes under the spotlight. The future tense appears also in the proems of *Purgatorio* and *Paradiso*, where it affects the usual dialectic between the *personaggio*'s past and the *poeta*'s present:

> Per correr miglior acque alza le vele
> omai la navicella del mio ingegno,
> che lascia dietro a sé mar sì crudele;
>   e *canterò* di quel secondo regno
> dove l'umano spirito si purga
> e di salire al ciel diventa degno.
>
>   [To run its course through smoother water
> the small bark of my wit now hoists its sail,
> leaving that cruel sea behind.
>   Now *I shall sing* the second kingdom,
> there where the soul of man is cleansed,
> made worthy to ascend to Heaven.]
>   (*Purg.* I, 1–6, italics mine)

In this proem, the narrator's extradiegetic time is expressed, as usual, in the present tense, when the narrator's *ingegno* (2) 'alza le vele' ['hoists its sail'] (1), and 'lascia dietro a sé' [literally, 'leaves behind'] (3) the cruel sea that has already been written about. This present tense, however, is set in counterpoint not with the past of Dante's journey, as again one might expect, but rather with the future (*canterò* ['I shall sing'], 4), the narrator's activity no longer retrospective but forward-oriented. *Paradiso* takes this one step further by doing away with the present tense altogether:

> Veramente quant'io del regno santo
> ne la mia mente potei far tesoro,
> *sarà* ora materia del mio canto.

> [Nevertheless, as much of the holy kingdom
> as I could store as treasure in my mind
> *shall* now become the subject of my song.]
>
> (*Par.* I, 10–12, italics mine)

Here again the emphasis is on futurity. The adverb *ora* ['now'] (12) does not simply mean the moment *now* but the stretch of time *from now on*. The present it appears to, but does not really, indicate is in fact absent from this terzina: the only two verbal tenses are simply the remembered past ('quant'io del regno santo |...*potei* far tesoro' ['as much of the holy kingdom | as I could store'], 10–11) and the future-oriented activity of writing ('*sarà* ora materia del mio canto' ['shall now become the subject of my song'], 12). The narrator thus straddles the present, with one foot in the journey he has concluded and the other in the writing he has begun.

The noun *canto* is similarly arched, its connotations ambiguously poised between the technical term for the poem's chapters (*canti*) and the progressive activity of singing a song (*canto*).[16] It is a significant ambiguity, as it represents the *Paradiso* at once as somehow already existing, independently of time, in the author's design, and as requiring time to unfold through the metaphorical act of singing—two perspectives that bear on questions of realism and authority that are always of paramount importance in the *Commedia*. Dante is counterpointing the *Commedia* as a material object that occupies a space with the activity of writing that takes time. This distinction can be approached in a number of ways, depending on whether we look at the text from the perspective of the writer or the reader, as a mental project or as a material object.[17] We can say, for instance, that at the time of writing this canto, the *Commedia* is envisaged as a complete book in the writer's mind, and yet its writing will take place over time. Or, equally, we can take the reader's perspective and say that the *Commedia* is a defined material object (*that* manuscript, *that* print book, *that* PDF), and yet reading it will

---

[16] Commenting on *canto* and its cognates in *Convivio* and *De vulgari eloquentia*, Margaret Bent notes that '[it] is sometimes hard to determine which of three possible levels Dante might be talking about: music as we understand it; musical terms as metaphors or analogies for poetry; undifferentiated terminology common to both and transferable between them' ('Songs Without Music in Dante's *De Vulgari Eloquentia*: *Cantio* and related terms', in *'Et facciam dolçi canti'*: *Studi in onore di Agostino Ziino in occasione del suo 65° compleanno*, ed. Bianca Maria Antolini, Teresa M. Gialdroni, and Annunziato Pugliese (Lucca: Libreria Musicale Italiana, 2004), I, pp. 161–81 (p. 166)).

[17] On this question of the design of a work as both mental project and material object, see Vittoria Fallanca, *The Design of Montaigne's 'Essays'* (unpublished doctoral thesis, University of Oxford, 2020).

take place over time.[18] This very ambiguity of Dante's *canto*—both complete, independent of time, and unfinished, still in progress; both ideal and material—gives a little taste of Dante's ambivalence on the risks and advantages of bringing the future into his poem. When Zygmunt Barański asks, 'why does he bother to use [the form of the *canto*] instead of an open-ended and continuous structure like that of the *romans*?,'[19] a possible answer is precisely the power of the term 'canto' to anticipate the complete poem in these ways. Barański suggests as much when commenting on the first occurrence of *canto* and *canzon* in *Inferno* XX (a canto which also expressly thematizes the future in its portrayal of false prophets, as I will show in Section 3.5 below):

> Di nova pena mi conven far versi
> e dar matera al ventesimo canto
> de la prima canzon ch'è d'i sommersi.
>
> [Of strange new pain I now must make my verse,
> giving matter to the canto numbered twenty
> of this first canzone, which tells of those submerged.]
>
> (*Inf.* XX, 1–3)

As Barański observes, '[t]he precision with which [Dante] affirms that we are about to read "il ventesimo canto | de la prima canzon" also reveals for the first time that this first canzone will have its numerical counterpart or counterparts elsewhere in the text. Up to this point, the poem provides no clue that it is to have such an unexpected and original design.'[20] If this is 'the twentieth *canto* of the first *canzon*', then the reader can reasonably expect more *canti* and *canzoni* to follow. Indeed, representing the *Commedia* as a complete work by highlighting a part to hint at the whole helps establish the poem as an intellectual and material unit. Prefiguring its unity is especially useful to Dante in the face of the adverse material conditions of its composition and transmission; it is a first step toward managing its interpretation as a complete work.[21] In the proem of *Paradiso*, this perspective is

---

[18] The distinction between the text in the writer's mind and the material manuscript is also alive in these lines in the secondary connotations of *mente* (10) and *materia* (11).

[19] Zygmunt G. Barański, 'The Poetics of Meter: *Terza rima*, "canto", "canzon", "cantica"', in *Dante Now: Current Trends in Dante Studies*, ed. Theodore J. Cachey Jr (Notre Dame, IN: University of Notre Dame Press, 1995), pp. 3–41 (p. 9).

[20] Barański, 'The Poetics of Meter', p. 6.

[21] On Dante's representation of the material unity of his work in the context of medieval material culture, see John Ahern, 'Binding the book: Hermeneutics and Manuscript Production

counterbalanced by the melic connotations of *canto* which turn the emphasis on the writing in progress. The advantage is that Dante can now stress, once again, the incompleteness and openness to the future that play such an important role in the *Commedia*, not least in the characterization of the narrator who has yet to write the work. These forms of the future thus help represent the poem and its writing, paradoxically, as both complete and in progress, both future-proof and future-facing. The last time Dante picks up the word *canto* in its technical connotation at the end of *Paradiso* V ('nel modo che 'l seguente canto canta' ['in the very manner that the next song sings'], 139), he underlines once more, with his etymological wordplay between noun (*canto*) and verb (*canta*), the two aspects of his writing that have interested him as early as the proems: the complete text and the act of writing it.[22]

As Barański argues, then, while Dante uses the term *canto* in the conventional poetic sense of 'song', he also overwrites it with a new technical meaning: a *canto* is a 'chapter' in the narrative poem *Commedia*. A similar case can be made about the narrator's use of the future tense in the proems. These futures—'dirò dell'altre cose ch'i' v'ho scorte' ['I will recount the other things I saw'] (*Inf.* I, 9), 'che ritrarrà la mente che non erra' ['which memory, unerring, shall retrace'] (*Inf.* II, 6), 'e canterò di quel secondo regno' ['Now I shall sing the second kingdom'] (*Purg.* I, 4), 'sarà ora materia del mio canto' [shall now become the subject of my song'] (*Par.* I, 12)—play a conventional role: the narrator is introducing the work's subject matter, in a tradition that spans from classical epic to academic writings such as this monograph. The programmatic future is even a trademark of many of the *Commedia*'s best-known embedded tales: the verb *dirò* is used by Virgil (*Inf.* II, 50), Francesca (*Inf.* V, 126), Ugolino (*Inf.* XXXIII, 15), and Buonconte (*Purg.* V, 103). Now, programmatic statements about the content of the work are nothing remarkable; what is more remarkable is the narrator's systematic use of the future tense. In Latin epic poetry circulating in Dante's times, in fact, narrators generally favoured the present, to the point where tense becomes an indicator of genre, distinguishing epic from other forms of poetry. Thus Virgil's narrator sings the epic *Aeneid* in the present ('Arma virumque cano' ['I sing arms and the man'], I, 1) but the didactic poetry of the *Georgics* in the future ('canere incipiam' [literally, 'I will begin to sing'],

---

in Paradiso 33', *PMLA* 97 (1982), 800–9. On his frustrated desire to see it implemented, see Elena Lombardi, *Imagining the Woman Reader in the Age of Dante* (Oxford: Oxford University Press, 2019), pp. 196–7.

[22] On 'the etymological figure' *canto/canta*, see also Barolini, *Undivine 'Comedy'*, p. 190.

THE FUTURE IN/OUT OF THE *COMMEDIA* 129

I, 5);[23] Ovid's narrator uses the present in the *Metamorphoses* ('fert animus...dicere' ['My mind is bent to tell'], I, 1) but the future in his didactic *Fasti* ('Tempora...[et] signa canam' ['The order of the calendar...and the starry signs...I'll sing'], I, 1–2);[24] and the narrators of Lucan and Statius's epics stick to the present ('Bella...plus quam civilia...canimus' ['Of war I sing, war worse than civil'], *Pharsalia* I, 1–2; 'Magnanimum Aeaciden... refer', ['tell of great-hearted Aeacides'], *Achilleid* I, 1–3),[25] while Horace's lyric persona feels free to sing in the future tense ('te canam' ['I shall sing of you'], *Odes* I, x, 2; 'Quid...dicam' ['What shall I sing'], I, xii, 13 and 25; etc.).[26] There are, of course, exceptions to this general distinction[27]—the most compelling of which will be discussed in a moment—but the fact remains, as classicist Matthew Leigh states, that 'employment of the future tense by the narrator in Latin epic is extremely rare and occurs in specific stylised contexts'.[28] Conversely, the future tense is altogether more popular in genres where the first-person narrator is part of the story, and there is a significant degree of overlap between the implied and historical author: I am thinking here specifically of classical lyric and elegiac poetry, but the definition equally applies to the *Commedia*.[29] In traditional epic, the story

---

[23] Virgil, *Eclogues. Georgics. Aeneid: Books 1–6*, trans. H. Rushton Fairclough, rev. G. P. Goold, Loeb Classical Library 63, new rev. edn (Cambridge, MA: Harvard University Press, 1999).
[24] Ovid, *Metamorphoses, Volume I: Books 1–8*, trans. Frank Justus Miller, rev. G. P. Goold, Loeb Classical Library 42, 3rd rev. edn (Cambridge, MA: Harvard University Press, 1977); and *Fasti*, trans. James G. Frazer, rev. G. P. Goold, Loeb Classical Library 253, 2nd rev. edn, repr. with corrections (Cambridge, MA: Harvard University Press, 1996).
[25] Lucan, *The Civil War (Pharsalia)*, trans. J. D. Duff, Loeb Classical Library 220 (Cambridge, MA: Harvard University Press, 1928), and Statius. *Thebaid, Volume II: Thebaid: Books 8–12. Achilleid*, ed. and trans. D. R. Shackleton Bailey, Loeb Classical Library 498 (Cambridge, MA: Harvard University Press, 2004).
[26] Horace, *Odes and Epodes*, ed. and trans. Niall Rudd, Loeb Classical Library 33, rev. edn (Cambridge, MA: Harvard University Press, 2012).
[27] Virgil's 'second proem' halfway through the *Aeneid* is the most notable one: 'dicam horrida bella | dicam acies actosque animis in funera reges' (VII, 41). Though not in a proem, Virgil, *Aeneid* X, 791–3 and Ovid, *Metamorphoses* X, 300, are in the future tense. Dante alludes to the latter ('Dira canam; procul hinc nate, procul este parentes') in *Inf.* XXX, 37–9 (see commentaries by Guido da Pisa, Gioachino Berthier, and Giacomo Poletto *ad loc.* (DDP)). My examples are limited to the poems available in Dante's times, and thus exclude notable classical proems in the present tense by the likes of Silius Italicus and Valerius Flaccus.
[28] Matthew Leigh, *Lucan: Spectacle and Engagement* (Oxford: Clarendon Press, 1997), p. 325. See his Appendix 3 on 'The Future Tense in Latin Epic Narrative', pp. 325–9.
[29] See Horace, *Odes* I, i, 36; and Ovid, *Ars Amatoria* I, 8, to limit examples to the proemial poems in each work (Ovid, *Art of Love. Cosmetics. Remedies for Love. Ibis. Walnut-tree. Sea Fishing. Consolation*, trans. J. H. Mozley, rev. G. P. Goold, Loeb Classical Library 232, 2nd rev. edn (Cambridge, MA: Harvard University Press, 1979)). See R. O. A. M. Lyne, *Collected Papers on Latin Poetry* (Oxford: Oxford University Press, 2007), p. 350, for further 'proud public, publishing futures' where the narrator is a fictionalized version of the author.

takes centre stage and the primary narrator recedes in the background, omniscient and disembodied; in lyric poetry, and in the *Commedia*, an embodied and affectively involved narrator is also the story's protagonist (or at least one half of it). Epic narrators eschew the future tense because it draws unwanted attention to them as historical authors, with wishes, fears, desires, regrets, however disguised or fictionalized; in contrast, the topical 'future of literary immortality'[30] appeals to lyric poets such as Horace and Ovid in their odes and elegies because it affords them the opportunity to reflect openly on the embodied activity of writing and the author's personal literary aspirations, thematizing the craft of writing that epic tends to prefer to eclipse. Lino Pertile has reflected on classical epic's separation between embodied characters and disembodied narrator that the *Commedia* subverts: 'Unlike Homer and Virgil who always say "he," never "I," and unlike Ulysses and Aeneas who went to Hell but did not write the stories of their own journeys, the protagonist and the narrator of the *Comedy* are one and the same.'[31] Indeed, in the *Aeneid* Virgil employs the future tense 'lyrically' precisely when he wants to draw attention to an internal narrator and his embodied and affective involvement in the story he is telling: this is the case of Aeneas's own narration of the fall of Troy, a tale which the hero begins, reluctantly and painfully, precisely in the future tense: 'incipiam' (*Aeneid* II, 13). Already one may argue from such instances that this is the kind of embodied narrator that provides a model for Dante-*poeta*; there is also, however, a further influence. Considering the epic tradition, it is not by chance that when Statius opens his *Thebaid* with meta-literary reflections of his own, he brings into the epic proem the very future tense that his precursors had ruled out. Statius taps into a relationship between the narrator's future and meta-literary themes that had long been established in other genres. As classicists have long noticed, the 'proem to the *Thebaid* and indeed the whole of the first book exhibit a self-conscious concern with the poetics of opening.'[32] All is sparked by the rhetorical question 'unde iubetis |

---

[30] Leigh, *Lucan*, p. 326.
[31] Lino Pertile, 'Introduction to *Inferno*', *The Cambridge Companion to Dante*, ed. Rachel Jacoff, 2nd edn (Cambridge: Cambridge University Press, 2007), pp. 67–90 (p. 67). On the 'lyric mode' in the *Commedia*, see most recently Francesca Southerden, 'The Lyric Mode', in *The Oxford Handbook of Dante*, ed. Manuele Gragnolati, Elena Lombardi, and Francesca Southerden (Oxford: Oxford University Press, 2021), pp. 546–62.
[32] K. Sara Myers, 'Statius on Invocation and Inspiration', in *Brill's Companion to Statius*, ed. William J. Dominik, Carole Elizabeth Newlands, and Kyle Gervais (Leiden and Boston: Brill, 2015), pp. 31–53, p. 32. Gianpiero Rosati makes a similar case about the epistolary preface of Statius's *Silvae* (it should be noted that Dante did not have access to this work, since it was only discovered by Poggio Bracciolini in 1417).

ire, deae?': where do you command me to begin, goddess?[33] Over the first forty-five lines of the poem, Statius proposes a dazzling array of possible beginnings:

> ...gentisne *canam* primordia dirae,
> Sidonios raptus et inexorabile pactum
> legis Agenoreae scrutantemque aequora Cadmum?
> ...
> atque adeo iam nunc gemitus et prospera Cadmi
> praeteriisse *sinam*: limes mihi carminis *esto*
> Oedipodae confusa domus,
> ...
> undarum terraeque potens, et sidera dones.
> tempus *erit*, cum Pierio tua fortior oestro
> facta *canam*:...
> quem prius heroum, Clio, *dabis*?

[*Shall I sing* the origins of the dire folk, the rape Sidonian, the inexorable compact of Agenor's ordinance, and Cadmus searching the seas?...No; already *shall I let* the sorrows and happy days of Cadmus be bygones. Let the limit of my lay be the troubled house of Oedipus....[O, Domitian,] a time will come when stronger in Pierian frenzy *I shall sing* your deeds....Clio, which of the heroes [*shall*] *you offer* first?] (*Thebaid* I, 4–6, 15–17, 31–33, and 41, italics mine)

The proem of the *Thebaid* is an extraordinarily rich text and has been closely studied;[34] but more can be said on its status as an important intertext for Dante's own proems in the *Commedia*. Dante must have taken note of how Statius 'conspicuously avoids a strong first-person presence by giving preference to conditional, interrogative and negative statements where his poetic program is concerned', thus underlying the narrator's uncertain relation to the open

---

[33] Statius, *Thebaid, Volume I: Thebaid: Books 1–7*, ed. and trans. D. R. Shackleton Bailey, Loeb Classical Library 207 (Cambridge, MA: Harvard University Press, 2003).

[34] For a recent bibliography, see *Brill's Companion to Statius*, ed. William J. Dominik, Carole Elizabeth Newlands, and Kyle Gervais (Leiden and Boston: Brill, 2015). For the historical Statius's influence on Dante, see Peter Heslin, 'Statius in Dante's *Commedia*', therein, pp. 512–26; as well as Winthrop Wetherbee, *The Ancient Flame: Dante and the Poets* (Notre Dame, IN: University of Notre Dame Press, 2008), pp. 159–202, according to whom 'One of the poem's most distinctive and disconcerting features is the continual tension between the remorseless forward movement of its narrative of historical disaster and the various means by which Statius seeks to arrest or transcend this movement' (p. 168).

future.[35] Statius's tentative futures are in stark contrast with the triumphalist certainty displayed by a traditional epic poet such as Virgil, notably in the future-tense prophecy of Rome's glorious imperial future in his epic *Aeneid*, which I discussed in Chapter 2. This use of the future tense was famously criticized by W. H. Auden as self-serving and 'political'; poetically, Auden claimed, 'hindsight as foresight makes no sense'.[36] In polemic with this colonization of the future, Statius's many possible beginnings undermine the very notion that the future tense can ever represent a single predetermined outcome, a point that cannot have escaped Dante and his sensitivity to alternative narratives.[37] The poet of the *Commedia* must have taken note of how Statius's 'multiple beginnings' in the future tense 'self-consciously [focus] our attention on the actual process and practice of narration and "the unavoidable *difficulty of beginning*"' not just his epic but virtually any writing,[38] and thus give a taste 'of the infinity of choices that were made in that text'.[39] The author of the *Commedia* himself is no stranger to problematizing beginnings:[40] Teodolinda Barolini has written about the ways in which the first cantos of the *Commedia* create 'multiple beginnings, so that each beginning undermines the absolute status of the previous beginning', thereby exorcizing the problem of starting.[41] The *Commedia* shares the same apotropaic goal as the *Thebaid* but follows a different tactic. Through false starts

[35] Donka D. Markus, 'The Politics of Epic Performance in Statius', in Anthony James Boyle and William J. Dominik, eds, *Flavian Rome: Culture, Image, Text* (Leiden: Brill, 2003), pp. 432–68 (p. 441).
[36] W. H. Auden, *Secondary Epic*, ll. 1–5, in *Homage to Clio* (London: Faber & Faber, 1960), p. 34.
[37] On the future tense in Virgil, see Sara Mack, *Patterns of Time in Vergil* (Hamden, CT: Archon Books, 1978). Robert Wilson takes Auden's *Secondary Epic* from Mack's book (*Prophecies and Prophecy*, p. 200). I am more sympathetic to Virgil's future than Auden is, as my brief discussion of the passage from *Aeneid* VI in the previous chapter hopefully demonstrates. For Virgil's less triumphalist voice: Adam Parry's seminal 'The Two Voices of Virgil's *Aeneid*', *Arion*, 2.4 (1963), 66–80; R. O. A. M. Lyne, *Further Voices in Vergil's 'Aeneid'* (Oxford: Clarendon Press, 1992); and Gian Biagio Conte, *Virgilio: L'epica del sentimento* (Turin: Einaudi, 2002), available in English as *The Poetry of Pathos: Studies in Virgilian Epic*, trans. Stephen J. Harrison (Oxford and New York: Oxford University Press, 2007), discussed in the Introduction.
[38] K. Sara Myers, 'Statius on Invocation and Inspiration', p. 32. The quotation and italics are from Gérard Genette, *Narrative Discourse* (Oxford: Basil Blackwell, 1980), p. 46.
[39] David Foster Wallace's words are taken from Bryan Garner and David Foster Wallace, *Quack This Way: David Foster Wallace & Bryan Gardner Talk Language and Writing* (Dallas: RosePen Books, 2013), p. 28.
[40] See Guglielmo Gorni, 'La teoria del "cominciamento"', in *Il nodo della lingua e il verbo d'amore: Studi su Dante e altri duecentisti* (Florence: Olschki, 1981), pp. 143–86; Teodolinda Barolini, *The Undivine 'Comedy': Detheologizing Dante* (Princeton, NJ: Princeton University Press, 1992), ch. 2, and her earlier essay on the *Vita nova* '"Cominciandomi dal principio infino a la fine" (V. N. XXIII, 15): Forging Anti-Narrative in the *Vita Nuova*', in *La gloriosa donna de la mente: A Commentary on the 'Vita Nuova'*, ed. Vincent Moleta (Florence: Olschki, 1994), pp. 119–40.
[41] Barolini, *Undivine 'Comedy'*, p. 22.

and delays, interruptions and new starts, Dante spreads out the proliferation of beginnings of Statius's proem across the space of several cantos, thus foregrounding the narrative and meta-literary implications that are so central to Statius's proem. Dante's own use of 'the future for the creation of a text' in the proems of the *Commedia*, as Matthew Leigh defines the kind of programmatic future we are discussing here,[42] remains as an indication that this is a trick out of Statius's book. The Latin poet's influence on the proems is unmistakable: the character Virgil alludes to Statius's proem in conversation with its fictionalized author ('tu cantasti le crude armi', *Purg.* XXII, 55),[43] and Dante may have cited it as early as the Latin incipit of the *Commedia*, reported by Boccaccio:

> Ultima regna *canam* fluvido contermina mundo,
> spiritibus que lata patent, que premia solvunt
> pro meritis cuicunque suis.[44]
>
> [*I will sing* the last realms, beyond the corruptible world, that open up wide to the souls, what rewards they offer each according to their merit...]

The author of this Latin proem chooses classical epic's 'expected verb of singing' (*cano*)[45] but conjugates it in the future tense (*canam*), thus following the lyricizing Statius rather than the epic authority of Virgil and Lucan. Although the question of the incipit's authenticity is, of course, still unresolved, the occurrence of the future tense is unquestionably in line with the lyricizing practice of the vernacular narrator of the *Commedia*.[46] If the author of the proem is not Dante, they certainly captured his future-tense poetics.

How to interpret the parallels between Statius's and Dante's proems, then? Characteristically of his relationship with the classics, Dante spins Statius's future to suit his own agenda.[47] The *Thebaid* narrates the power struggle between the brothers Eteocles and Polynices over the city of Thebes, a theme

---

[42] Leigh, *Lucan*, p. 327.
[43] As noted by a number of commentators, from Francesco da Buti (*ad Purg.* XXII, 55–63) to Nicola Fosca (*ad* ll. 55–60) (DDP). See Bosco Reggio, *ad* ll. 55–7: 'Cfr. "Fraternas acies" e "gentisne canam primordia *dirae*" [*Theb.* I, 1 and 4]' (DDP).
[44] Boccaccio, introductory note to *Inferno* (DDP). The translation of the Latin incipit is mine.
[45] Myers, 'Statius on Invocation and Inspiration', p. 33.
[46] See Saverio Bellomo, 'Il sorriso di Ilaro e la prima redazione in latino della "Commedia"', in *Studi sul Boccaccio*, XXXII (2004), 201–35.
[47] See Roberto Mercuri, 'Dante nella prospettiva intertestuale', in *Dante: For Use, Now: Atti del Convegno internazionale su La presenza di Dante nella poesia contemporanea nordamericana*, ed. Annalisa Goldoni and Andrea Mariani (Rome: Euroma, 2000), pp. 75–92.

which, according to classicist K. Sara Myers, is anticipated in the poem's multiple beginnings: 'the competing authority over the very nature and direction of the poem at its commencement suggests a parallel between the poetics and themes of the narrative'.[48] In contrast, the structural use of the future tense in the *Commedia* complicates the narrator's retrospective authority (the 'position backwards') by drawing attention to his embodied presence and implicating him personally in the 'position forward' that constitutes the existential perspective expressed in the poem. Statius's dilemma as to what to write is thus especially significant to Dante as an author who dramatizes the tentative, progressive, open-ended experience of writing in a moral universe of freedom.

When associated with writing, then, the future tense has two obvious advantages. On the one hand, it works in agreement with Dante's teleological masterplot, as it envisions the complete poem before its completion and thus gives the impression that there already is an end from which the poem will be judged. By planting evidence of the journey's predetermined conclusion early on, it supports the validity of the retrospective interpretation of Dante's making. In parallel with this teleological working, however, the future serves another, less expected purpose. It tempers the hegemony of the masterplot by contextualizing the *poeta* within the existential condition of those living forward and thus involves him in the hermeneutic limitations attached to it. It declares, in other words, the narrator's participation in Kierkegaard's hermeneutic caveat that 'temporal life can never properly be understood precisely because I can at no instant find complete rest in which to adopt a position: backwards'. Whether as an attempt to control the poem's reception, or simply as the wishful thinking of an author who suspected, correctly, that he would never see his work bound in a single volume, the strategy of writing in the future tense is inseparable from the workings of the *Commedia*'s masterplot. Dante's use of the future of writing constitutes, as always in the *Commedia*, a gamble. Will appealing to the future pay off? Or will it only undermine the narrator as someone whose retrospective understanding is also partial and fleeting?

The future we have discussed so far involves the writing of the *Commedia*'s text, and thus ends with the poem's conclusion. This kind of future is fictionalized and self-enclosed within the text itself. But there is another future, a more unpredictable future that knocks at the poem's door and

---

[48] Myers, 'Statius on Invocation and Inspiration', p. 32.

demands entrance. It is the future outside the text about which the author is in the dark, a future that concerns and fascinates him throughout the poem. The problem arises as early as the first occurrence of the future tense in the proem's programmatic future of writing, and inevitably takes the shape of a question: what if the real future outside of the text breaks Dante's promise? Considering the author's own literary career, this is more than just a possibility.

3.3 Unfinished Writing

At the time of writing the *Commedia*, Dante had already made promises, but they had not always paid off. The number of his works that are left unfinished are a simple demonstration of precisely what can go wrong with the future of writing. Dante himself was aware of the risks. The first book of *Convivio* promised fourteen *canzoni* and as many additional books (*Conv.* I, i, 14), but as far as we know it delivered only a total of four before it was abandoned. In that work, Dante also anticipated 'un libello ch'io intendo di fare, Dio concedente, di Volgare Eloquenza' ['a book I intend to write, God willing, on Eloquence in the Vernacular'] (I, v, 10), where the incidental 'Dio concedente' ['God willing'] conceded, in one of many such concessions throughout Dante's career, that future writing does not always go to plan. And indeed, the *De vulgari eloquentia* realized the *Convivio*'s promise only in part, while failing to fulfil a few promises of its own: notably, when the treatise was abandoned in the second of the four books originally planned. Even as late as the second book of the *Monarchia*, Dante was acknowledging the tentative nature of writing in the future tense:

> Hec equidem duo fient sufficienter, si secundam partem presentis propositi prosecutus fuero, et instantis questionis veritatem ostendero.
>
> [These two things will be sufficiently accomplished when I have brought to completion the second part of my present project and shown the truth of the question we are now considering.] (*Mon.* II, i, 6)

Prue Shaw's translation, cited here, is worth analysing. Notably, Shaw translates the cautious hypothetical adverb 'si' into the temporal 'when', ostensibly making a certainty out of what was to Dante only a possibility. Moreover, she translates the open futures 'prosecutus fuero' and 'ostendero' ['I *will* have brought to completion', 'I *will* show'], respectively, into past perfect and present continuous tenses ('I *have* brought to completion', 'we *are* now *considering*'), which make it look as though the book has already been written. This is a telling choice: it shows the translator's awareness of the fact that the book was indeed brought to completion, its promise fulfilled. It is for this reason, I think, that Shaw places author and reader in the same boat, enjoying each other's company in a common present ('*we* are *now* considering'), even though the narrator is conspicuously isolated in the singular future tense 'ostendero', the uncertain future of writing still weighing on him. Thus, affected perhaps by the prophetic tone of the passage, the translation performs a little teleology of its own as it imposes the knowledge of the end of the *Monarchia* on earlier parts of the text. In so doing, it attributes to Dante a confidence that is not exactly philological, and which the author learned the hard way not to claim for himself.

Expressions of caution abound in the most famous promise of future writing in Dante's other works: the ending of the *Vita nova*.[49] A book featuring the unfinished canzone 'Sì lungiamente' (*VN* XXVII) and the sonnet with alternative beginnings 'Era venuta ne la mente mia' (*VN* XXXIV), the *Vita nova* is the first of Dante's works to reflect on the uncertainties of writing.[50] The promise of future writing contained in its last chapter is worded as tentatively as the ones in the other works:

> io vidi cose che mi fecero proporre di non dire più di questa benedetta infino a tanto che io potesse più degnamente dire di lei. E di venire a ciò io studio *quanto posso*....Sì che, *se piacere sarà* di colui a cui tutte le cose vivono, che la mia vita duri per alquanti anni, *io spero* di dicer di lei quello

---

[49] Jennifer Rushworth writes on the relationship between the promise of future writing at the end of the *Vita nova* and its hermeneutic implications in her *Discourses of Mourning in Dante, Petrarch and Boccaccio* (Oxford: Oxford University Press, 2016), pp. 126–61: '*Vita nova* is notably open-ended, coming to a close with a promise of future writing' (p. 135).

[50] Harrison, *The Body of Beatrice*, draws attention to the metonymic relation between these lyrics within the *Vita nova* and the *libello*'s own 'unfinished'-like macrostructure. H. Wayne Storey offers an interesting reading of the interrupted 'Sì lungiamente' as a false start, the trace of a narrative trajectory that could have been but 'is no longer tenable': 'Because of its narratological status as a fragmented text, necessarily interrupted by the story the *Vita nova* has to tell, "Sì lungiamente" is subsequently defined by its poetic representation of a narrative trajectory no longer tenable in the context of the *libello*. Instead, its role in the *libello* is, narratively speaking, a place to which the poet's story can never return' ('Early Editorial Forms of Dante's Lyrics', in *Dante for the New Millennium*, ed. Teodolinda Barolini and H. Wayne Storey (New York: Fordham, 2003), pp. 16–44 (p. 33)).

che mai non fue detto d'alcuna. E poi *piaccia* a colui che è sire de la cortesia, che la mia anima se ne *possa* gire a vedere la gloria de la sua donna....

[I saw things that made me resolve to say no more about this blessed one until I would be capable of writing about her in a nobler way. To achieve this I am striving as hard as I *can*....Accordingly, *if it be* the pleasure of Him through whom all things live that my life continue for a few more years, *I hope* to write of her that which has never been written of any other woman. And then *may it please* the One who is the Lord of graciousness that my soul [*may*] ascend to behold the glory of its lady....

(*VN* XLII, 1–3, emphases mine)

The passage offers a series of disclaimers and reminders of the contingent nature of this and all promises, which could be variously interpreted as humble, falsely modest, matter-of-fact, or wise. These take the shape of the phrases 'quanto posso' ['as hard as I can'] (1), 'io spero' ['I hope'] (2), and 'se ne possa gire' [literally, 'may ascend'] (3), the hypothetical clause 'se piacere sarà' ['if it be the pleasure'] (2), and its optative variation 'piaccia a colui' ['may it please'] (3). With the benefit of hindsight, scholars have been tempted to identify the promised work with virtually all of those that have come down to us, but as Jennifer Rushworth's text-centric approach reminds us, 'this other work, *qua* promise, is not reducible to a prescient announcement of the *Commedia*'.[51] Following Rushworth's approach further, it can be pointed out that, unlike all other promises of future writing in Dante's works, the one in the *Vita nova* appears at the book's very end. This creates a unique mimetic coincidence between the book's temporal framework and the time outside the fiction, whereby fiction imitates life: the book starts in the present tense and purports to be a linear, retrospective narrative; as we read on, we gradually catch up with the narrator's past, and once we near the end of the *Vita nova* we come to the same position of its writer, at work on the last few sentences. It is at this point that, by promising future writing at the end of the book, the last chapter anticipates by a few words, as mimetically as possible, the act of moving into the future beyond the book's end: 'the *libello* comes to a conclusion, but the author projects its story beyond the bounds of the narrative'.[52] The play of tenses in the passage captures precisely this movement from past-tense retrospective narrative ('apparve'

---

[51] Rushworth, *Discourses of Mourning*, p. 140, and bibliographical references.
[52] Harrison, *The Body of Beatrice*, p. 130.

[literally, 'appeared']; 'io vidi' ['I saw']; 'mi fecero' ['made me']; and the imperfect subjunctive 'potesse' ['I would be capable'], *VN* XLII, 1) to the present tense of writing ('io studio' ['I am striving']; 'posso' ['I can']; 'ella sae' ['she...knows'], 2) to the future tense 'sarà' [literally, 'it will be'] (2) and the other future-oriented constructs noted above that gesture beyond the end of the text (2–3).[53] From this text's mimetic perspective, the future is, simply, what happens after writing and reading the text itself.[54]

This is a rare case in which Dante uses the future of writing to point beyond and outside the fiction in which it is contained. The proems of the *Commedia* ostensibly use it in the same way, but their position within the work has a markedly different effect. While in the *Vita nova* the future of writing is mimetically located at the end of the book, waiting to give way to a future work, in the *Commedia* it is anticipated strategically at the beginning of the poem and of each cantica, thus making the future coincide with the text itself. Through their placing in the proems, the future tenses of writing create the illusion that there is, somehow *a priori* of it having been written, a story to be told in the near future, with a planned form and a proper endpoint, or at least their design—wishful or controlling—in the writer's mind: and that story is none other than the *Commedia*. It is only by locating the future of promised writing at the beginning of the ideal work or material book that the *Commedia* can hold the illusion that the future—the only future that counts—lies in the content of its fiction, tamed and self-contained; not, crucially, in the other future of what lies beyond the text, open and uncontrollable.[55] This simple editorial choice, comparable to ones Dante experimented with as early as the *Vita nova*, helps him limit the future to the confines of his poem, while blurring the more problematic future beyond it.

It will be clear, by now, that the relationship between futures and ends which I am tracing is essentially double-edged. In the teleological master narrative of the *Commedia* the futures are a source of fascination and fear.

---

[53] For an impassioned analysis of the moods and tenses of this passage, see Harrison, *The Body of Beatrice*, pp. 133–8. Harrison notes how the future tense, typically of Dante's ambivalence when it comes to this time, simultaneously serves a teleological purpose: 'the new life is projected along a linear, teleological axis that grants it direction as well as a determinate, if deferred, closure' (p. 135).

[54] Singleton on 'visione' as a term referring to the future (as opposed to 'imaginazione'); quoted in Harrison, *The Body of Beatrice*, p. 8, who says the distinction is incorrect.

[55] It should be noted that Dante does imagine future works, following in the wake of the *Commedia* (*Paradiso* I, 34–6, and XXX, 34–6). Unlike in the *Vita nova*, however, these imaginary works are by other authors.

The future becomes both a means of envisioning, imagining, inhabiting, or controlling definitive endpoints, and a threat to their very possibility. If the future allows Dante to take a peek beyond the poem's reach, then it also, by that very act, undermines the conclusiveness of all ends, since it makes it possible for them to be always one step removed. As long as we are able to use a future tense, we also always raise doubts over the end's ability to have the last word. The representation of the future in the *Commedia*, therefore, is inevitably problematic, precisely in that it exposes the blind spots and fault lines of the poem's teleological workings. It is no wonder that the issue of the future has preoccupied Dante scholars for such a long time, under the guise of the question of prophecy and prophets.[56] In the reading offered in the present chapter, this question is but a special case of the *Commedia*'s wider concerns with what lies beyond the masterplot's reach. Dante appears to be keenly aware of the problems inherent in the future, as he dramatizes them by embroiling in futurity first the protagonist, then the narrator, and lastly his text.

3.4 Vulnerable Narrator, Vulnerable Text

The poet of the *Commedia*, author of at least two unfinished treatises, a sonnet with two beginnings, and an interrupted canzone, writing in exile and circulating his writing in batches—should it surprise us that he represents his poem as vulnerable to the future? In the address to the reader of *Paradiso* V, Dante calls upon them to envision precisely 'the event of a sudden interruption of the canticle':[57]

> Pensa, lettor, se quello che qui s'inizia
> non procedesse, come tu avresti
> di più savere angosciosa carizia;
> e per te vederai come da questi
> m'era in disio d'udir lor condizioni,
> sì come a li occhi mi fur manifesti.

---

[56] For a recent review of the subject, see Wilson, *Prophecies and Prophecy*.
[57] Elena Lombardi, *The Syntax of Desire: Language and Love in Augustine, the Modistae, Dante* (Toronto: University of Toronto Press, 2007), p. 156. Lombardi discusses the triangulation of desires between the pilgrim, the souls, and the reader at pp. 156–7. On premature endings, see also the figure of Carlo Martello, in Chapter 2 above.

> [Merely consider, reader, if what I here begin
> went on no farther, how keen would be
> your anguished craving to know more.
> But you shall see for yourself what great desire
> I felt to hear about their state from them
> as soon as they appeared to me.]
>
> (*Par.* V, 109–14)

The possibility of the poem's interruption is given as a known quantity, conceivably part of the everyday experience of both the poet and his readers, whom the 'veiled threat of narrative interruption', as Barolini calls it, concerns in equal measure.[58] The readers may be counted upon to entertain a scenario where the poem is unfinished or its manuscript transmission incomplete; all the more so, if they are familiar with the precarious material culture of the time, not to mention its author's track record and well-publicized circumstances. Moreover, the two elements of the pseudo-simile are the *personaggio*'s journey and that of the *poeta*, once again blurring the line between the two when it comes to the desire to move forward. In the *Commedia*, of course, *personaggio* and *poeta* 'undertake separate journeys within the poem: the journey of the character from the dark forest to the Empyrean heaven…; and the journey of the narrator through the one-hundred cantos of the poem, from canto I of the *Inferno* to canto XXXIII of the *Paradiso*. The first journey lasts one week; the second, to the best of our knowledge, took at least a dozen years (circa 1307–20).'[59] The parallels extend to the fact that both journeys are represented as vulnerable to the uncertainties of the future. The vulnerability of narration is evoked also at the beginning of this same canto, where Dante, incidentally, plays twice on the equivocal meaning of *canto* as both metaphorical song and chapter of the *Commedia* (at lines 16 and 139):

> Sì cominciò Beatrice questo canto:
> e sì com'uom che suo parlar non spezza
> continuò così 'l processo santo.

---

[58] Barolini, *Undivine 'Comedy'*, p. 190. See also Rushworth, *Discourses of Mourning*, p. 147, on 'the possibility of resistance of any form of closure'.

[59] Pertile, 'Introduction to *Inferno*', p. 67. Barolini often notes the compresence of the two journeys in the ambiguous expressions of 'alto passo' (*Inferno* II, 12; XXVI, 132) and 'corso' (*Inferno* XV, 88): 'The text is also…a voyage' (*Undivine 'Comedy'*, p. 22).

> [Thus did Beatrice begin this canto and,
> like a man who does not interrupt his speech,
> continued thus her holy discourse.]
>
> (*Par.* V, 16–18)

Treading 'the margin between fiction and textuality', this terzina seems to entrust the fictional Beatrice with the act of beginning the canto: the chapter of the book that contains her as a character.[60] The demonstrative *questo* seems to confirm this interpretation, as it appears to be written from the perspective of the *poeta* and his reader, not hers. Underlining this promiscuity between narrators and characters, extradiegesis and diegesis, textuality and fiction, is the threat of broken narrative expressed by the line 'e sì com'uom che suo parlar non spezza' ['like a man who does not interrupt his speech'] (17), evoked here only to be negated, but evoked nonetheless. Interruptions of this kind haunt the *Commedia*'s storytelling, often in the softer forms of hypotheticals and negations. Thus, the character Thomas Aquinas is represented as toying with the possibility of interrupting his explanation:

> Or s'i' non procedesse avanti piùe,
> 'Dunque, come costui fu sanza pare?'
> cominicerebber le parole tue.
>
> [Now, if I went no farther,
> 'How, then, was that other without equal?'
> would be the first words from your mouth.]
>
> (*Par.* XIII, 88–90)

Interruption is here suggested benignly, in the subjunctive mood of hypotheticals ('s'i' non procedesse' ['if I went no farther'], 88), as a way to stimulate the protagonist into dialogue. It is a rhetorical interruption. What if the speech were to end before its proper end? Aquinas indicates that he has not quite reached the conclusion of his spiel but is truncating it in the middle,

---

[60] Lombardi notices the conflation of roles between Beatrice and Dante in the attribution of the masculine 'uom' to the lady (*Imagining the Woman Reader*, ch. 4). Teodolinda Barolini discusses the dynamic in *Undivine 'Comedy'*, pp. 188–9, making a similar point about gender. Barolini seems to share in practice Margaret Bent's opinion that the word *canto* here 'refers unambiguously to the unit of a *canto*' ('Songs Without Music', p. 179, n. 38), whereas Barański, 'Terza Rima', is more cautious. In their commentary *ad Par.* V, 16–18, Umberto Bosco and Giovanni Reggio register the aesthetic discrepancy between fiction and reality by commenting that '"canto" o "materia del canto" appartiene alla struttura del poema e stona se riferito come didascalia al discorso di Beatrice' (DDP).

for suspense. As ever in the *Commedia*—readers of this chapter are familiar, by now, with the ambiguity of this dynamic—this kind of suspense works teleologically as desire for the revelation that lies ahead in the text; but it also evokes, however briefly, the real risk of premature ends and the threat they pose to writing. In *Paradiso* XXX, it is the narrator that summons this ghost, when he boasts that the continuative act of his singing/writing (*cantar* [literally, 'singing'], *Par.* XXX, 30) has never been interrupted before (a boast that nobody, to my knowledge, has called out as the lie it is—as I mentioned, Dante left unfinished a number of works).[61] Dante then declares that this time he must give up on his attempt to describe Beatrice's beauty:

> Dal primo giorno ch'i' vidi il suo viso
> in questa vita, infino a questa vista,
> non m'è il seguire al mio cantar preciso;
>   ma or convien che mio seguir desista
> più dietro a sua bellezza, poetando,
> come a l'ultimo suo ciascuno artista.
>
> [From the first day, when in this life I saw
> Until my vision of her now, pursuit
> of her in song has never been cut off.
>   But now I must desist in my pursuit,
> no longer following her beauty in my verse,
> as every artist, having reach his limit, must.]
>
> (*Par.* XXX, 28–33)

Of course, the *Commedia* continues for three more cantos beyond this interruption, which is routinely seen as rhetorical, on a par with Aquinas's dialectical move, a hyperbole or a ploy to create suspense—a suspense whose substance is, nevertheless, once again, the genuine possibility of interruption.[62] This risk is more often evoked in connection with the *personaggio*'s journey, as exemplified by the broken bridge in *Inferno* XX, or the episode in *Purgatorio* IV when the beginning of the actual journey is con-

---

[61] I am referring here, of course, to Dante's sonnets with alternative beginnings, his interrupted canzone, and the last chapter of the *Vita nova*; not to mention, if we are taking his statement as open to interruptions in general, the unfinished *De vulgari* and *Convivio*. Hollander understands the passage as limited to the theme of Beatrice, and still ponders on the 'marked deviation from singing of Beatrice in *Convivio*'. See Robert Hollander, '*Paradiso* XXX', *Studi Danteschi*, 60 (1988), 1–33 (11, n. 26).

[62] On the passage, see Barolini, *Undivine 'Comedy'*, pp. 241–4.

stantly delayed. One need look no further than the first two cantos of *Inferno* to find multiple threats to the poem's beginning: the three beasts *lonza, leone,* and *lupa* (*Inf.* I); and the protagonist's *viltade* (*Inf.* II).[63] But even in those cases, the threats to the journey can have verbal repercussions. In *Inferno* VIII–IX, for instance, when the journey itself seems to be threatened with a premature end, as the protagonist and his guide are locked outside of the city of Dis and unable to continue on their journey, the possibility of interruption exerts its pressure on Virgil's very words and cuts off his speech:

> 'Pur a noi converrà vincer la punga',
> cominciò el, 'se non... Tal ne s'offerse.
> Oh quanto tarda a me ch'altri qui giunga!'
>   I' vidi ben sì com'ei ricoperse
> lo cominciar con l'altro che poi venne,
> che fur parole a le prime diverse;
>   ma nondimen paura il suo dir dienne,
> perch'io traeva la parola tronca
> forse a peggior sentenzia che non tenne.
>
> ['Yet we must win this fight,' he began,
> 'or else... Such help was promised us.
> How long it seems to me till someone comes!'
>   I clearly saw that he had covered up
> His first words with the others that came after,
> Words so different in meaning.
>   Still I was filled with fear by what he said.
> Perhaps I understood his broken phrase
> To hold worse meaning than it did.]
>
>   (*Inf.* IX, 7–15)

Scholars have noticed how this passage is engineered to expose Virgil's limits as a guide in the new poetic universe of the *Commedia*. It is not by chance that the pagan poet's fallibility is emphasized rhetorically by a failed future tense. Virgil's sentence begins combatively ('Pur a noi converrà vincer la punga' ['Yet we must win this fight'], 7), stressing 'necessity' through the future *converrà* ['we must'], and employing specific Latinisms virtually synonymous with the martial epic he is identified with ('vincer la

[63] Ibid., pp. 21–47.

punga' ['win this fight']). And yet the epic march of the sentence is cut short in an ellipsis, exploiting interruption for dramatic effect: 'se non...' ['or else...'] (8). The brief suggestion that things might go differently is enough to wreck the sentence, throwing into disarray the previous sentence's carefully crafted rhetoric. It is a clash of poetics as much as worldviews, with prophetic future tenses (which Auden maligned as 'history in the future tense')[64] beset by the new existential future of the *Commedia* and the uncertainties and interruptions it brings into the poem's universe. Virgil quickly springs to cover up the silence but cannot refrain from appearing emotionally affected by this tentative temporality of hesitation and delay. He sighs and even drops the first-person plural *ne* [literally, 'to us'] (8) for the solitary singular *a me* ('Oh quanto tarda a me ch'altri qui giunga' ['How long it seems to me till someone comes!'], 9). Virgil is uncertain, dismayed, isolated. When the pagan poet's speech reveals its vulnerability to the new future, Dante's imagination begins to fill in the gaps left by his guide. These begin to take on dark tones.[65] The void left by 'la parola tronca' (14) fills the protagonist with fear, the sentence's continuation growing worse in his imagination than perhaps was originally meant ('perch'io traeva la parola tronca | forse a peggior sentenzia che non tenne' ['Perhaps I understood his broken phrase | To hold worse meaning than it did'], 14–15). This kind of *reticentia* is not unique in the *Commedia*;[66] here it offers a limpid example of the risks of interruption, and it is all the more interesting for having Dante as its embodied protagonist, affectively involved in the business of filling in the gaps and trying to envision a future after the interruption.

This reading of the *Commedia* as a text threatened by interruption was first made by one of the poem's most responsive early readers, Giovanni Boccaccio, an author himself concerned with the future reception of his works. In the *Trattatello in laude di Dante*, Boccaccio reflects, with 'his own innate talent for narrative', on the difficult circumstances of the *Commedia*'s composition:[67]

---

[64] Auden, *Secondary Epic*, 3.

[65] For a reading of this passage's 'anacoluthon' and Dante's 'pessimistic fantasy', see Justin Steinberg, *Dante and the Limits of the Law* (Chicago: University of Chicago Press, 2013), p. 106.

[66] Nicola Gardini reflects on this passage in his *Lacuna* (Turin: Einaudi, 2014), p. 46, and dedicates a chapter to instances of *reticentia* in the *Commedia* (pp. 46–55). With his usual insightfulness, Contini calls Dante 'lo scrittore, i cui silenzî, le cui reticenze, le cui oscurità e ambiguità sono ferree quanto tutto il resto' (Gianfranco Contini, 'Cavalcanti in Dante', in *Un'idea di Dante*, pp. 143–57 (p. 143)).

[67] Martin McLaughlin, 'Biography and Autobiography in the Italian Renaissance', in *Mapping Lives: The Uses of Biography*, ed. Peter France and William St Clair (Oxford: Oxford University Press, 2004), pp. 37–65 (pp. 47–8).

Ma, sì come noi veggiamo le gran cose non potersi in brieve tempo comprendere, e per questo conoscere dobbiamo così alta, così grande, così escogitata impresa...non essere stato possibile in picciolo spazio avere il suo fine recata; e massimamente da uomo, il quale da molti e varii casi della Fortuna, pieni tutti d'angoscia e d'amaritudine venenati, sia stato agitato.[68]

[But just as we see that it is not possible to understand greater events in a short time, so we must understand that it was not possible...to bring to its conclusion such a lofty, great, and designed undertaking; and especially on the part of a man who was troubled by the many and varied chances of Fortune, which were all full of anguish and poisoned with bitterness.]

Writing an ambitious poem such as the *Commedia* takes a long time, as Boccaccio testifies; all the more so for a poet in Dante's situation. Showing the ways in which both the author and his poem were once vulnerable to time, in chapter XXVI Boccaccio proceeds to relate two 'accidenti intorno al principio e alla fine di quella [la *Commedia*] avvenuti' ['two accidents, which occurred surrounding the beginning and ending of the *Commedia*'] that nearly prevented the poem from reaching its conclusion ('il suo fine'). The first accident is exile ("l gravoso accidente della sua cacciata, o fuga che chiamar si convegna' ['the terrible accident of his exile, or escape, whatever one should called it']), which forces Dante to abandon the first seven cantos in Florence as he wanders throughout Italy in perpetual insecurity ('...per lo quale egli e quella e ogni altra cosa abandonata, incerto di se medesimo, più anni con diversi amici e signori andò vagando' ['which, after he abandoned both Florence and all other things, caused him to meander and stay by several friends and lords, in personal uncertainty']). The practical writer that he is, Boccaccio does not see exile as a fortifying experience nor as an allegory of Dante's spiritual journey but as a concrete problem in the practice of writing. Through a suspenseful narration, Boccaccio tells us that the interruption was only resolved sometime later when Dante's protector, Marquis Morello Malaspina, happened to get his hands on the early cantos and, led on by the *plaisir du texte*, entreated Dante to pick up where he left off so as to avoid leaving the work unfinished ('che gli piacesse di non lasciare senza debito fine sì alto principio' ['that it may please him to not leave such a lofty beginning without a proper conclusion']).

---

[68] Giovanni Boccaccio, *Trattatello in laude di Dante*, ed. Vittore Branca (Milan: Mondadori, 1974), XXVI.

The second accident that threatens the integrity of the *Commedia* is the loss of the last thirteen cantos of *Paradiso*, as death catches the poet before he can finish his work ('prima nol sopragiugnesse la morte che egli tutta publicare la potesse'). Even if apocryphal, the tale is significant: it responds to Dante's concerns about leaving his text unfinished and unbound, while giving us an insight into what could plausibly be believed to be the material conditions of the *Commedia*'s composition and transmission in times of exile.[69] Thus Boccaccio reflects on the ways in which the loss of the final cantos affects so systematic, structured a poem as the *Commedia*. He has a keen sense that the *Commedia* is, in its design, a strong coherent whole and repeatedly refers to the idea of a 'proper end' to the poem, which, though materially lost, still informs and constricts its architecture.[70] So strong is this ideal completeness, that, in Boccaccio's tale, Dante's sons Iacopo and Pietro Alighieri feel compelled to reconstruct the integrity of their father's text based on what is left of the poem, in an attempt to 'supplire la paterna opera, acciò che imperfetta non procedesse' ['to supplement their father's work, so as to avoid leaving it incomplete']. Their attempt not to let the *Commedia* remain 'imperfect' confirms the fundamental tension between the vulnerability of the material text and the integrity of its architectural design.[71] The teleological *Commedia* is perceived to both require and already contain the proper conclusion.

This idea of the proper conclusion is the recurring theme in Boccaccio's narrative. The term *fine* ['conclusion'] has already quietly appeared in the quotations of the last few pages, but Boccaccio refers to this chimeric entity a few more times in his account of Dante's writing. Although the conclusion is at this point only imaginary ('lo 'mmaginato fine' ['the conclusion he had imagined']), it is somehow due to the poem ('il debito fine' ['the conclusion it deserved'], twice) and inherent in it ('il suo fine' ['its proper conclusion']).[72] This is, in other words, a necessary end that guides the text teleologically from its inception. Crucially, the conclusion is invoked once more, when Boccaccio applies it not to the poem, but to its author's life:

---

[69] Ahern, 'Binding the Book', p. 801.

[70] On the ways to mark the proper end of works of literature in the Middle Ages, see John Ahern, 'Dante's Last Word: The Comedy as a *liber coelestis*', *Dante Studies*, 102 (1984), 1–14.

[71] On the 'sort of idealism' implicit in scribal attempts to reconstitute the completeness of a text, see Daniel Wakelin, *Scribal Correction and Literary Craft: English Manuscripts 1375–1510* (Cambridge: Cambridge University Press, 2014), pp. 246–74 (p. 246).

[72] Boccaccio, *Trattatello*, XXVI.

Ma la Fortuna, volgitrice de' nostri consigli e inimica d'ogni umano stato, come che per alquanti anni nel colmo della sua rota gloriosamente reggendo il tenesse, assai diverso fine al principio recò a lui, in lei fidantesi di soperchio.[73]

[But Fortune, who overturns our intentions and is the enemy of every form of stability in human life, despite the fact that for many years she gloriously held him high in the turning of her wheel, nonetheless brought him, who trusted in her above all, a very different conclusion to his beginning.]

The master of narrative that he is, Boccaccio conceives of Dante's life in the same narrative terms as his fiction: as though infringing an aesthetic principle, Fortune is said to bring 'assai diverso fine al principio' ['a very different conclusion to the beginning'] of the poet's life. Thus, Boccaccio blurs the line between the poet and the poem, the narrator and his narrative, in a manner attuned to the ways in which the *Commedia* embroils the *poeta* in the perilous and open-ended journey of writing. In Boccaccio's depiction, of course, Fortune and premature ends do not threaten the pilgrim of the afterlife—his journey is fictional after all—but, rather, the *Commedia*'s embodied author and his fragile material writing.

3.5 Future's Messes in the *Inferno*

Representing the future, then, is a problem for this most teleological of poems. Bringing it into the work stresses everything that is yet unfinished about the *Commedia*, from the protagonist's journey to the poet's life, to the poem's writing. The future helps express the forward-oriented perspective of the living, as we have seen, but also endangers the poem's meaning, if not its very existence. Tampering with the future in the *Commedia*, however, ends up creating its own set of issues. This is most evident in the first cantica, where the end of the work is still distant and nightmares of futurity weigh heavily on Dante's imagination, at times strangely deforming, with their gravitational pull, the fabric of the poem, as this section will now show.

The future plays an active role in the punishment of a number of sins, most notably in the rather straightforward *contrapasso* of the soothsayers of

[73] Ibid., VI.

Inferno XX: guilty of gazing impudently into the future (like Anfiarao who 'volse veder troppo avante' ['he aspired to see too far ahead'], *Inf.* XX, 38), the soothsayers have their heads twisted backward and are thus deprived of the ability to look ahead ('e in dietro venir li convenia, | perché 'l veder dinanzi era lor tolto' ['they came on walking backward, | since seeing forward was denied to them'], 14–15). For people who used to rely on the ability to foresee for their living, it is quite a punishment to have one's gaze averted from the future—a condition that the canto literalizes through its virtuoso avoidance of future tenses. Having described the soothsayer's fate, the narrator draws attention to himself as he calls on the reader to imagine what he must have felt at their distorted sight:

> Se Dio ti lasci, lettor, prender frutto
> di tua lezione, or pensa per te stesso
> com'io potea tener lo viso asciutto,
>   quando la nostra imagine di presso
> vidi sì torta, che 'l pianto de li occhi
> le natiche bagnava per lo fesso.
>
> [Reader, so may God let you gather fruit
> from reading this, imagine, if you can,
> how I could have kept from weeping
>   when I saw, up close, our human likeness
> so contorted that tears from their eyes
> ran down their buttocks, down into the cleft.]
>
> (*Inf.* XX, 19–24)

Commentators have noted the protagonist's affective involvement in the scene, with some going as far as Jacopo della Lana in speculating that Dante must have been once 'inviluppato in questo peccato di divinazione' ['enveloped in this sin of divination'].[74] Leaving speculation aside, it can be pointed out how the protagonist participates affectively in the punishment he is witnessing, unable to help himself from crying with the sinners (Dante: 'com'io potea tener lo visa asciutto' ['how I could have kept from weeping'], 21; the soothsayers: ''l pianto de li occhi | le natiche bagnava' ['so contorted

---

[74] Jacopo della Lana, *ad Inf.* XX, 19–24 (DDP). Robert Hollander *ad Inf.* XX, 19–24, proposes a more normative interpretation, stating that the point of the address to the reader may be 'that Dante was wrong to weep for these creatures' (DDP).

that tears from their eyes | ran down their buttocks, down into the cleft'], 23-4).[75] He is soon rebuked for his pity by Virgil: 'Ancor se' tu degli altri sciocchi?' ['Are you still witless as the rest?'] (27).[76] In light of Virgil's words, it is perhaps surprising that Dante's compassion is not confined to the *personaggio*'s past but infects the *poeta*: the narrator not only steps onstage with his address to the reader but also drops the impartial description of the damned in the third person for a first-person plural involving readers, sinners, and the narrator alike ('nostra imagine' ['our human likeness'], 22). Perhaps Virgil's lesson was not so conclusive after all. The gravitational pull of the future drags the poet into the *Inferno*: indeed, as Benvenuto da Imola is the first to suggest, if Dante is involved in soothsaying, it is not necessarily as astrologer but rather as 'autor': witness the *Commedia* ('sicut patet in libro isto' ['as is evident in this book']).[77]

This is not the only instance of punishments involving the future, and the future involving the narrator in turn. In *Inferno* X future tenses are abounding. The canto of the heretics hosts the Epicureans, who rejected the (eschatological) future by questioning the immortality of the soul; fittingly, it opens with a future-tense prophecy of the resurrection of the body. The sepulchres in which the heretics lie, as Virgil explains, 'Tutti *saran serrati* | quando di Iosafàt qui *torneranno* | coi corpi che là sù hanno lasciati' ['All *will be shut and sealed* | when the souls [*will*] *return* from Jehosaphat | with the bodies they have left above'] (*Inf.* X, 10–12, emphases mine throughout). This is the last endpoint imaginable, at the end of both history and all possible interpretations. Halfway through the canto, a second more personal endpoint, closer to home, is afforded by one of the earliest prophecies of Dante's exile, Farinata degli Uberti's menacing prediction that the protagonist will soon experience in person what it means to never return to his city:

---

[75] For the pilgrim's participation in the punishments he witnesses in the *Purgatorio*, see Heather Webb, *Dante's Persons: An Ethics of the Transhuman* (Oxford: Oxford University Press, 2017).

[76] For a discussion of Virgil's rebuke as mitigated by paradox, see Chapter 1.

[77] Benvenuto da Imola, ad *Inf.* XX, 19–24, speaks clearly here of *autor* and the *libro* he is writing: 'praesens negotium tangebat autorem ipsum, qui…voluit praedicere aliqua futura, sicut patet in libro isto' (DDP). See also Robert Hollander, 'The Tragedy of Divination in *Inferno* XX', in *Studies in Dante* (Ravenna: Longo, 1980), pp. 131–218. Teodolinda Barolini also draws a parallel between soothsaying and textuality: 'their attempt to read the future in God's "magno volume" (*Par.* XV, 50) is an attempt to reach a vantage from which they, like God, "Colui che mai non vide cosa nova," will never see a new thing. And so, these sinners, who would have obliterated by foretelling all the new things before they occurred…are reduced to being one more instance of the new on the poet's narrative path: "Di nova pena mi conven far versi" (*Inf.* XX, 1)' (*Undivine 'Comedy'*, p. 58).

'Ma non cinquanta volte *fia* raccesa | la faccia de la donna che qui regge | che tu *saprai* quanto quell'arte pesa' ['But the face of the lady reigning here | *will be rekindled* not fifty times before you too | *shall know* how difficult a skill that is to learn'] (79–81). Farinata's obscure words of a dark future trouble Dante. Realizing this, Virgil uses the last future tenses of the canto, referring to another significant step in the protagonist's journey: his anticipated encounter with Beatrice, in the Garden of Eden, and her clarification of the prophecies he will hear ('quando *sarai* dinanzi al dolce raggio | di quella il cui bell'occhio tutto vede, | da lei *saprai* di tua vita il viaggio' ['When you *shall stand* before the radiance | of her whose fair eyes see and understand, | from her *you'll learn* the journey of your life'], 130–2). The anticipation turns out to be inaccurate, given that the task is left to Cacciaguida—but such are the risks of writing in the future tense.[78]

This list of fast-approaching futures, each bringing an important endpoint from which to understand the past, is a perfect example of how the *Commedia* employs the future teleologically. In contrast with this productive usage, at the heart of this very canto lie the disturbing encounter with Cavalcante Cavalcanti, his over-reading of Dante's use of tenses, and Dante's ensuing doubts about the idiosyncratic ways in which the damned experience temporality, which I will now turn to. In the picture Farinata paints, futures and presents are mutually necessary in making life intelligible (just as they are in the wider canto). But as Farinata explains to the protagonist, the damned, or, on a more restricted interpretation, the heretics, are not able to see their relation.[79] Before Judgement Day, the damned experience time as those who have 'mala luce' ['faulty vision'] (100): they are far-sighted, aware of the future but blind to the present. After the end of time, however, the future will cease, and with it its power to illuminate the present. The blindness of the damned will be absolute, then: 'tutta *morta* | *fia* nostra conoscenza da quel punto | che del futuro *fia chiusa* la porta' ['all our knowledge | *will perish* at the very moment | the portals of the future [*will*] *close*'] (107–8). In the metatextual nuance of the terzina, nothing can be known after the last full stop (*punto*, 107).

---

[78] The canto's short-term anticipations of the plot in the future tense also include 'Però a la dimanda che mi faci | quinc'entro satisfatto sarà tosto' (16–17) and 'da la cintola in sù tutto 'l vedrai' (33).
[79] Supporting the idea that the *mala luce* 'si direbbe poeticamente "inventata qui"' in the significantly specific context of *Inferno* X, Pasquale Stoppelli notices that Ciacco does show knowledge of the present when he refers to 'tal che *testè* piaggia' (*Inferno* VI, 69) ('La talpa dei bestiari e la "mala luce" dei dannati', in *Studi di letteratura italiana: In memoria di Achille Tartaro*, ed. Giulia Natali and Pasquale Stoppelli (Rome: Bulzoni, 2009), pp. 51–65 (p. 59)).

This account of far-sightedness is exclusive to the damned, but it offers an interesting counterpoint to the canto's wider appreciation of predictive futures. Even more interestingly, the entire conceit of the 'mala luce' ['faulty vision'] seems to arise as a justification of Dante's exchange with Cavalcante, when the protagonist is misunderstood in his explanation of his son Guido's absence from the otherworldly journey. When Dante replies to Cavalcante, saying 'Da me stesso non vegno: | colui ch'attende là, per qui mi mena | forse cui Guido vostro ebbe a disdegno' ['I come not on my own: | he who stands there waiting leads me through, | perhaps to one Your Guido held in scorn'] (61–3), Cavalcante famously reads too much into Dante's use of the past tense 'elli ebbe' ['he held'] (62):

> Di subito drizzato gridò: 'Come?
> dicesti "elli ebbe"? non viv'elli ancora?
> non fiere li occhi suoi lo dolce lume?'.
> Quando s'accorse d'alcuna dimora
> ch'io facea dinanzi a la risposta,
> supin ricadde e più non parve fora.
>
> [Suddenly erect, he cried: 'What?
> Did you say "he held"? Lives he not still?
> Does not the sweet light strike upon his eyes?'
> When he perceived that I made some delay
> before I answered, he fell backward
> and showed himself no more.]
>
> (*Inf.* X, 67–72)

In Cavalcante's over-reading, Dante's phrase 'elli ebbe' ['he held'] (62) seems to consign Guido to the past tense of storytelling, a time that is self-contained and most unlike the open-ended present of the living. As in the case of Dante's own dark over-reading of Virgil's ellipsis in the previous canto, discussed in Section 3.4 above, the uncertain future left open by Dante's hesitation is immediately and pessimistically filled in by Cavalcante. Why does Dante hesitate? The readers, of course, know that Dante's friend and Cavalcante's son, the poet Guido Cavalcanti, died at the end of August 1300; in other words, his death, according to the fictional time frame of Dante's otherworldly journey, lay still a few months in the future. Centuries after it dismayed Cavalcante in *Inferno*, Guido's overt absence from the poem continues to mystify readers. 'Having disappeared in the blind spot (less than five months) close to the imaginary journey', as Gianfranco

Contini writes, Dante's former friend 'is shielded both from the final sentence and from the prophecies', thus impervious to the two most common forms of conclusive judgement in the *Commedia*. As such, Guido 'half-lives in an interval or suspended limbo in the great account of the afterlife that revolves around his death on earth, which is avoided'.[80] Dante's obstinate avoidance of any endpoint whatsoever—be it of divine judgement, of prophecy, or of any other account of Guido's death—causes his friend to vanish in the poem's most remarkable blind spot. The historical Dante Alighieri, author of the *Commedia*, could not have ignored the fate that awaited Guido Cavalcanti right around the corner of his fiction's time frame; and his reader cannot but know that Dante knew. Until an explanation comes to restore the *Commedia*'s space-time continuum (109–14), the protagonist's hesitation opens a rare wormhole in the poem. As Robert Wilson puts it, 'it is almost as if, in some strange way, Cavalcante has asked Dante *personaggio* why he refers to Guido from the viewpoint of Dante *uomo*'.[81] Thus, under the gravitational pull of Dante's knowledge of what lay ahead in his character's future, the texture of the poem is warped, and the protagonist blinks. In this *contaminatio* of roles, the fictional *personaggio* momentarily appears to have an insight into the perspective of the historical *uomo* outside the fiction, the boundaries between the two Dantes more porous than ever.[82]

While the future that lies outside of the fiction has this warping effect when included in the poem, cutting it out altogether is no less problematic. *Inferno* XXXIII—the canto of Ugolino—is neatly divided into two halves. The first and more famous part (1–78) is devoted to Ugolino della Gherardesca's first-person narration of his and his sons' tragic incarceration and death in the Torre della Muda. This half relies on the conventions of oral storytelling by an embodied, diegetic narrator: in Ugolino's suspenseful tale, the future of promised narration *dirò* (15), discussed in Section 3.1 above, is enhanced by a whole host of future tenses related to the

---

[80] 'Scomparso nell'angolo morto (meno di cinque mesi) a ridosso del viaggio immaginato,' Guido 'è sottratto alla sentenza finale, sottratto anche alle profezie'; 'semivive in un intervallo o limbo sospensivo del gran rapporto sull'oltretomba, che ruota attorno all'evitata sua fine terrena' (Gianfranco Contini, 'Cavalcanti in Dante', in *Un'idea di Dante*, pp. 143–57 (p. 143), trans. mine).
[81] Robert Wilson, *Prophecies and Prophecy*, p. 165.
[82] For a rational (all too rational?) scrutiny of the tenses in the episode, see John Freccero, 'Epitaph for Guido: *Inferno* X', *Religion & Literature*, 39.3 (2007), 1–29.

performance of storytelling: 'parlare e lagrimar *vedrai* insieme' ['then *you will see* me speak and weep together'] (9, emphases mine throughout) and 'come la morte mia fu cruda, | *udirai*, e *saprai* s'e' m'ha offeso' [literally, 'the cruelty of my death | *you shall hear*, and *you shall know* if he has wronged me'] (20–1); a further forward-oriented element is offered by Ugolino's prognostic dream.[83] In this skilful narrator's speech, the future goes as planned. Ugolino is perfectly able to fulfil all his promises; and, if his last infamous *reticentia* means what we fear, then so are his children, when they exclaim in the future tense, 'Padre, assai ci *fia* men doglia | se tu mangi di noi' ['Father, *we would suffer* less | if you would feed on us'] (61–2).[84] In this oral performance of storytelling, then, the embodied narrator seems to have narration under absolute control.

Set in counterpoint with Ugolino's oral narrative, the second, less celebrated half of *Inferno* XXXIII features another tale based on promises and futures. Frate Alberigo only embarks on his narration of his treacherous life and strange *pre-mortem* damnation with the aim of getting Dante to clear the tears that freeze over his eyes. Dante swears an equivocal oath ('Se vuo' ch'i' ti sovvegna, | dimmi chi se', e s'io non ti disbrigo, | al fondo de la ghiaccia ir mi convegna' ['If you want my help, let me know your name,' | I answered. 'Then, if I do not relieve you, | may I have to travel to the bottom of the ice'], 115–17), knowing perfectly well that he must journey to the bottom of Lake Cocytus regardless as a stage in his pilgrimage. This half-lie persuades Alberigo to fulfil his side of the pact (118–20), even throwing in the story of Branca Doria's fate as an extra (129–47), hoping thus better to entice Dante into obliging him ('perché tu più volentier mi rade | le 'nvetriate lagrime dal volto' ['So that you may be all the more inclined | to scrape these tear-drops glazed upon my face'], 127–8). Once the tale is over,

---

[83] On the relation of oral and written storytelling, Barolini comments: 'The writerly context that has absorbed the originally oral "canto" is denoted by the adverb "suso"; the poet refers to the children whose names are registered "above," in the written text' (*Undivine 'Comedy'*, p. 247, n. 49).

[84] On the question of cannibalism, first proposed by Iacopo della Lana, see Robert Hollander's bibliographical note 'Ugolino's Supposed Cannibalism: A Bibliographical Note and Discussion', *Quaderni d'italianistica*, 6 (1985), 64–81. The strongest case in favour of this option are in Marianne Shapiro, 'An Old French Source for Ugolino?', *Dante Studies*, 91 (1974), 129–47, and Ronald B. Herzman, 'Cannibalism and Communion in *Inferno* XXXIII', *Dante Studies*, 98 (1980), 53–78. See, more recently, Saverio Bellomo's review of the question in 'Il canto XXXIII dell'*Inferno*', in *Lectura Dantis 2002–2009, omaggio a Vincenzo Placella per i suoi settanta anni*, ed. Anna Cerbo and Mariangela Semola (Naples: Università degli Studi di Napoli 'L'Orientale', 2011), pp. 1369–86.

however, Alberigo's third and final request does not have the expected outcome, as Dante reneges on his word:

> 'Ma distendi oggimai in qua la mano;
> aprimi li occhi'. E io non gliel'apersi;
> e cortesia fu lui esser villano.
>
> ['But now extend your hand and open
> my eyes for me.' I did not open them;
> And to be rude to him was courtesy.]
>
> (*Inf.* XXXIII, 148–50)

Commentators debate Dante's uncharacteristic mercilessness and its epigrammatic justification, often relating this episode to that of Bocca degli Abati in the previous canto, whom the protagonist similarly abuses (*Inf.* XXXII, 73–139). In *Inferno* XXXIII, Dante's broken promise appears to be part of the canto's concern with treachery, the sin punished in this ninth circle. It manifests Dante's continuing interest in the inconsistencies between presents and futures in the *Inferno*, explored in cantos X and XX. Indeed, narrative promises, kept or broken, play an important role in this discourse, and the canto pushes it even further. Through Frate Alberigo's words, Dante introduces in the poem the unprecedented theological idea that the sin of treachery punished in the Ptolomaea is so grave that the souls of those who commit it are immediately plunged into Hell while their bodies remain on Earth, possessed by a demon (121–47; 154–7).[85] In stark contrast with the *Commedia*'s distinctively open soteriology, exemplified by the tales of last-minute damnations and redemptions of the various Montefeltros and Manfredis, this theological novelty appears idiosyncratic, suspending for a fearful moment the poem's radical embrace of possibility as the cornerstone of human existence and morality. Frate Alberigo explains this dismaying new information thus:

> tosto che l'anima trade
> come fec'io, il corpo suo l'è tolto

[85] Maurizio Fiorilla writes, 'non è ancora...del tutto risolta la questione della possibile *auctoritas* presente dietro l'idea dell'eccezionale castigo inflitto ai dannati della Tolomea, contrario alla dottrina cristiana che lascia a tutti uno spazio per il pentimento fino all'ultimo', before reviewing the sources traditionally proposed and suggesting a further possible intertextual reference ('"Et descendant in inferum": *Inf.* XXXIII, 109–157 e il salmo 54', *L'Alighieri*, 27 (2006), 133–9 (135)).

> da un demonio, che poscia il governa
> mentre che 'l tempo suo tutto sia vòlto.
>
> [the moment when a soul betrays
> as I did, its body is taken by a devil,
> who has it then in his control
> until the time allotted it has run.]
>
> (*Inf.* XXXIII, 129-32)

As soon as a soul commits treachery, they are sent to Hell. Thus, they are stripped not only of their body ('il corpo suo l'è tolto' ['its body is taken'], 130) but also of their time on Earth ("'l tempo suo' [literally, 'its time'], 132). Their body, although nominally belonging to them, is taken from them; similarly, their time on Earth, although still perceived as 'theirs', continues on without them. But if their body and their time go on without them, how can they be said to be 'theirs'? Therein lies the passage's tragic irony. One's time, as the repetition of *suo* communicates (130 and 132), is as dear to one's person as is one's body; and yet both are here shown to be vulnerable to alienation through any of life's violences: sin and *pre-mortem* damnation, in this case, but also more generally chance, accident, coercion, exile. I have shown, in the previous section, how Boccaccio uses the possessive as richly in the expression 'suo fine', which he employs in the *Trattatello* to highlight the discrepancy between Dante's ideal end—the glory that Dante wished for and deserved—and Dante's actual end—his exile; between the *Commedia*'s designed conclusion and its near material loss. Analogously, Frate Alberigo's phrase "'l tempo suo' (132) compels the reader to reflect on the vital yet fragile relationship between what we cherish as 'our time' and the fact that it is only considered 'ours' affectionately through a wishful fiction and by some ongoing lucky coincidence, and at any rate only until something happens that demonstrates how easily stripped from our hands it is. Voiced by a character who discovered in his punishment the rift between his affective and actual futures, Alberigo's phrasing begs the question: was that time ever his? Was that body ever his? The damned soul is only able to speak of 'his time' and 'his body' because, for whatever reason, he still cherishes the fiction that his own time and body belong to him, even when his very presence in Hell points to the grotesque absurdity of that very belief. In any case, what his expressions 'corpo suo' and 'tempo suo' express is that alongside the real future lies a more personal future that can be affectionately called one's own, a future that is imagined and wished for, as inseparable from one's self as his, your, my body.

It is that personal future that the damned are stripped of so brutally in *Inferno* XXXIII. Dante must have been aware of the effect that the theological invention of *pre-mortem* damnation would have had on his readers. It is unmistakable: as Emilio Pasquini writes, 'all ancient commentators marvel at it'.[86] The various explanations of this dilemma offered by early commentators all have something in common: 'they insist on it as an instance of *fictio* (Pietro, Graziolo, Benvenuto etc.) or on the arbitrariness inherent in placing limits on God's mercy (Lana, Anonimo fiorentino, Guido da Pisa, etc.'[87] In other words, commentators find the passage's theological violence to personal lives and possibilities jarring ('the fact that once the soul is separated from the body the body can manage itself and live in any way is false, and against nature and the faith', protests L'Ottimo).[88] When they explain the violence away, unanimously, they stress the fact the 'auctor' is only speaking 'poetizzando' ['poetically'] (Jacopo della Lana), 'immaginando' ['imaginatively'] (Anonimo Fiorentino), 'figurative' ['figuratively'] (Benvenuto da Imola); this is a 'locuti[o] poetic[a] colorat[a] auctoris hujus' ['a colourful poetic expression of this author'] (Pietro Alighieri), or even better a 'poetica narratio seu fictio' ['poetic narration or fiction'] (Guido da Pisa); in our words, just a narrative poem, a fiction. If early commentators rebel against what they see as an arbitrary narrative-theological novelty, modern commentators find it suspicious in its very intentions. As Casini notes, Dante's invention has an obvious practical advantage: 'it allows Dante to mark notes of infamy on the people that were still alive in 1300, without always having to resort to prophecies (cf. *Inf.* XVII, 68; XIX, 79–87; XXVIII, 55–60, 76–90) or invectives (cf. *Inf.* XVII, 72; XIX, 52–57; XXX, 76–78; XXXII, 69) made by the dead regarding the living.'[89] The explanation is neat but immediately creates problems of its own. Why not resort here also to the

---

[86] 'Se ne meravigliano...tutti i commentatori antichi' (Emilio Pasquini, 'Il canto XXXIII dell'*Inferno*', *Letture classensi*, 10–11 (1982), 191–216 (213, n. 55), trans. mine).

[87] 'Insistono sul suo carattere di *fictio* (Pietro, Graziolo, Benvenuto ecc.) o sull'arbitrio insito nel porre un limite alla misericordia divina (Lana, Anonimo fiorentino, Guido da Pisa ecc.)' (ibid.). Jacopo della Lana, *ad Inf.* XXXIII, 127–35 allusively contrasts *Inferno* XXXIII with Manfredi's last-minute salvation: 'Questa allegoria non è altro a dire se non che su nel mondo, largo modo, elli si puonno giudicare dannati; vero è che *la misericordia di Dio è tanta, ed ha sì ampio lo suo abbracciare, che* d'ogni peccato si può *tornare* a penitenzia e non essere per quello perduto' (DDP, emphases mine). Jacopo is clearly thinking here about the Manfredi episode, whose language he unmistakably echoes ('ma la bontà infinita ha sì gran braccia, | che prende ciò che si rivolge a lei', *Purg.* III, 121–3).

[88] 'egli è falso, e contro natura e fede, che partita l'anima dal corpo il corpo per alcuno modo si governi e viva' (L'Ottimo, *ad Inf.* XXXIII, 129 (DDP), trans. mine).

[89] 'permette a Dante di segnar note d'infamia su uomini viventi ancora nel 1300, senza ricorrere sempre alla forma delle predizioni (cfr. *Inf.* XVII, 68; XIX, 79–87; XXVIII, 55–60,

proven methods of prophecies and invectives? Why risk, for the sake of one episode, the *Commedia*'s entire representation of human existence as on the perennial verge of redemption or salvation? There is no need to speculate on authorial intentions, I think, to register the sheer conspicuousness of the author's intervention in this narrative decision. Dante's overbearing presence in the canto offers a decisive clue. In *Inferno* XXXIII, readers find a distorted image of what the universe of the *Commedia* would be like if the desire for self-enclosed futures and definitive endings under the author's control had its way. Cutting the future out of characters' lives, in practice, produces a dystopian theological vision, which erases moral freedom and consigns the poem's universe to an arbitrarily deterministic Hell. It would be ridiculous to argue that *Inferno* XXXIII is somewhat less or more a part of the *Commedia* or closer to/further from Dante Alighieri's artistic vision—this whole monograph is after all a critique of the very desire to arbitrarily subordinate one part of the work to another—but it is nonetheless arguable that this episode exposes in its inescapable consequences the drive to control interpretations by controlling ends; the very drive, in other words, that is at the heart of the *Commedia*'s dominant narrative. If you stick to the masterplot to the very end, this is what you get: a dystopian universe where humanity is stripped of its affective and personal dimension, deprived of its future and damned before death, its moral freedom voided—all in the name of a definitive, controlling end.

In *Inferno* X, XX, and XXXIII we thus have three episodes where the future is represented as problematic, if not an outright nightmare, within the poem's plot. Most importantly, all three episodes embroil Dante himself in the question of the future, severely testing, once again, the compartmentalization between *personaggio* and *poeta*. In *Inferno* X, Farinata's explanation of far-sightedness in Hell is elicited by the extreme compression of the poem's time frame, whereby the *personaggio* seems to share the *poeta*'s knowledge regarding Guido's death. In *Inferno* XX, the *personaggio* is rebuked for his pity for the soothsayer's punishment and their attempt to know the future, yet, despite his vantage point, the *poeta* does not appear to know any better. Lastly, when in *Inferno* XXXIII Frate Alberigo introduces the narrative-theological invention of *pre-mortem* damnation—a caricature of the masterplot in its extreme implications—the *personaggio* seems to

76–90) o delle imprecazioni (cfr. *Inf.* XVII, 72; XIX, 52–7; XXX, 76–8; XXXII, 69) fatte dai dannati rispetto ai vivi', Tommaso Casini and S. A. Barbi, *ad Inf.* XXXIII, 124 (DDP).

perform the episode's theological brutality, as he breaks his promise to Alberigo and thus makes himself complicit in sabotaging the continuity between presents and futures. In these episodes, then, *Inferno* thematizes the dark side of the future in general; but it also, more specifically, gives a taste of its destabilizing consequences for the *Commedia* and its author. Whenever it is conjured up, the future ends up putting pressure on the building blocks of the *Commedia*: its fictional time frame, its masterplot, the division of labour between *poeta* and *personaggio*.

3.6 The Ageing Author

Future tenses of promised writing, risks of precarious transmission, threats of unfinished works, infernal nightmares of futurity—these are reminders in the *Commedia* that, alongside Dante the masterful author with an assured grip on his fiction and its interpretation, there is another Dante, preoccupied with the very future that he indefatigably strives to tame. This is the vulnerable Dante that this chapter is concerned with, and whom we begin to see more and more of as the *Commedia* progresses. Manuele Gragnolati has written about the protagonist's embodied experience of the afterlife, arguing that alongside the traditional reading of the *Commedia* as *itinerarium mentis in Deum*—the allegorical journey of the soul to God famously advocated by Charles S. Singleton—the poem can also be read as 'a journey of the body'.[90] The protagonist's own body, as Gragnolati shows, 'goes through several stages of transformation as he moves through the otherworld', from the 'heavy, mortal body' of *Inferno*, to the progressively lighter body of *Purgatorio*, made ever lighter by the transformative 'experience of pain' as Dante climbs the mountain.[91] In *Paradiso*, significant episodes mark the body's transformation and the progressive strengthening of its faculties, through Dante's repeated efforts, failures, and renewed attempts to experience the transhuman reality of Heaven with his mortal body. The journey culminates in the last cantos of *Paradiso*, where the protagonist appears to

---

[90] Manuele Gragnolati, *Experiencing the Afterlife: Soul and Body in Dante and Medieval Culture* (Notre Dame: The University of Notre Dame Press, 2005), p. 168, and see pp. 168–78 for his account of the journey of the body. For the *itinerarium mentis*, see Charles S. Singleton, 'The Allegorical Journey', in *Dante Studies: Vol. 2. Journey to Beatrice* (Cambridge, MA: Harvard University Press, 1958), pp. 3–14. John Freccero writes about Dante's 'corpo lasso' in *Inferno* I, 28 as the 'sudden incarnation, the presence of a body on this journey of the mind' which 'marks Dante's poetic originality' (Freccero, *Poetics of Conversion*, p. 33).

[91] Gragnolati, *Experiencing the Afterlife*, p. 170.

have gained the augmented faculties of the resurrected body and is finally 'granted the vision of the mysteries of the universe and the Trinity'.[92] The protagonist's journey of the body, then, is one of increasing strength and faculties, a quintessentially teleological progression towards the fullness of experience that characterizes the resurrected body of the blessed.[93]

The *poeta*'s journey of the body is a different matter. It proceeds in parallel with that of the *personaggio*, yet its arc is not an ascending one, and the end toward which it moves is far from glorious. As Pertile writes, 'we are given to understand along the way' that the journey of the narrator 'is in a sense a far more difficult undertaking, a task that costs him "hunger, cold and vigils" (*Purg.* XXIX, 37–8)'.[94] Pertile quotes a passage in which the narrator dwells on his own embodied presence for the first time; indeed, this is one of the very few details in the poem that give us an insight, however indirect, into Dante's appearance in general:[95]

> O sacrosante Vergini, se fami,
> freddi o vigilie mai per voi soffersi,
> cagion mi sprona ch'io mercé vi chiami.
>
> [O sacred Virgins, if fasting, cold, or sleepless nights
> I've ever suffered for your sake,
> Necessity drives me to call for my reward.]
>
> (*Purg.* XXIX, 37–9)

'Fasting, cold, or sleepless nights' (37): Dante's travels test him physically in the otherworld as much as after his return, whether he ascends through the afterlife or meanders through Italy's courts. Here his plights are portrayed as implicitly redeeming and 'productive'; they have a purpose ('per voi [sacrosante Vergini]' ['for your sake [O sacred Virgins]'], 37), and give him reason to call on the

---

[92] Ibid., p. 178.
[93] In his *Amor che move: Linguaggio del corpo e forma del desiderio in Dante, Pasolini e Morante* (Milan: Il Saggiatore, 2013), pp. 139–61, Gragnolati revisits the conclusion of *Paradiso* as non-linear and anti-narrative, by placing further emphasis on the ways in which the return of the body, both of Dante and the blessed, resists sublimation, 'non si dissolve ma continua a essere parte integrante della gloria' (p. 161).
[94] Pertile, 'Introduction to *Inferno*', p. 67, quoted above (italics his).
[95] In *Inferno* XVI, 106–8, we learn that Dante was wearing a 'corda intorno cinta'; in *Purgatorio* XXXI, 68, Beatrice admonishes him to lift his 'barba', although most commentators take this to be a synecdoche for his chin ('chin up!'), tinged with a reproach of immaturity, rather than a reference to facial hair. On the question of Dante's beardedness, see R. A. Shoaf, 'Dante's Beard: *Sic et non* [*Purgatorio* XXXI, 68]', in *Magister Regis: Studies in Honor of Robert E. Kaske*, ed. Arthur Groos et al. (New York: Fordham University Press, 1986), pp. 171–7, and bibliographical references therein.

Muses for help (38). Yet Dante is not always so confident in the meaning and productivity of his exilic wanderings. Already in *Inferno* XXVI the narrator expressed his mixed feelings about a future he feared and anticipated in equal measure, as we have seen in Section 3.1:

> E se già fosse, non saria per tempo.
> Così foss'ei, da che pur esser dee!
> ché più mi graverà, com'più m'attempo.
>
> [Were it already come, it would not be too soon.
> But let it come, since come indeed it must,
> and it will weigh the more on me the more I age.]
>
> (*Inf.* XXVI, 10–12)

The verb *attemparsi*, a common word in modern-day Italian meaning 'to grow old', is Dante's neologism. It refers to the ageing that will weigh the narrator down as time goes by. Its construction (*ad* + *temporem* + reflexive form) is a trademark of the *Commedia*: it links *attemparsi* to the family of 'parasynthetic verbs [i.e., constructed with prefix + noun], reflexive or, more precisely, of middle voice, that is, referred to the subject, whose ontological action they set in motion metaphorically, without however falling within the category of action proper' (Contini lists as examples the likes of 's'inmilla', 's'interna', 's'insempra', etc.), which form Dante's 'grammar of metamorphosis'.[96] In Dante's hands, *attemparsi* becomes a verb worthy of Heidegger: transforming oneself into something which rushes towards time. This metamorphosis, however, does not have an aim, much less a glorious one. Compare it to the analogously constructed *infuturarsi* used by Cacciaguida in the renowned prophecy concerning Dante's exile in *Paradiso* XVII:

> poscia che s'infutura la tua vita
> vie più là che 'l punir di lor perfidie.
>
> [since your life shall far outlast
> the punishment of their treachery.]
>
> (*Par.* XVII, 98–9)

---

[96] 'Verbi parasintetici...riflessivi, o più esattamente medi, cioè riferiti al soggetto, di cui perciò movimentano metaforicamente la descrizione ontologica, senza propriamente cadere nell'azione'; 'grammatica delle metamorfosi' (Gianfranco Contini, 'Un esempio di poesia dantesca (Il canto XXVIII del *Paradiso*)', in *Un'idea di Dante*, pp. 191–213 (p. 200). Contini also notices how these neologisms often occurs as rhyme-words, as in this case: 'la posizione in rima, punto accusato del ritmo, quando non addirittura in rima finale di terzina, esalta la portata del neologismo' (ibid.).

Here the future that Dante envisions is a textbook case of teleology. Dante's life 's'infutura' (98), that is, will advance further into the future than the punishment of those who have been cruel to him. With a firm footing in the future, Dante will have the teleological vantage point, which will enable him to have the last word and make sense of his sufferings. Later in the canto Dante recreates the same dynamic, as he expresses the fear that he might be despised by posterity: 'temo di perder viver tra coloro | che questo tempo chiameranno antico' ['I fear I shall not live on for those | to whom our times shall be the ancient days'] (*Par.* XVII, 119–20). As Piero Boitani writes, the expression 'implies a keen sense of the future on Dante's part, and also gives the future a very peculiar connotation, that of an age which looks as it were mainly to the past'.[97] The roles have changed slightly, but the teleological dynamic remains the same, this time with posterity in a position to judge Dante's life after his death. With 'm'attempo', however, time affords no such advantages. In *Inferno* XXVI, temporality shows instead its dark side; it does not exalt Dante's body but weighs him down with age ('graverà', 12). The verb is used much to the same effect by Cacciaguida in a further point of contact between the two cantos:

> Tu proverai sì come sa di sale
> lo pane altrui, e come è duro calle
> lo scendere e 'l salir per l'altrui scale.
>
> E quel che più ti graverà le spalle
> sarà la compagnia malvagia e scempia
> con la qual tu cadrai in questa valle;
>
> ['You shall learn how salt is the taste
> of another man's bread and how hard is the way,
> going down and then up another man's stairs.
>
> But the heaviest burden your shoulders must bear
> shall be the companions, wicked and witless,
> among whom you shall fall in your descent.]
>
> (*Par.* XVII, 58–63)

Part of the reason why the poetry of the first terzina is so poignant and memorable is that Dante chooses to express exile, helplessness, and the

---

[97] Piero Boitani, 'Those who will call these times ancient: The Futures of Prophecy and Poetry', in *Medieval Futures: Attitudes to the Future in the Middle Ages*, ed. John Anthony Burrow and Ian P. Wei (Woodbridge: Boydell Press, 2000), pp. 51–65 (p. 52). A further instance of this dynamic occurs in very similar terms in *Purgatorio* XXIII, 91–111, where Forese prophesies: 'Tempo futuro m'è già nel cospetto, | cui non sarà quest'ora molto antica' (98–9).

experience of being on the receiving end of charity through the use of concrete terms rather than abstractions. Salty bread and walking up and down a stranger's stairs are descriptions of what exile means in everyday life, and the phrase 'graverà le spalle' ['burden your shoulder'] (61) carries part of this loaded literality into the following terzina. From a dramaturgic point of view, however, this justly celebrated passage does nothing new. By the time Dante is told of 'lo scendere e 'l salir' ['going down and then up'] (60) that awaits him, we have seen him practise these steps about fifty-six times in the poem, and in roughly that order. The verb *scendere* (and *discendere*) occurs forty-one times in *Inferno*, twenty-four in *Purgatorio*, and twenty-nine in *Paradiso*; the verb *salire* (and *risalire*) respectively ten, forty-two, and fourteen times. Unsurprisingly, most descending takes place in the valley of Hell and most ascending on the mountain of Purgatory, and Dante does more of it than any other single character or subject. However, whereas the pilgrim's ascending and descending steps have a precise aim in sight, their trajectory after the end of his otherworldly journey loses this teleological optimism. The journey will be equally corporeal, as the concrete language states plainly, but in this case it will follow the natural course of any journey on Earth, where time is more ungrateful and the immediate end in sight is not so welcome: first rise, then fall. The imaginative universe of the *Commedia* is oriented toward this earthly end; and the protagonist himself shows an acute awareness of the kind of world that awaits him after the conclusion of his journey. In *Purgatorio* XX the protagonist refers to his return to Earth cautiously with the lines 's'io ritorno a compiér lo cammin corto | di quella vita ch'al termine volà' ['if I return to finish my brief journey | in that life which rushes to its ending'] (*Purg.* XX, 38–9): his return may be uncertain ('s[e]'), but the journey's brevity, rushing speed, and conclusion are painfully clear. Further, in the Garden of Eden, when Beatrice urges the protagonist to fulfil his destiny with the famous lines 'così queste parole segna a' vivi | del viver ch'è un correre alla morte' ['set these words down for those | who live the life that is a race to death'] (*Purg.* XXXIII, 53–4), she is once again complicating the passage's prophetic tone, addressing the protagonist and perhaps including him in the kind of journey that, unlike comedies, promises no happy ending. Even if the pilgrim were somehow immune to the melancholy tale of mortality, his exile will await him with its own special violence:

> Ben veggio, padre mio, sì come sprona
> lo tempo verso me, per colpo darmi
> tal, ch'è più grave a chi più s'abbandona;

> [I can see, father, that time is spurring toward me
> to deal me such a blow as falls most heavily
> on one proceeding heedless on his way.]
>
> (*Par.* XVII, 106–8)

The terzina is reminiscent of the line 'che più mi graverà, com' più m'attempo' ['it will weigh the more on me the more I age'] (*Inf.* XXVI, 12). While Dante pictured himself rushing towards time in *Inferno* XXVI ('m'attempo' ['I age']), in *Paradiso* XVII time rushes towards him ('sprona | lo tempo verso me' ['time is spurring toward me'], 106). It does not bring Dante any advantage but only a heavy blow, more imminent now that it relinquishes the future tense ('che più mi graverà' ['it will weigh more'], *Inf.* XXVI, 12) in favour of the present ('ch'] più grave' ['falls most heavily'], *Par.* XVII, 108).

3.7 Between Vulnerability and Performance: *Paradiso* XXV

The narrator's time-worn body is last seen in the address to the reader of *Paradiso* XXV:

> Se mai continga che 'l poema sacro
> al quale ha posto mano e cielo e terra,
> sì che m'ha fatto per molti anni macro,
> vinca la crudeltà che fuor mi serra
> del bello ovile ov'io dormi' agnello,
> nimico ai lupi che li danno guerra;
> con altra voce omai, con altro vello
> ritornerò poeta, e in sul fonte
> del mio battesmo prenderò 'l cappello.
>
> [Should it ever come to pass that this sacred poem
> to which both Heaven and earth have set their hand
> so that it has made me lean for many years,
> should overcome the cruelty that locks me out
> of the fair sheepfold where I slept as a lamb,
> for of the wolves at war with it,
> with another voice then, with another fleece,
> shall I return a poet and, at the font
> where I was baptized, take the laurel crown.]
>
> (*Par.* XXV, 1–9)

The famous incipit of the canto in which the protagonist is examined on the cardinal virtue of Hope—'"Spene," dissi'io, "è uno attender certo | de la gloria futura"' ['"Hope," I said, "is the certain expectation | of future glory"'] (*Par.* XXV, 67–8)—presents the future in all the ambiguity that we have traced throughout the *Commedia*. The meaning of the passage is inseparable from the tone one reads into it. Do we voice it triumphantly, emphasizing the *gravitas* of the biblical references and elevated rhetorical construction, and the cosmological vastness involving Heaven and Earth?[98] Or do we voice it more cautiously as the delicate hope of an ageing and emaciated man, placing the emphasis, rather, on tentative hypotheticals and subjunctives and the fact that this (pseudo-?)prophecy is voiced by the narrator on Earth, unlike all other prophecies bar the opening of *Inferno* XXVI analysed above?[99] A hallmark of Dante's narrative pluralism, the incipit alternates these major and minor chords. It appears to make a prophecy through the future indicatives of the third terzina ('ritornerò poeta' ['shall I return a poet'], 8; 'prenderò 'l cappello' ['[I shall] take the laurel crown'], 9) but modulates it through the subjunctives on which they are conditional ('Se mai continga' ['Should it ever comes to pass'], 1; 'vinca la crudeltà' ['should overcome the cruelty'], 4), a movement which is anticipated within each of the first two terzinas (from hypothetical ('Se mai continga') to present indicative ('sì che m'ha fatto'); from subjunctive ('vinca la crudeltà') to past historical ('ov'io dormii') and present ('li danno guerra').[100]

Reading the incipit after Dante's death, it is impossible to suspend one's knowledge that, even if these lines were meant to be prophetic, they failed— one of very few such failures in Dante's oeuvre.[101] We may never know (and

---

[98] For the biblical intertext in *Paradiso* XXV, see Giuseppe Ledda, 'L'esilio, la speranza, la poesia: Modelli biblici e strutture autobiografiche nel canto XXV del *Paradiso*', *Studi e Problemi di Critica Testuale*, 90.1 (2015), 257–77.

[99] From these very details, Robert Wilson rules out the possibility that this is a prophecy: 'I do not consider *Par.* XXV, 1–9, prophetic or predictive. It is expressed in the form of the conditional, and represents, at best, Dante's future hope. It is also expressed by Dante *poeta*, who, as we have seen, does not prophesy directly' (Wilson, *Prophecies and Prophecy*, p. 205, n. 19). Albert Russell Ascoli reflects that the Dante described here is '"human, all too human". Dante's coronation…is posited as radically contingent, subject to the constraints of history' (Ascoli, *Dante and the Making of a Modern Author*, p. 402).

[100] Claire Honess and Matthew Treherne discuss the shift in mood in the first terzina: 'if the return to Florence imagined here is hypothetical ("Se mai *continga*…"), the divine agency in the poem's composition is presented as unassailably true ("al quale ha posto mano…"), as the move from subjunctive to indicative mood confirms' ('Introduction' to *Se mai continga…: Exile, Politics and Theology in Dante*, ed. Claire E. Honess and Matthew Treherne (Ravenna: Longo, 2013), pp. 7–10 (p. 8)).

[101] Robert Wilson writes how Dante prefers obscurity and ambiguity to the possibility of incorrect prophecy, especially when it comes to *ante eventum* prophecies such as this one. An

can only imagine) whether the 'molti anni' ['many years'] spent in exile did render Dante as *macro* ['lean'] as he paints himself (3), and whether age did alter his *voce* ['voice'] and *vello* ['fleece', i.e., 'hair'] (7);[102] what we do know is that he never returned to Florence, and he was never poet laureate as he hoped. From this perspective at least, a more cautious reading of *Paradiso* XXV seems justified: Dante's hypotheticals and subjunctives, showing the vulnerability of his text, proved more truthful than his prophetic future.

Yet in a sense Dante did return to Florence as poet laureate.[103] Not just in the shape of 'the words of his poetry' and thus 'only in a metaphorical sense', as Claire Honess has argued, but, as it were, in person and in a way that seems to respond to *Paradiso* XXV.[104] Whereas the earliest depictions of Dante in manuscripts, panels, or frescos represent him as 'giovanile, sereno, chiaro d'incarnato' and wearing his recognizable cap, two iconographic innovations begin to appear in the fifteenth century: on the one hand, Dante appears more mature and gaunt, as he already did in such early fifteenth-century manuscripts as Strozzi 174 (held in the Biblioteca Medicea Laurenziana, Florence, fol. 4v) and Riccardiano 1040 (Biblioteca Riccardiana, Florence, fol. 1v); on the other, he wears the laurel that alludes to his poetic coronation.[105] The earliest representation to feature both iconographic innovations is perhaps the best known one: the fresco painted by Domenico di Michelino in the Duomo of Florence in 1465 for the bicentenary of Dante's birth (see Figure 3.1). Here Dante appears at the centre of the frame, gaunt and laurelled, holding his *Commedia*, surrounded by Hell

---

example of failed prophecy is offered by both *Epistle* VI and *Purgatorio* XIII, 91–111: 'The detail about mourning is shared by both texts. The letter predicts the imminent attack on Florence by Henry VII, so that, in this instance, Dante's prediction in his letter was not realised, since Henry ended his six week siege of the city in October 1312 and withdrew his army, never to return.' (Wilson, *Prophecies and Prophecy*, pp. 96–7). Note that the epistle too resorts to one of Dante's disclaimers about futurity: 'si praesaga mens mea non fallitur' (*Ep.* VI, 17).

[102] On the subject of Dante's leanness, Giuseppe Ledda reflects on whether it should be considered a case of autobiographical realism versus the symbolic significance of a prophetic persona based on 'il modello della magrezza apostolico'. Ledda preserves the ambiguity in his answer: 'Nel caso di Dante questi elementi topici assumono poi un intenso valore di vissuto autobiografico' (Ledda, 'L'esilio, la speranza, la poesia', p. 261, n. 1 and bibliographical references therein). The case for seeing the adjective as referring to the *magrezza apostolica* would be reinforced by reference to *Inferno* XXVII, 92–3; see Nick Havely, *Dante and the Franciscans: Poverty and the Papacy in the 'Commedia'* (Cambridge: Cambridge University Press, 2004), p. 56 with n. 82 and 177 with nn. 153–4.

[103] For a powerful argument in favour of the interpretation that Dante intended the incipit of *Paradiso* XXV to mean his wish to be poet laureate, see Ledda, 'L'esilio, la speranza, la poesia', p. 262.

[104] 'Ritornerò poeta...': Florence, Exile, and Hope', in *Se mai continga...*, pp. 85–103, p. 102.

[105] Anna Maria Francini Ciaranfi, 'Iconografia', in *ED*.

166 DANTE'S MASTERPLOT AND ALTERNATIVE NARRATIVES

Figure 3.1 Domenico di Michelino, *Dante and his Poem* (1465). Fresco. Cathedral of Santa Maria del Fiore, Florence. Copyright: Wikimedia Commons.

to the left, Purgatory in the background, and the spheres of Heaven above him. On the right-hand side of the composition lies his home town Florence, showing its walls to the poet, who stands outside the gates. Behind the city walls, the skyline is dominated by the Duomo that in real life contains this very fresco where Dante is represented. Through this *mise en abyme*—the fresco of Dante in the Duomo representing the Duomo that contains the fresco—the poet can be seen or imagined both outside and inside the city: outside, because we see him standing outside of the city walls; inside, because we know the painted Duomo inside the gates to hold the poet's portrait. Thus the painting preserves the ambiguity of *Paradiso* XXV and all of Dante's futures, remaining faithful to the poet's own uncertainty and open-endedness when using the future tense at the time of writing. As Catherine Keen notes, 'return' in this episode is 'understood to bring not closure but change and rebirth, extended indefinitely towards the future.'[106]

---

[106] Catherine Keen, 'Florence and Faction in Dante's Lyric Poetry: Framing the Experience of Exile', in *Se mai contigna...*, pp. 63–83 (p. 82).

The 'resilient validation of the spiritually, politically and poetically transformative nature of Dante's experience of banishment from Florence' that Keen writes of coincides, specifically, with Dante's laureation and ageing, both performed by his poetry in the future tense and performing the two complementary sides of it—authorial mastery and authorial vulnerability. Robert Hollander comments that 'it is notable that Dante, on both occasions on which he considers the prospect of his own laureation (see *Par.* I, 26, "coronarmi" ["crowning myself"]), imagines the wreath, not as being bestowed upon him by some benevolent figure, but as being taken by himself'.[107] As the last five centuries of Dante iconography demonstrate, his *Commedia* gained him the poetic laurel with which he is now always represented, but also left a trace of the arduous and uncertain journey of its writing.

---

[107] Robert Hollander, *ad Par.* XXV, 1–9. See also Daniele Mattalia, *ad Par.* XXV, 9.

Epilogue
Dante's Narrative Pluralism

In her review of the promise and problems of biographical studies of Dante, Elisa Brilli raises the question of how those examining Dante's autobiographical statements should deal with the fact that the author 'changed his mind quite often about the general plot and details of his life. Should we try to establish which of these contrasting statements is historically "truer" than the others? Should we instead attempt the impossible, yet frequently undertaken, mission of reconciling them? Given that palinode and *retractatio* are common tools in this scholarly quest for a unitary meaning, do those declarations...have the same specific testimonial weight?'[1] In their search for the historical truth on the man and author, Dante's biographers are indeed particularly aware of his talent for proposing teleological narratives and exploiting them to turn even the most sceptical of his interpreters into the keenest of teleologians. Faced with the task of disentangling fact from idealized fiction, biographers have adopted different strategies: some have conceded that contesting Dante's self-narrative is no longer possible; others have proposed leaning on it unreservedly;[2] others have advocated a more radical return to historical documents as a way forward;[3] but all

---

[1] Elisa Brilli, 'Dante's Biographies and Historical Studies: An *Ouverture*', *Dante Studies*, 136 (2018), 133–42 (138). Cf. also the entire 'Forum: Dante and Biography' therein, pp. 133–231.

[2] As Gorni writes, '[L]'assenza, quasi provvidenziale, di documenti ha conferito un valore astratto, astorico ed esemplare, all'esperienza del poeta, modello ed eroe italiano moderno' (Guglielmo Gorni, *Dante: Storia di un visionario* (Bari: Laterza, 2009), p. 27). On leaning on Dante's self-narrative: 'Un seule possibilité semble se présenter: s'appuyer sur l'autobiographie dantesque' (Jacqueline Risset, *Dante: Une Vie* (Paris: Flammarion, 1995), p. 9); 'la soluzione migliore per cogliere il segreto di un artista è tentare di ripercorrerne il cammino, ponendoci per così dire dal suo punto di vista' (Emilio Pasquini, *Vita di Dante: I giorni e le opere* (Milan: BUR, 2007), p. 10).

[3] On the proposal of a historical turn aimed at the 'svincolamento dall'onnipresenza della voce di Dante nella costruzione della biografia dantesca', see Giuliano Milani and Antonio Montefusco, '"Prescindendo dai versi di Dante?" Un percorso negli studi tra testi, biografia e documenti', in *Dante attraverso i documenti. I. Famiglia e patrimonio (secolo XII–1300 circa)*, ed. Giuliano Milani and Antonio Montefusco. Special issue of *Reti Medievali Rivista*, 15.2 (2014).

accompanied their statements with methodological caveats that are worth pondering for all readers of Dante. Giorgio Inglese put the matter clearly when he wrote: 'autobiographical references, which are of great importance within Dante's oeuvre…, must be confronted with the intention to stylize them, and even idealize them, which is typical of the literary strategy that they are part of'.[4] The teleological trajectory, with its exemplary narrative arc and inspiring message, is precisely an instance of such a stylized and idealized narrative. On the heels of this realization, Inglese decides to write a less linear, more pluralistic narrative of Dante's life: one possible biography among the various equally possible alternatives—as valid as Dante's dominant one. 'Rather than attempting the umpteenth linear reconstruction—of a novelistic kind—of Dante's life,' writes Inglese, 'it seemed to me more appropriate to propose a not altogether coherent combination of elements that are certain, probable, or merely plausible.'[5] The lines are drawn: on the one hand, the influence of the linear narrative, novelistic plotting, and fictionality proposed by Dante; on the other, a methodological open-mindedness about a lack of coherence and of pre-established design.[6]

In the present study, I have taken a similar approach to Dante's *Commedia* from a literary perspective. I fully acknowledge the importance of Dante's teleological masterplot in the textual construction of the *Commedia*, with its ideological, literary, and ethical projects. At the same time, however, I have tried to consider the masterplot for what it is: an artefact on a par with any other part of the text and thus equally demanding of critical scrutiny. In my analysis of alternative narratives, therefore, I have resisted the impulse to subordinate them to teleology, showing how this impulse is produced by the teleological masterplot itself with its man-made hierarchy of *before* and *after*. I have tried, in other words, to take the *master* out of the *masterplot*, and study it just as any other plot in the poem.

The picture of the *Commedia* that emerges from this study questions three important assumptions underlying Dante's teleological masterplot. First, the

---

[4] 'i riferimenti autobiografici, rilevantissimi nell'opera dantesca…, dev[ono] essere pur sempre mess[i] a confronto con gli intenti di stilizzazione, e persino di idealizzazione, propri della strategia letteraria entro la quale essi sono proposti' (Giorgio Inglese, *Vita di Dante: Una biografia possibile* (Rome: Carocci, 2015), p. 11, trans. mine).

[5] '[P]iù che tentare l'ennesima ricostruzione lineare—di tenore romanzesco—della vita di Dante', writes Inglese, 'mi è parso conveniente proporre una combinazione non troppo coerente fra elementi certi, probabili o solo plausibili' (ibid., trans. mine). Gorni agrees: 'Bisogna rassegnarsi al fitto mistero, che obbliga a emettere ipotesi, nient'altro che ipotesi, sulla vita, sulla cronologia delle opere e sul loro stesso canone' (*Dante: Storia di un visionario*, p. 27).

[6] On this point, see also Zygmunt G. Barański, 'The "New Life" of 'Comedy': The *Commedia* and the *Vita Nuova*', *Dante Studies*, 113 (1995), 1–29 (20).

oxymora and long-range paradoxes explored in Chapter 1 question 'the interpretive assumption...of "total coherence" in the *Commedia*'.[7] In this respect, I agree with those scholars who argue that not everything is resolved in the *Commedia* but that paradox is part of the poem's design.[8] The body of this monograph has shown this in practice, by focusing variously on how God's justice is represented as inflexible, and yet his mercy is portrayed as infinite; how figuring Heaven is said to be an impossible task, and yet the experience of its paradoxes is performed for the reader; how the poem's narrative necessity can coexist in the text with the freedom of centrifugal and parallel narratives; and how the poet's prophetic persona coexists with that of a man vulnerable to time and circumstance. As these and other instances demonstrate, paradox and contradiction are not only very much at home in the poetic universe of the *Commedia*; they are structural components of it. Dante's desire for coherence does not overrule his respect for the theological, moral, and narrative otherness that a dominant narrative risks sacrificing.

This respect for otherness extends to Dante's relationship with his readers, with whom the interpretation of his poem will eventually rest. The precise nature of this relationship is open to debate.[9] Some scholars characterize it as authoritative and controlling, as they draw attention to Dante's assured command of the narrative, and emphasize the ways in which the text 'manipulate[s] the reader' and 'manages our...reactions'.[10] The gendered

---

[7] Albert Russell Ascoli, *Dante and the Making of a Modern Author* (Cambridge: Cambridge University Press, 2008), p. 45. Ascoli is alluding here to Gianfranco Contini's dismissal of 'l'illusione della cosiddetta lettura totale' of the *Commedia* ('Filologia ed esegesi dantesca', repr. in *Un'idea di Dante: Saggi danteschi* (Turin: Einaudi, 1970), pp. 113–42 (p. 114)).

[8] See, most recently, Manuele Gragnolati and Francesca Southerden, 'From Paradox to Exclusivity: Dante and Petrarch's Lyrical Eschatologies', in *The Unity of Knowledge in the Pre-Modern World: Petrarch and Boccaccio between the Middle Ages and Renaissance*, ed. Igor Candido (Berlin: De Gruyter, 2018).

[9] 'Dante appeals to the reader ('lettore') more frequently than any other classical or medieval author' (Elena Lombardi, *The Wings of the Doves: Love and Desire in Dante and Medieval Culture* (Montreal: McGill-Queen's University Press, 2012), p. 215). On the *Commedia*'s addresses to the reader: Erich Auerbach, 'Dante's Addresses to the Reader', *Romance Philology*, 7 (1954), 268–78, and *Literary Language and its Public in Late Antiquity and in the Middle Ages*, trans. Ralph Mannheim (New York: Pantheon, 1965); Leo Spitzer, 'The Addresses to the Reader in the *Commedia*', *Italica*, 32 (1955), 143–65; William Franke, *Dante's Interpretive Journey* (Chicago: University of Chicago Press, 1996), pp. 37–80.

[10] Teodolinda Barolini, *Undivine 'Comedy'*, p. 16, and the rest of ch. 1. Although not always agreeing with Barolini's method and rhetoric, other scholars share her view of the author's control of his text's reception: see, for instance, Albert Russell Ascoli's account of Dante's construction of his authorial persona in *Dante and the Making of the Modern Author* (Cambridge: Cambridge University Press, 2008); and Heather Webb's case for the ways in which the *Commedia* makes the reader participate in the narrative through gestures and posture (*Dante's Persons: An Ethics of the Transhuman* (Oxford: Oxford University Press, 2016).

term *masterplot*, as used here, will hopefully be seen to make fun of this very portrait with its connotations of dominance, superiority, and a particular brand of macho *bravura*.[11] It parodies what the rampant success of the teleological narrative model in the reception of the *Commedia* has made its author look like.[12] While Dante does exert unprecedented control over his poem and its reception, he does not shy away from representing his own failings. In fact, as Chapter 3 argues, the *Commedia* and its narrator systematically remind readers of their vulnerability, an aspect of Dante's self-representation which demands serious critical consideration. By exploring Dante's vulnerability further, in the face of an over-authoritative image of the poet, readers will be able to appreciate the ways in which his relationship with his reception is more open-ended and generous. In this light, the *Commedia*'s openness to the future can be read as evidence of how the poem 'remain[s] in some ways incomplete, or...unfulfilled';[13] the many paradoxes and moral quandaries in the poem often make the *Commedia* an 'undecidable text' which bestows 'solely upon [the reader] the (in)decisions of interpretation'.[14]

Lastly, this monograph demonstrates how Dante's masterplot, although rampant in the reception of the *Commedia*, is far from uncontested within the text. In the body of this study, I have identified three alternative narrative models, afforded respectively by paradoxes, alternative endings and parallel lives, and the problem case of the future—pioneering work by Albert Russell Ascoli, Teodolinda Barolini, Elisa Brilli, Manuele Gragnolati, Elena Lombardi, and Gennaro Sasso demonstrates that these are likely not the only ones, nor is this the only way to conceptualize them. In line with

---

[11] Proving this point, such connotations are indeed discernible throughout T. K. Seung's *The Fragile Leaves of the Sibyl: Dante's Master Plan* (Westminster, MD: Newman Press, 1961).

[12] Reflecting on gendered understandings of 'narrative authority', feminist scholar Alison Case finds 'a larger gendered pattern, in which self-conscious narrative mastery is coded as a masculine attribute, while credibility for female narrators tends to be associated with unself-consciously embodying or reflecting social truths' ('Gender and History in Narrative Theory: The Problem of Retrospective Distance in *David Copperfield* and *Bleak House*', in *A Companion to Narrative Theory*, ed. James Phelan and Peter J. Rabinowitz (Malden, MA: Blackwell, 2005), pp. 312–21 (p. 320)).

[13] Robert Wilson, *Prophecies and Prophecy in Dante's 'Commedia'*, p. 121.

[14] Elena Lombardi, *The Wings of the Doves*, pp. 4 and 11 (see also her 'Introduction', pp. 3–19). Cf. also Sara Fortuna and Manuele Gragnolati's discussion of the *Commedia* as a 'multi-stable image' involving the reader's interpretation in 'Dante after Wittgenstein: "Aspetto", Language, and Subjectivity from *Convivio* to *Paradiso*', in Sara Fortuna, Manuele Gragnolati, and Jürgen Trabant, *Dante's Plurilingualism: Authority, Knowledge, Subjectivity* (Oxford: Legenda, 2010), pp. 223–47. On open-endedness in the *Commedia*, Nicolò Crisafi, 'Interrupted and Unfinished: The Open-ended Dante of the *Commedia*', in *Openness in Medieval Culture*, ed. Almut Suerbaum and Manuele Gragnolati (Berlin: ICI Berlin Press, forthcoming).

this volume's pluralistic understanding of Dante and of the poetic universe of the *Commedia*, I believe that further narrative models can, and should, be explored.[15] It would be this work's proudest accomplishment if, alongside the established notions of Dante's *plurilingualism* and *pluristylism*, an appreciation of Dante's *narrative pluralism* could come to play a key role in contemporary and future readings of his *Commedia*.

---

[15] I propose 'bad infinity'—an endless succession of episodes without meaning or aim—as a further, nightmarish, narrative model in Nicolò Crisafi, 'Problemi narrativi nella cornice dei superbi (*Purgatorio* X–XII): Teleologia, cattiva infinità, e possibilità', *Chroniques Italiennes*, 39.2 (2020), 242–60.

Bibliography

Works by Dante

Alighieri, Dante, *De vulgari eloquentia*, ed. Pio Rajna (Florence: Società Dantesca Italiana, 1960).
Alighieri, Dante, *Rime*, ed. Michele Barbi (Florence: Società Dantesca Italiana, 1960).
Alighieri, Dante, *Vita Nuova*, ed. Michele Barbi (Florence: Società Dantesca Italiana, 1960).
Alighieri, Dante, '*La Commedia*' *secondo l'antica vulgata*, ed. Giorgio Petrocchi, 3 vols (Florence: Società Dantesca Italiana, 1966–8).
Alighieri, Dante, *Dante's Lyric Poetry*, ed. and trans. Kenelm Foster and Patrick Boyd, 2 vols (Oxford: Clarendon Press, 1967).
Alighieri, Dante, *The Divine Comedy*, trans. Charles S. Singleton, 3 vols (Princeton, NJ: Princeton University Press, 1975).
Alighieri, Dante, *The Banquet*, trans. Richard Lansing (New York: Garland, 1990).
Alighieri, Dante, *Vita Nuova*, trans. Mark Musa (Oxford: Oxford University Press, 1992).
Alighieri, Dante, *Convivio*, ed. Franca Brambilla Ageno (Florence: Le Lettere, 1995).
Alighieri, Dante, *Rime*, ed. Gianfranco Contini (Turin: Einaudi, 1995).
Alighieri, Dante, *De vulgari eloquentia*, trans. Steven Botterill (Cambridge: Cambridge University Press, 1996).
Alighieri, Dante, *Vita nova*, ed. Guglielmo Gorni (Turin: Einaudi, 1996).
Alighieri, Dante, *Inferno*, trans. Jean and Robert Hollander (New York: Anchor, 2000).
Alighieri, Dante, *Purgatorio*, trans. Jean and Robert Hollander (New York: Anchor, 2003).
Alighieri, Dante, *Paradiso*, trans. Jean and Robert Hollander (New York: Doubleday: 2007).
Alighieri, Dante, *Paradiso*, trans. Robin Kirkpatrick (London: Penguin, 2007).
Alighieri, Dante, *Rime giovanili e della 'Vita Nuova'*, ed. Teodolinda Barolini (Milan: Rizzoli, 2009).
Alighieri, Dante [?], 'Epistola a Cangrande', ed. Claudia Villa, in *Opere*, ed. Marco Santagata, 3 vols (Milan: Mondadori, 2011–), III, pp. 1417–592.
Alighieri, Dante, *Rime*, ed. Claudio Giunta, in *Opere*, ed. Marco Santagata, 3 vols (Milan: Mondadori, 2011–), I, pp. 5–744.
Alighieri, Dante, *Dante's Lyric Poetry: Poems of Youth and of the 'Vita Nuova'*, ed. Teodolinda Barolini, trans. Richard Lansing (Toronto: University of Toronto Press, 2014).
Alighieri, Dante, Epistola XIII, ed. Luca Azzetta, in *Le Opere*, vol. V. *Epistole, Egloge, Questio de aqua et terra*, ed. Marco Baglio, Luca Azzetta, Marco Petoletti, Michele Rinaldi (Rome: Salerno, 2016), pp. 271–487.

Primary Texts

Antonelli, Roberto, ed., *I poeti della scuola siciliana*, 3 vols (Milan: Mondadori, 2008).
Ariosto, Ludovico, *Orlando Furioso*, ed. Edoardo Sanguineti and Marcello Turchi (Milan: Garzanti, 1964).
Aristotle, *Metaphysics*, trans. Hugh Tredennick and George Cyril Armstrong, rev. edn, 2 vols (Cambridge, MA: Harvard University Press, 2014).
Auden, W. H., *Homage to Clio* (London: Faber & Faber, 1960).
Augustine of Hippo, *Confessions*, trans. William Watts, 2 vols (Cambridge, MA: Harvard University Press, 2006).
Bernard of Clairvaux, *Liber de diligendo deo* (Turnhout: Brepols, 2010).
Biblia Sacra Vulgata and The King James Version, http://biblehub.com/.
Boccaccio, Giovanni, *Decameron*, ed. Vittore Branca, in *Tutte le opere*, ed. Vittore Branca, Antonio Enzo Quaglio, Alberto Limentani, Giorgio Padoan, 10 vols (Milan: Mondadori, 1964–98), IV.
Boccaccio, Giovanni, *Rime, Carmina, Epistole*, ed. Ginetta Auzzas, in *Tutte le opere*, ed. Vittore Branca, Antonio Enzo Quaglio, Alberto Limentani, Giorgio Padoan, 10 vols (Milan: Mondadori, 1964–98), V, 1.
Boccaccio, Giovanni, *Trattatello in laude di Dante*, ed. Vittore Branca (Milan: Mondadori, 1974).
Boethius, *The Theological Tractates and The Consolation of Philosophy*, trans. Hugh F. Stewart, Edward K. Rand, and S. Jim Tester (Cambridge, MA: Harvard University Press, 1973).
Bonaventure, *Journey of the Soul into God: Itinerarium Mentis in Deum*, ed. Philotheus Boehner, trans. Zachary Hayes (Saint Bonaventure, NY: Franciscan Institute Publications, 2002).
Cavalcanti, Guido, *Rime. Con le rime di Iacopo Cavalcanti*, ed. Domenico De Robertis (Turin: Einaudi, 1986).
Cavalcanti, Guido, *The Poetry of Guido Cavalcanti*, trans. Lowry Nelson Jr. (New York: Garland, 1986).
Cicero, *Brutus; Orator*, trans. George L. Hendrickson and Harry M. Hubbell (Cambridge, MA: Harvard University Press, 1952).
Cicero, *Rhetorica ad Herennium*, trans. Harry Caplan (Cambridge, MA: Harvard University Press, 1954).
Cicero, *De re publica, De legibus*, trans. Clinton Walker Keynes, rev. edn (Cambridge, MA: Harvard University Press, 2000).
Contini, Gianfranco, ed., *Poeti del duecento*, 2 vols (Naples: Ricciardi, 1995).
Daniel, Arnaut, *The Poetry of Arnaut Daniel*, ed. and trans. James J. Wilhelm (New York: Garland Publishing, 1981).
da Tempo, Antonio, *Summa artis rithimici vulgaris dictaminis*, ed. Richard Andrews (Bologna: Commissione per i testi di lingua, 1977).
Eliot, T. S., *Four Quartets* (New York: Harcourt, Brace & Co., 1943).
Francesco da Barberino, *Reggimento e costumi di donna*, ed. Giuseppe Sansone, 2nd edn (Rome: Zauli, 1995).
Francesco da Barberino, *Documenti d'Amore*, ed. Marco Albertazzi (Lavis: La finestra, 2008).

Frost, Robert, *The Mountain Interval* (New York: Quinn & Boden Co., 1916).
Herodotus, *The Histories*, trans. G. C. Macaulay, rev. Donald Lateiner (New York: Barnes & Noble Classics, 2004).
Horace, *Odes and Epodes*, ed. and trans. Niall Rudd, Loeb Classical Library 33, rev. edn. (Cambridge, MA: Harvard University Press, 2012).
John of Garland, *Poetria magistri Johannis Anglici de arte prosayca metrica et rithmica*, ed. Giovanni Mari, in *Romanische Forschungen*, 13 (1902), 883–965.
Kierkegaard, Søren, *Journals and Papers*, ed. Howard V. Hong and Edna H. Hong (Charlottesville, VA: InterLex Corporation, 1995).
Lerner, Ben, *10:04* (London: Granta, 2014).
Lucan, *The Civil War (Pharsalia)*, trans. J. D. Duff, Loeb Classical Library 220 (Cambridge, MA: Harvard University Press, 1928).
Marti, Mario, ed., *Poeti del Dolce stil nuovo* (Florence: Le Monnier, 1969).
Montaigne, Michel de, *Les Essais*, ed. Jean Balsamo, Michel Magnien, and Catherine Magnien-Simonin (Gallimard: Paris, 2007).
Ovid, *Metamorphoses, Volume I: Books 1–8*, trans. Frank Justus Miller, rev. G. P. Goold, Loeb Classical Library 42, 3rd rev. edn (Cambridge, MA: Harvard University Press, 1977).
Ovid, *Art of Love. Cosmetics. Remedies for Love. Ibis. Walnut-tree. Sea Fishing. Consolation*, trans. J. H. Mozley, rev. G. P. Goold, Loeb Classical Library 232, 2nd rev. edn (Cambridge, MA: Harvard University Press, 1979).
Ovid, *Fasti*, trans. James G. Frazer, rev. G. P. Goold, Loeb Classical Library 253, 2nd rev. edn, repr. with corrections (Cambridge, MA: Harvard University Press, 1996).
Petrarch, Francis, *Il Canzoniere*, ed. Gianfranco Contini (Turin: Einaudi, 1964).
Proust, Marcel, *Un amour de Swann*, in *Du côté de chez Swann* (Paris: Grasset, 1913). Available in English as *In Search of Lost Time. Volume I: Swann's Way*, trans. C. K. Scott Moncrieff and Terence Kilmartin, rev. R. J. Enright (New York: Modern Library, 1992).
Saba, Umberto, *Mediterranee* (Milan: Mondadori, 1946).
Statius, *Thebaid, Volume I: Thebaid: Books 1–7*, ed. and trans. D. R. Shackleton Bailey, Loeb Classical Library 207 (Cambridge, MA: Harvard University Press, 2003).
Tasso, Torquato, *Gerusalemme Liberata*, ed. Lanfranco Caretti (Milan: Mondadori, 1957).
Thomas Aquinas, *Summa theologiae*, in *Opera Omnia iussu impensaque Leonis XIII P. M. edita* (Rome: Typographia Polyglotta, 1882–), vols. 4–12 (1888–1906). Available in English as *Summa theologica*, trans. Fathers of the English Dominican Province, 5 vols (Allen, TX: Christian Classics, 1948).
Thomas Aquinas, *Commentary on the Metaphysics of Aristotle*, trans. John P. Rowan, 2 vols (Chicago: Regnery, 1964); repr. in 1 vol. with revisions as *Commentary on Aristotle's Metaphysics* (Notre Dame, IN: Dumb Ox Books, 1995).
Thomas Aquinas, *Quaestiones disputatae*, <http://www.corpusthomisticum.org/iopera.html> (2019).
Uguccione da Pisa, *Derivationes*, ed. Enzo Cecchini and Guido Arbizzoni (Florence: SISMEL-Edizioni del Galluzzo, 2004).

Virgil, *Eclogues, Georgics, Aeneid: Books 1-6*, trans. H. Rushton Fairclough, rev. G. P. Goold, Loeb Classical Library 63, new rev. edn (Cambridge, MA: Harvard University Press, 1999).
Virgilio, *Eneide*, ed. with notes by Ettore Paratore, trans. Luca Canali (Milan: Mondadori, 1985).

Secondary Sources

Abbott, H. Porter, *The Cambridge Introduction to Narrative* (Cambridge: Cambridge University Press, 2002).
Ahern, John, 'Binding the Book: Hermeneutics and Manuscript Production in *Paradiso* XXXIII', *PMLA*, 97 (1982), 800-9.
Ahern, John, 'The New Life of the Book: The Implied Reader of the *Vita Nuova*', *Dante Studies*, 110 (1992), 1-16.
Antonelli, Roberto, 'La morte di Beatrice e la struttura della storia', in *Beatrice nell'opera di Dante e nella memoria europea, 1290-1990*, ed. Maria Picchio Simonelli (Florence: Cadmo, 1994), pp. 35-56.
Antonelli, Roberto, 'Bifrontismo, pentimento e forma-canzoniere', in *La palinodia: Atti del XIX Convegno interuniversitario, Bressanone, 1991*, ed. Gianfelice Peron and Gianfranco Folena (Padua: Esedra, 1998), pp. 35-49.
Ascoli, Albert Russell, 'Palinode and History in the Oeuvre of Dante', in *Dante Now: Current Trends in Dante Studies*, ed. Theodore J. Cachey Jr (Notre Dame, IN: University of Notre Dame Press, 1995).
Ascoli, Albert Russell, *Dante and the Making of a Modern Author* (Cambridge: Cambridge University Press, 2008).
Auerbach, Erich, 'Dante's prayer to the Virgin (*Paradiso* XXXIII) and earlier eulogies', *Romance Philology*, 3.1 (1949), 1-26.
Auerbach, Erich, 'Farinata and Cavalcanti', in *Mimesis: The Representation of Reality in Western Thought* (Princeton, NJ: Princeton University Press, 1953), pp. 174-202.
Auerbach, Erich, *Dante: Poet of the Secular World*, trans. Ralph Manheim (Chicago: University of Chicago Press, 1961).
Auerbach, Erich, 'Introduction: Purpose and Method', in *Literary History & Its Public in Late Latin Antiquity and in the Middle Ages* (Princeton, NJ: Princeton University Press, 1965).
Auerbach, Erich, 'Figura', in *Time, History, and Literature: Selected Essays of Erich Auerbach*, ed. James I. Porter, trans. Jane O. Newman (Princeton, NJ: Princeton University Press, 2014), pp. 65-113.
Auerbach, Erich, '*Passio* as passion' [1941], in *Time, History, and Literature: Selected Essays of Erich Auerbach*, ed. James I. Porter, trans. Jane O. Newman (Princeton, NJ: Princeton University Press, 2014), pp. 165-87.
Auerbach, Erich, *Time, History, and Literature: Selected Essays of Erich Auerbach*, ed. James I. Porter, trans. Jane O. Newman (Princeton, NJ: Princeton University Press, 2014).

Auerbach, Erich, 'Typological Symbolism in Medieval Literature' [1952], in *Time, History, and Literature: Selected Essays of Erich Auerbach*, ed. James I. Porter, trans. Jane O. Newman (Princeton, NJ: Princeton University Press, 2014), pp. 114–23.

Baldini, Massimo, *Il linguaggio dei mistici* (Brescia: Queriniana, 1986), pp. 47–54.

Barański, Zygmunt G., '"Significar per verba": Notes on Dante and plurilingualism', in *The Italianist*, 6 (1986), 5–18, repr. in *'Sole nuovo, luce nuova.' Saggi sul rinnovamento culturale in Dante* (Turin: Scriptorium, 1996), pp. 41–77.

Barański, Zygmunt G., 'Structural Retrospection in Dante's *Comedy*: The Case of *Purgatorio* XXVII', *Italian Studies*, 41.1 (1986), 1–23.

Barański, Zygmunt G., 'Dante's Biblical Linguistics', *Lectura Dantis*, 5 (1989), 105–43.

Barański, Zygmunt G., 'Dante commentatore e commentato: Riflessioni sullo studio dell'iter ideologico di Dante', *Letture classensi* 23 (1994), 9–39.

Barański, Zygmunt G., 'The "New Life" of "Comedy": The *Commedia* and the *Vita Nuova*', *Dante Studies*, 113 (1995), 1–29.

Barański, Zygmunt G., 'The Poetics of Meter: *Terza rima*, "canto", "canzon", "cantica"', in *Dante Now: Current Trends in Dante Studies*, ed. Theodore J. Cachey Jr (Notre Dame, IN: University of Notre Dame Press, 1995), pp. 3–41.

Barański, Zygmunt G., *Dante e i segni: Saggi per una storia intellettuale di Dante Alighieri* (Naples: Liguori, 2000).

Barański, Zygmunt G., '"Comedìa": Dante, l'*Epistola a Cangrande* e la commedia medievale', in *Chiosar con altro testo: leggere Dante nel Trecento* (Florence: Cadmo, 2001), pp. 41–76.

Barański, Zygmunt G., 'Dante Alighieri: Experimentation and (Self-)exegesis', in *The Cambridge History of Literary Criticism. Volume II: The Middle Ages*, ed. Alastair Minnis and Ian Johnson (Cambridge: Cambridge University Press, 2005), pp. 561–82.

Barański, Zygmunt G., 'Dante *poeta* e *lector*: "poesia" e "riflessione tecnica" (con divagazioni sulla *Vita nova*)', *Critica del testo*, 14.1 (2011), 81–110.

Barański, Zygmunt G., 'Without any Violence', in *Vertical Readings in Dante's 'Comedy': Vol. 1*, ed. George Corbett and Heather Webb (Cambridge: Open Book Publishers, 2015), pp. 181–202.

Barolini, Teodolinda, *Dante's Poets: Textuality and Truth in the 'Comedy'* (Princeton, NJ: Princeton University Press, 1984).

Barolini, Teodolinda, 'True and False See-ers in *Inferno* XX', *Lectura Dantis*, 4 (1989), 42–54.

Barolini, Teodolinda, *The Undivine 'Comedy': Detheologizing Dante* (Princeton, NJ: Princeton University Press, 1992).

Barolini, Teodolinda, '"Cominciandomi dal principio infino a la fine" (*V.N.* XXIII, 15): Forging Anti-Narrative in the *Vita Nova*', in *La gloriosa donna de la mente: A Commentary on the 'Vita Nuova'*, ed. Vincent Moleta (Florence: Olschki, 1993), pp. 119–40.

Barolini, Teodolinda, 'Dante and Cavalcanti (On Making Distinctions in Matters of Love): *Inferno* V in its Lyric Context', *Dante Studies*, 116 (1998), 31–63.

Barolini, Teodolinda, *Dante and the Origins of Italian Literary Culture* (New York: Fordham University Press, 2006).

Barolini, Teodolinda, 'Dante's Sympathy for the Other, or The Non-Steretyping Imagination: Sexual and Racialized Others in the *Commedia*', *Critica del Testo*, 14.1 (2011), 177–204.

Barolini, Teodolinda, 'The Case of the Lost Original Ending of Dante's *Vita Nuova*: More Notes Toward a Critical Philology', *Medioevo letterario d'Italia*, 11 (2014), 37–43.

Barry, Raymond W., and A. J. Wright, *Literary Terms: Definitions, Explanations, Examples* (San Francisco: Chandler Publishing Co., 1966).

Barthes, Roland, *S/Z*, trans. Richard Miller (New York: Noonday Press, 1974).

Basile, Bruno, 'Dante e l'idea di *peregrinatio*', in *Il tempo e le forme: Studi letterari da Dante a Gadda* (Modena: Mucchi, 1990), pp. 9–36.

Beall, Chandler B., 'Dante and his Reader', *Forum Italicum*, 13 (1979), 299–343.

Bellomo, Saverio, 'Il sorriso di Ilaro e la prima redazione in latino della "Commedia"', in *Studi sul Boccaccio*, XXXII (2004), 201–35.

Bellomo, Saverio, 'Il canto XXXIII dell'*Inferno*', in *Lectura Dantis 2002–2009, omaggio a Vincenzo Placella per i suoi settanta anni*, ed. Anna Cerbo, Mariangela Semola (Naples: Università degli Studi di Napoli 'L'Orientale', 2011), pp. 1369–86.

Bent, Margaret, 'Songs Without Music in Dante's *De vulgari eloquentia*: *Cantio* and Related Terms', in *'Et facciam dolçi canti': studi in onore di Agostino Ziino*, ed. Bianca Maria Antolini, Teresa Maria Gialdroni, and Annunziato Pugliese, 2 vols (Lucca: LIM, 2003), I, pp. 161–82.

Bersani, Leo, *The Freudian Body: Psychoanalysis and Art* (New York: Columbia University Press, 1986).

Bezzola, Reto R., 'L'opera di Dante: Sintesi poetica dell'antichità e del Medioevo cristiano', in *Studi danteschi*, ed. Martina Albertini and Johannes Bartuschat (Locarno: Pro Grigioni Italiano, Armando Dadò, 2015), pp. 133–51.

Bigi, Emilio, *Il canto XXX dell'*Inferno'' (Florence: Le Monnier, 1963).

Bisi, Monica, *Poetica della metamorfosi e poetica della conversione: Scelte formali e modelli del divenire nella letteratura* (Bern: Peter Lang, 2012).

Boitani, Piero, 'Those who will call these times ancient: The Futures of Prophecy and Poetry', in *Medieval Futures: Attitudes to the Future in the Middle Ages*, ed. John Anthony Burrow and Ian P. Wei (Woodbridge: Boydell Press, 2000), pp. 51–65.

Bolzoni, Lina, 'Memory', in *The Oxford Handbook of Dante*, ed. Manuele Gragnolati, Elena Lombardi, and Francesca Southerden (Oxford: Oxford University Press, 2021), pp. 17–33.

Borsellino, Nino, *Il poeta giudice: Dante e il tribunale della 'Commedia'* (Turin: Aragno, 2011).

Boswell, John E., 'Dante and the sodomites', *Dante Studies*, 112 (1992), 63–76.

Botterill, Steven, '"Quae non licet homini loqui": The Ineffability of Mystical Experience in *Paradiso* I and the "Epistle to Can Grande"', *Modern Language Review*, 83.3 (1988), 332–41.

Botterill, Steven, '"Però che la divisione non si fa se non per aprire la sentenza de la cosa divisa" (*V.N.*, XIV. 13): The *Vita Nuova* as Commentary', in *'La gloriosa donna de la mente': A Commentary on the 'Vita Nuova'*, ed. Vincent Moleta (Florence: Olschki, 1994), pp. 61–76.

Bowe, David, *Poetry in Dialogue in the Duecento and Dante* (Oxford: Oxford University Press, 2021).

Boyde, Patrick, *Perception and Passion in Dante's 'Comedy'* (Cambridge: Cambridge University Press, 1993).
Brilli, Elisa, *Firenze e il profeta: Dante fra teologia e politica* (Roma: Carrocci, 2012).
Brooks, Cleanth, *The Well-Wrought Urn: Studies in the Structure of Poetry* (New York: Harcourt Brace, 1947).
Brooks, Peter, *Reading for the Plot: Design and Intention in Narrative* (Cambridge, MA: Harvard University Press, 1984).
Canettieri, Paolo, *Iacopone e la poesia religiosa del Duecento* (Milan: Rizzoli, 2001).
Casadei, Alberto, 'Il titolo della *Commedia* e l'*Epistola a Cangrande*', in *Dante oltre la 'Commedia'* (Bologna: ll Mulino, 2013), pp. 15–43.
Case, Alison, 'Gender and History in Narrative Theory: The Problem of Retrospective Distance in *David Copperfield* and *Bleak House*', in *A Companion to Narrative Theory*, ed. James Phelan and Peter J. Rabinowitz (Malden, MA: Blackwell, 2005), pp. 312–21.
Cherchi, Paolo, and Selene Sarteschi, 'Il cielo del Sole: Per una lettura della *Commedia* a "lunghe campate"', *Critica del Testo*, 14.2 (2011), 311–31.
Chimenz, Siro A., *Il canto XXXIII del 'Paradiso'* (Rome: Signorelli, 1951).
Ching, Marvin K. L., 'A Linguistic Analysis of Compact Verbal Paradox in Literature: A Semantic Interpretation of the Oxymoron' (unpublished doctoral thesis, Florida State University, 1975).
Colombo, Manuela, *Dai mistici a Dante: Il linguaggio dell'ineffabilità* (Florence: Nuova Italia, 1987).
Conte, Gian Biagio, *Virgilio: L'epica del sentimento* (Turin: Einaudi, 2002). Available in English as *The Poetry of Pathos: Studies in Virgilian Epic*, trans. Stephen J. Harrison (Oxford and New York: Oxford University Press, 2007).
Contini, Gianfranco, 'Cavalcanti in Dante', in *Un'idea di Dante: Studi danteschi* (Turin: Einaudi, 1970), pp. 143–57.
Contini, Gianfranco, 'Dante come personaggio-poeta della *Commedia*', in *Un'idea di Dante: Studi danteschi* (Turin: Einaudi, 1970), pp. 33–62.
Contini, Gianfranco, 'Filologia ed esegesi dantesca', in *Un'idea di Dante: Studi danteschi* (Turin: Einaudi, 1970), pp. 113–42.
Contini, Gianfranco, 'Introduzione alle *Rime* di Dante', in *Un'idea di Dante: Studi danteschi* (Turin: Einaudi, 1970), pp. 3–20.
Contini, Gianfranco, 'Preliminari sulla lingua del Petrarca', *Paragone*, 2.16 (1951), 3–26, repr. in *Varianti e altra linguistica: Una raccolta di saggi* (Turin: Einaudi, 1970), pp. 169–92.
Contini, Gianfranco, 'Un esempio di poesia dantesca (Il canto XXVIII del *Paradiso*)', in *Un'idea di Dante: Studi danteschi* (Turin: Einaudi, 1970), pp. 191–213.
Crisafi, Nicolò, 'Problemi narrativi nella cornice dei superbi (*Purgatorio* X–XII): Teleologia, cattiva infinità, e possibilità', *Chroniques Italiennes*, 39.2 (2020), 242–60.
Crisafi, Nicolò, 'Defascistizzare Dante', *Jacobin Italia*, 2 June 2021, <https://jacobinitalia.it/defascistizzare-dante/> [accessed 29 June 2021].
Crisafi, Nicolò, 'Interrupted and Unfinished: The Open-ended Dante of the *Commedia*', in *Openness in Medieval Culture*, ed. Almut Suerbaum and Manuele Gragnolati (Berlin: ICI Berlin Press, forthcoming).

Crisafi, Nicolò, and Elena Lombardi, 'Lust and Law: Reading and Witnessing in *Inferno* V', in *Ethics, Politics and Law in Dante*, ed. Catherine Keen and Giulia Gaimari (London: UCL Press, 2019).

Croce, Benedetto, *La poesia di Dante* (Bari: Laterza, 1921).

Curtius, Ernst Robert, *European Literature and the Latin Middle Ages*, trans. Willard R. Trask (Princeton, NJ: Princeton University Press, 1990).

Dasenbrock, Reed Way, '"Paradiso ma non troppo": The Place of the Lyric Dante in the Late *Cantos* of Ezra Pound', *Comparative Literature*, 57.1 (2005), 45–60.

Delcorno, Carlo, '"Ma noi siam peregrin come voi siete": Aspetti penitenziali del Purgatorio', in *Da Dante a Montale: Studi di filologia e critica letteraria in onore di Emilio Pasquini*, ed. Gian Mario Anselmi (Bologna: Gedit, 2006), pp. 11–30.

Dell'Aquila, Michele, 'Gli spiriti amanti del cielo di Venere (*Par*. canti VIII e IX)', in *Al millesmo del vero: Letture dantesche* (Fasano: Schena, 1989), pp. 146–58.

Demaray, John, *Dante and the Book of the Cosmos* (Philadelphia: American Philosophical Society, 1987), pp. 1–60.

Dictionary of World Literary Terms: Forms, Techniques, Criticism, ed. Joseph T. Shipley, new rev. edn (London: Allen & Unwin, 1970).

Druker, Jonathan, *Primo Levi and Humanism After Auschwitz* (New York: Palgrave Macmillan, 2009).

Eliot, T. S., 'Dante' [1929], in *Selected Essays*, 3rd rev. edn (London: Faber & Faber, 1951), pp. 237–77.

Enciclopedia dantesca, ed. Umberto Bosco, 6 vols (Rome: Istituto della Enciclopedia Italiana, 1970–8).

Fallanca, Vittoria, *The Design of Montaigne's 'Essays'* (unpublished doctoral thesis, University of Oxford, 2020).

Fels, Heinrich, 'Dante und Meister Eckhart', *Deutsches Dante-Jahrbuch*, 27 (1948), 171–87.

Ferrucci, Franco, *Le due mani di Dio: Il cristianesimo e Dante* (Rome: Fazi, 1999).

Fiorilla, Maurizio, '"Et descendant in inferum" *Inf*. XXXIII, 109–57 e il salmo 54', *L'Alighieri*, 27 (2006), 133–9.

Fortuna, Sara, and Manuele Gragnolati, 'Dante after Wittgenstein: "Aspetto", Language, and Subjectivity from *Convivio* to *Paradiso*', in *Dante's Plurilingualism: Authority, Knowledge, Subjectivity*, ed. Sara Fortuna, Manuele Gragnolati, and Jürgen Trabant (Oxford: Legenda, 2010), pp. 223–47.

Franke, William, *Dante's Interpretive Journey* (Chicago: University of Chicago Press, 1996), pp. 37–80.

Freccero, John, 'Casella's Song: *Purgatorio* II, 112', repr. in *Dante: The Poetics of Conversion*, ed. Rachel Jacoff (Cambridge, MA: Harvard University Press, 1986), pp. 186–94.

Freccero, John, 'Dante's Ulysses: From Epic to Novel', in *Dante: The Poetics of Conversion*, ed. Rachel Jacoff (Cambridge, MA: Harvard University Press, 1986), pp. 136–51.

Freccero, John, *Dante: The Poetics of Conversion*, ed. Rachel Jacoff (Cambridge, MA: Harvard University Press, 1986).

Freccero, John, 'Infernal Irony: The Gates of Hell', repr. in *Dante: The Poetics of Conversion*, ed. Rachel Jacoff (Cambridge, MA: Harvard University Press, 1986), pp. 93–109.

Freccero, John, 'The Dance of the Stars: *Paradiso* X', repr. in *Dante: The Poetics of Conversion*, ed. Rachel Jacoff (Cambridge, MA: Harvard University Press, 1986), pp. 221–44.
Freccero, John, 'The Significance of *Terza Rima*', repr. in *Dante: The Poetics of Conversion*, ed. Rachel Jacoff (Cambridge, MA: Harvard University Press, 1986), pp. 258–71.
Freccero, John, 'Epitaph for Guido: *Inferno* X', *Religion & Literature*, 39.3 (2007), 1–29.
Fubini, Mario, *Due studi danteschi* (Florence: Sansoni, 1951).
Gardini, Nicola, *Lacuna* (Turin: Einaudi, 2014).
Garner, Bryan, and David Foster Wallace, *Quack This Way: David Foster Wallace & Bryan Gardner Talk Language and Writing* (Dallas: RosePen Books, 2013).
Genette, Gérard, *Narrative Discourse* (Oxford: Basil Blackwell, 1980).
Gilson, Étienne, *The Philosophy of St. Bonaventure*, trans. Illtyd Trethowan and F. J. Sheed (London: Sheed & Ward, 1938).
Gilson, Simon A., 'Sincretismo e scolastica in Dante', in *Studi e Problemi di Critica Testuale*, 90.1 (2015), 317–39.
Gilson, Simon A., 'The Wheeling Sevens', in *Vertical Readings in Dante's 'Comedy'*: Vol. 1, ed. George Corbett and Heather Webb (Cambridge: Open Book Publishers, 2015), pp. 143–60.
Giorgi, Rubina, *Dante e Meister Eckhart: Letture per il tempo della fine* (Salerno: Ripostes, 1987).
Giunta, Claudio, *La poesia italiana nell'età di Dante: La linea Bonagiunta-Guinizzelli* (Bologna: Il Mulino, 1998).
Gorni, Guglielmo, 'La teoria del "cominciamento"', in *Il nodo della lingua e il verbo d'amore: Studi su Dante e altri duecentisti* (Florence: Olschki, 1981), pp. 143–86.
Gorni, Guglielmo, *Dante: Storia di un visionario* (Bari: Laterza, 2009).
Gragnolati, Manuele, 'From Plurality to (Near) Unicity of Forms: Embryology in *Purgatorio* 25', in *Dante for the New Millennium*, ed. Teodolinda Barolini and H. Wayne Storey (New York: Fordham University Press, 2003), pp. 192–210.
Gragnolati, Manuele, *Experiencing the Afterlife: Soul and Body in Dante and Medieval Culture* (Notre Dame, IN: University of Notre Dame Press, 2005).
Gragnolati, Manuele, 'Authorship and Performance in Dante's *Vita nova*', in *Aspects of the Performative in Medieval Culture*, ed. Manuele Gragnolati and Almut Suerbaum (Berlin and New York: de Gruyter, 2010), pp. 123–40.
Gragnolati, Manuele, *Amor che move: linguaggio del corpo e forma del desiderio in Dante, Pasolini e Morante* (Milan: Il Saggiatore, 2013).
Gragnolati, Manuele, and Francesca Southerden, 'From Paradox to Exclusivity: Dante and Petrarch's Lyrical Eschatologies', in *The Unity of Knowledge in the Pre-Modern World: Petrarch and Boccaccio between the Middle Ages and Renaissance*, ed. Igor Candido (Berlin: De Gruyter, 2018).
Harmless, William, *Mystics* (Oxford: Oxford University Press, 2008).
Harrison, Robert Pogue, *The Body of Beatrice* (Baltimore and London: Johns Hopkins University Press, 1988).
Hartley, Julia Caterina, *Reading Dante and Proust by Analogy* (Cambridge: Legenda, 2019).

Havely, Nick, *Dante and the Franciscans: Poverty and the Papacy in the 'Commedia'* (Cambridge: Cambridge University Press, 2004).

Hawkins, Peter S., 'Dante's *Paradiso* and the dialectic of ineffability', in *Ineffability: Naming the Unnamable*, ed. Peter S. Hawkins and Anne Howland Schotter (New York: AMS Press, 1984), pp. 5–21.

Hawkins, Peter S., 'Crossing over: Dante and Pilgrimage', in *Dante's Testaments. Essays in Scriptural Imagination* (Stanford: Stanford University Press, 1999), pp. 247–64.

Herzman, Ronald B., 'Cannibalism and Communion in *Inferno* XXXIII', *Dante Studies*, 98 (1980), 53–78.

Heslin, Peter, 'Statius in Dante's *Commedia*', in *Brill's Companion to Statius*, ed. William J. Dominik, Carole Elizabeth Newlands, and Kyle Gervais (Leiden and Boston: Brill, 2015), pp. 512–26.

Hindmarsh, D. Bruce, *The Evangelical Conversion Narrative: Spiritual Autobiography in Early Modern England* (Oxford: Oxford University Press, 2005).

Hollander, Robert, *Allegory in Dante's 'Commedia'* (Princeton, NJ: Princeton University Press, 1969).

Hollander, Robert, 'The Tragedy of Divination in *Inferno* XX', *Studies in Dante* (Ravenna: Longo, 1980), pp. 131–218.

Hollander, Robert, 'Ugolino's Supposed Cannibalism: A Bibliographical Note and Discussion', *Quaderni d'italianistica*, 6 (1985), 64–81.

Hollander, Robert, '*Paradiso* XXX', *Studi Danteschi*, 60 (1988), 1–33.

Hollander, Robert, 'The 'Canto of the Word' (*Inferno* 2)', in *Lectura Dantis Newberryana*, ed. Paolo Cherchi and Antonio C. Mastrobuono, 2 vols (Evanston, IL: Northwestern University Press, 1990), II, pp. 98–100.

Holloway, Julia Bolton, *The Pilgrim and the Book* (New York: Peter Lang, 1992), esp. pp. 57–84.

Holmes, Olivia, *Dante's Two Beloveds: Ethics and Erotics in the Divine Comedy* (New Haven, CT: Yale University Press, 2008).

Holsinger, Bruce, 'Sodomy and Resurrection: The Homoerotic Subject of the Divine Comedy', in *Premodern Sexualities*, ed. Louise Fradenburg and Carla Freccero (New York: Routledge, 1996), pp. 243–74.

Honess, Claire E., 'Expressing the Inexpressible: The Theme of Communication in the Heaven of Mars', *Lectura Dantis*, 14–15 (1994), 42–60.

Honess, Claire E., '"Ritornerò poeta...": Florence, Exile, and Hope', in *Se mai continga...: Exile, Politics and Theology in Dante*, ed. Claire E. Honess and Matthew Treherne (Ravenna: Longo, 2013), pp. 85–103.

Honess, Claire E., and Matthew Treherne, eds, *Se mai continga...: Exile, Politics and Theology in Dante* (Ravenna: Longo, 2013).

Iannucci, Amilcare A., 'Autoesegesi dantesca: La tecnica dell'episodio parallelo', repr. in *Forma ed evento nella 'Divina Commedia'* (Rome: Bulzoni, 1984), pp. 83–114.

Inglese, Giorgio, *Vita di Dante: Una biografia possibile* (Rome: Carocci, 2015).

Jacoff, Rachel, 'The Post-Palinodic Smile', *Dante Studies*, 98 (1980), 111–22.

Jacomuzzi, Angelo, 'Il topos dell'ineffabile nel *Paradiso*', in *L'imago al cerchio e altri saggi sulla 'Divina Commedia'* (Milan: Angeli, 1995) pp. 78–113.

Jacomuzzi, Angelo, 'Ond'io son fatto scriba', in *L'imago al cerchio e altri saggi sulla 'Divina Commedia'* (Milan: Angeli, 1995), pp. 29–100.

Jameson, Fredric, *Archaeologies of the Future: The Desire Called Utopia and Other Fictions* (London and New York: Verso, 2005).
Janz, Denis R., 'Syllogism or Paradox: Aquinas and Luther on Theological Method', *Theological Studies*, 59 (1998), 3–21.
Kay, Tristan, *Dante's Lyric Redemption. Eros, Salvation, Vernacular Tradition* (Oxford: Oxford University Press, 2016).
Keen, Catherine, 'The Language of Exile in Dante', *Reading Medieval Studies*, 27 (2001), 79–102.
Keen, Catherine, 'Florence and Faction in Dante's Lyric Poetry: Framing the Experience of Exile', in *Se mai continga...: Exile, Politics and Theology in Dante*, ed. Claire E. Honess and Matthew Treherne (Ravenna: Longo, 2013), pp. 63–83.
Kermode, Frank, *The Sense of an Ending: Studies in the Theory of Fiction* (Oxford: Oxford University Press, 1966).
Kirkpatrick, Robin, *Dante's 'Paradiso' and the Limitations of Modern Criticism: A Study of Style and Poetic Theory* (Cambridge: Cambridge University Press, 1978).
Kirkpatrick, Robin, *Dante's 'Inferno': Difficulty and Dead Poetry* (Cambridge: Cambridge University Press, 1987).
Ladner, Gerhardt B., '*Homo viator*: Medieval Ideas on Alienation and Order', *Speculum*, 42.2 (1967), 233–59.
Ledda, Giuseppe, '*Tópoi* dell'indicibilità e metaforismi nella *Commedia*', *Strumenti Critici*, 83.1 (1997), 117–41.
Ledda, Giuseppe, *La guerra della lingua: Ineffabilità, retorica e narrativa nella 'Commedia' di Dante* (Ravenna: Longo, 2002).
Ledda, Giuseppe, 'Immagini di pellegrinaggio e di esilio nella Commedia di Dante', *Annali Online di Ferrara: Lettere*, 1 (2012), 295–308.
Ledda, Giuseppe, 'L'esilio, la speranza, la poesia: Modelli biblici e strutture autobiografiche nel canto XXV del *Paradiso*', *Studi e Problemi di Critica Testuale*, 90.1 (2015), 257–77.
Ledda, Giuseppe, 'Teologia e retorica dell'ineffabilità nella *Commedia* di Dante', in *Le teologie di Dante*, ed. Giuseppe Ledda (Ravenna: Centro Dantesco dei Frati Minori Conventuali, 2015), pp. 261–92.
Leigh, Matthew, *Lucan: Spectacle and Engagement* (Oxford: Clarendon Press, 1997).
Lentricchia, Frank, *Modernist Quartet* (Cambridge: Cambridge University Press, 1994).
Levers, Toby, 'The Image of Authorship in the Final Chapter of the *Vita Nuova*', in *Italian Studies*, 57 (2002), 6–10.
Lia, Pierluigi, *Poetica dell'amore e conversione: Considerazioni teologiche sulla lingua della 'Commedia' di Dante* (Florence: Olschki, 2015).
Lombardi, Elena, *The Syntax of Desire: Language and Love in Augustine, the Modistae, Dante* (Toronto: Toronto University Press, 2007).
Lombardi, Elena, 'Plurilingualism *sub specie aeternitatis* and the Strategies of a Minority Author', in *Dante's Plurilingualism: Authority, Knowledge, Subjectivity*, ed. Sara Fortuna, Manuele Gragnolati, and Jürgen Trabant (Oxford: Legenda, 2010), pp. 133–47.
Lombardi, Elena, *The Wings of the Doves: Love and Desire in Dante and Medieval Culture* (Montreal: McGill-Queen's University Press, 2012).

Lombardi, Elena, '"Che libido fe' licito in sua legge"': Lust and Law, Reason and Passion in Dante', in *Dantean Dialogues: Engaging with the Legacy of Amilcare Iannucci*, ed. Maggie Kilgour and Elena Lombardi (Toronto: University of Toronto Press, 2013), pp. 125–54.

Lombardi, Elena, *Imagining the Woman Reader in the Age of Dante* (Oxford: Oxford University Press, 2019).

Lombardi, Elena, 'Purgatorio 22', in *Lectura Dantis Andreapolitana*, ed. Claudia Rossignoli and Robert Wilson (Notre Dame, IN: University of Notre Dame Press, forthcoming).

Lukács, György, *The Theory of the Novel: A Historico-Philosophical Essay on the Forms of Great Epic Literature*, trans. Anna Bostock (London: Merlin Press, 1971).

Lyne, R. O. A. M., *Further Voices in Vergil's 'Aeneid'* (Oxford: Clarendon Press, 1992).

Lyne, R. O. A. M., *Collected Papers on Latin Poetry* (Oxford: Oxford University Press, 2007).

Mack, Sara, *Patterns of Time in Vergil* (Hamden, CT: Archon Books, 1978).

McLaughlin, Martin, 'Biography and Autobiography in the Italian Renaissance', in *Mapping Lives: The Uses of Biography*, ed. Peter France and William St Clair (Oxford: Oxford University Press, 2004), pp. 37–65.

Markus, Donka D., 'The Politics of Epic Performance in Statius', in *Flavian Rome: Culture, Image, Text*, ed. Anthony James Boyle and William J. Dominik (Leiden: Brill, 2003), pp. 432–68.

Mazzoni, Francesco, *Saggio di un nuovo commento alla 'Divina Commedia': 'Inferno' Canti I–III* (Florence: Sansoni, 1967).

Mazzotta, Giuseppe, 'Musica e storia nel *Paradiso* 15–17', *Critica del testo*, 14.2 (2011), 333–48.

Mazzotta, Giuseppe, *Reading Dante* (New Haven, CT: Yale University Press, 2014).

Mercuri, Roberto, *Semantica di Gerione: Il motivo del viaggio nella 'Commedia' di Dante* (Rome: Bulzoni, 1984).

Mercuri, Roberto, 'Dante nella prospettiva intertestuale', in *Dante: For Use, Now: Atti del Convegno internazionale su La presenza di Dante nella poesia contemporanea nordamericana*, ed. Annalisa Goldoni and Andrea Mariani (Rome: Euroma, 2000), pp. 75–92.

Mercuri, Roberto, 'Il metodo intertestuale nella lettura della *Commedia*', *Critica del testo*, 14.1 (2011), 111–51.

Mikics, David, *New Handbook of Literary Terms* (New Haven, CT: Yale University Press, 2007).

Milani, Giuliano, and Antonio Montefusco, '"Prescindendo dai versi di Dante?" Un percorso negli studi tra testi, biografia e documenti', in *Dante attraverso i documenti. I. Famiglia e patrimonio (secolo XII-1300 circa)*, ed. Giuliano Milani and Antonio Montefusco. Special issue of *Reti Medievali Rivista*, 15.2 (2014), <http://rivista.retimedievali.it>.

Miller, James, 'Introduction: Retheologizing Dante', in *Dante and the Unorthodox: The Aesthetics of Transgression*, ed. James Miller (Waterloo, ON: Wilfrid Laurier University Press, 2005).

Moevs, Christian, *The Metaphysics of Dante's Comedy* (Oxford and New York: Oxford University Press, 2005).

Montemaggi, Vittorio, 'On Unknowability as Love: The Theology of Dante's *Commedia*', in *Dante's 'Commedia': Theology as Poetry*, ed. Vittorio Montemaggi and Matthew Treherne (Notre Dame, IN: Notre Dame University Press, 2010), pp. 60–94.

Muscetta, Carlo, 'Canto VIII', in *Lectura Dantis Scaligera: III. 'Paradiso'* (Florence: Le Monnier, 1966), pp. 255–92.

Myers, K. Sara, 'Statius on Invocation and Inspiration', in *Brill's Companion to Statius*, ed. William J. Dominik, Carole Elizabeth Newlands, and Kyle Gervais (Leiden and Boston: Brill, 2015), pp. 31–53.

O'Connell Baur, Christine, *Dante's Hermeneutics of Salvation* (Toronto: University of Toronto Press, 2006).

Ossola, Carlo, 'Apoteosi ed ossimoro: Retorica della "traslazione" e retorica dell"unione' nel viaggio mistico a Dio: Testi italiani dei secoli XVI–XVII', in *Mistica e retorica: Studi*, ed. Franco Bolgiani (Florence: Olschki, 1977), pp. 46–103.

Paolazzi, Carlo, *Dante e la 'Comedia' nel Trecento: Dall"Epistola a Cangrande' all'età di Petrarca* (Milano: Vita e Pensiero, 1989).

Parodi, Ernesto, G. 'La critica della poesia classica del ventesimo canto dell'*Inferno*', *Atene e Roma*, 11 (1908), 183–95.

Parry, Adam, 'The Two Voices of Virgil's *Aeneid*', *Arion*, 2.4 (1963), 66–80.

Pasquini, Emilio, 'Il canto XXXIII dell'*Inferno*', *Letture classensi*, 10–11 (1982), 191–216.

Pasquini, Emilio, *Vita di Dante: I giorni e le opere* (Milan: BUR, 2007).

Pequigney, Joseph, 'Sodomy in Dante's *Inferno* and *Purgatorio*', *Representations*, 36 (1991), 22–42.

Pertile, Lino, 'Dante e l'ingegno di Ulisse', *Stanford Italian Review*, 1 (1979), 35–65.

Pertile, Lino, '*Paradiso*: A Drama of Desire', in *Word and Drama in Dante: Essays on the Divina Commedia*, ed. John C. Barnes and Jennifer Petrie (Dublin: Irish Academy Press, 1993), pp. 143–80.

Pertile, Lino, 'La *Comedìa* tra il dire e il fare', in *Sotto il segno di Dante: Scritti in onore di Francesco Mazzoni*, ed. Leonella Coglievina and Domenico De Robertis (Florence: Le Lettere, 1998) pp. 233–47.

Pertile, Lino, 'Does the *Stilnovo* Go to Heaven?', in *Dante for the New Millennium*, ed. Teodolinda Barolini and H. Wayne Storey (New York: Fordham University Press, 2003), pp. 104–14.

Pertile, Lino, *La punta del disio: semantica del desiderio nella 'Commedia'* (Florence: Cadmo, 2005).

Pertile, Lino, 'Introduction to *Inferno*', in *The Cambridge Companion to Dante*, ed. Rachel Jacoff, 2nd edn (Cambridge: Cambridge University Press, 2007), pp. 67–90.

Pertile, Lino, '"Trasmutabile per tutte guise": Dante in the *Comedy*', in *Dante's Plurilingualism: Authority, Knowledge, Subjectivity*, ed. Sara Fortuna, Manuele Gragnolati, and Jürgen Trabant (Oxford: Legenda, 2010), pp. 164–78.

Pertile, Lino, 'Dante e la Shoah', in *The Oxford Handbook of Dante*, ed. Manuele Gragnolati, Elena Lombardi, and Francesca Southerden (Oxford: Oxford University Press, 2021), pp. 651–67.

Petrocchi, Giorgio, 'Itinerari nella *Commedia*', in *Itinerari Danteschi*, ed. Carlo Ossola (Milan: Francoangeli, 1994), pp. 9–20.

Picone, Michelangelo, ed., *L'enciclopedismo medievale: Atti del Convegno, San Gimignano, 8–10 ottobre 1992* (Ravenna: Longo, 1994).
Picone, Michelangelo, 'Dante and the Classics', in *Dante: Contemporary Perspectives*, ed. Amilcare A. Iannucci (Toronto: University of Toronto Press, 1996), pp. 51–73.
Picone, Michelangelo, 'Inferno VIII: Il viaggio contrastato', *L'Alighieri*, 9 (1997), 35–50.
Picone, Michelangelo, 'Dante come autore/narratore della *Commedia*', *Nuova rivista di letteratura italiana*, 2.1 (1999), 9–26.
Picone, Michelangelo, 'Canto VIII', in *Lectura Dantis Turicensis: 'Paradiso'*, ed. Georges Güntert and Michelangelo Picone (Florence: Cesati, 2002), pp. 119–32.
Picone, Michelangelo, 'La teoria dell'*Auctoritas* nella *Vita nuova*', *Tenzone*, 6 (2006), 173–91.
Pirovano, Donato, *Dante e il vero amore: Tre letture dantesche* (Pisa: Fabrizio Serra, 2009).
Polimeni, Giuseppe, 'Grammatica e stile dell'ineffabile: Spitzer legge Dante', in *Leo Spitzer: Lo stile e il metodo*, ed. Ivano Paccagnella and Elisa Gregori (Padua: Esedra, 2010), pp. 371–9.
Pozzi, Giovanni, 'L'alfabeto delle sante', in *Scrittrici mistiche italiane*, ed. Giovanni Pozzi and Claudio Leonardi (Turin: Einaudi, 1988), pp. 21–42.
Prince, Gerald, 'Narrative pragmatics, message, and point', *Poetics*, 12.6 (1983), 527–36.
Prince, Gerald, 'The Disnarrated', *Style*, 22.1 (1988), 1–8.
Prince, Gerald, *Narrative as Theme: Studies in French Fiction* (Lincoln, NE: University of Nebraska Press, 1992).
Psaki, F. Regina, 'Love for Beatrice: Transcending Contradiction in the *Paradiso*', in *Dante for the New Millennium*, ed. Teodolinda Barolini and H. Wayne Storey (New York: Fordham University Press, 2003), pp. 114–30.
Raffa, Guy P., *Divine Dialectic: Dante's Incarnational Poetry* (Toronto: University of Toronto Press, 2000).
Ragni, Eugenio, 'Il canto VIII del *Paradiso*', in *I primi undici canti del 'Paradiso'*, ed. Attilio Mellone (Rome: Bulzoni, 1992), pp. 157–75.
Riccobono, Maria Grazia, *Dante Poeta-Profeta, Pellegrino, Autore: Strutturazione Espressiva della Commedia e Visione Escatologica Dantesca* (Rome: Aracne, 2012).
Risset, Jacqueline, *Dante: Une Vie* (Paris: Flammarion, 1995).
Rorem, Paul, *Pseudo-Dionysius: A Commentary on the Texts and an Introduction to their Influence* (New York and Oxford: Oxford University Press, 1993).
Rushworth, Jennifer, 'Conversion, Palinode, Traces', in *The Oxford Handbook of Dante*, ed. Manuele Gragnolati, Elena Lombardi, and Francesca Southerden (Oxford: Oxford University Press, 2021), pp. 529–45.
Rushworth, Jennifer, *Discourses of Mourning in Dante, Petrarch and Boccaccio* (Oxford: Oxford University Press, 2016).
Sabbatino, Pasquale, 'Dante lettore e critico di se stesso nel canto XXX del *Purgatorio*', in *Dante in lettura*, ed. Giuseppe De Matteis (Ravenna: Longo, 2005), pp. 231–42.
Sasso, Gennaro, *Le autobiografie di Dante* (Naples: Bibliopolis, 2008).
Seung, T. K., *The Fragile Leaves of the Sibyl: Dante's Master Plan* (Westminster, MD: Newman Press, 1961).

Shapiro, Marianne, 'An Old French Source for Ugolino?', *Dante Studies*, 91 (1974), 129-47.
Shaw, Prue, *Reading Dante: From Here to Eternity* (New York: Liveright, 2014).
Shen, Yeshayahu, 'On the Structure and Understanding of Poetic Oxymoron', *Poetics Today*, 8.1 (1987), 105-22.
Shoaf, R. A., 'Dante's Beard: *Sic et non* [*Purgatorio* XXXI, 68]', in *Magister Regis: Studies in Honor of Robert E. Kaske*, ed. Arthur Groos et al. (New York: Fordham University Press, 1986), pp. 171-77.
Singleton, Charles S., *Dante Studies: Vol. 1. 'Commedia': Elements of Structure* (Baltimore, MD: Johns Hopkins University Press, 1954).
Singleton, Charles S., *Dante Studies: Vol 2. Journey to Beatrice* (Cambridge, MA: Harvard University Press, 1958).
Singleton, Charles S., 'The Vistas in Retrospect', *MLN* 81.1 (1966), 55-80.
Southerden, Francesca, 'Lost for Words: Recuperating Melancholy Subjectivity in Dante's Eden', in *Dante's Plurilingualism: Authority, Knowledge, Subjectivity*, ed. Sara Fortuna, Manuele Gragnolati, and Jürgen Trabant (Oxford: Legenda, 2010) pp. 193-210.
Southerden, Francesca, 'The Lyric Mode', in *The Oxford Handbook of Dante*, ed. Manuele Gragnolati, Elena Lombardi, and Francesca Southerden (Oxford: Oxford University Press, 2021), pp. 546-62.
Spitzer, Leo, 'Note on the Poetic and the Empirical "I" in Medieval Authors', *Traditio*, 4 (1946), 414-22.
Spitzer, Leo, 'The Addresses to the Reader in the *Commedia*', *Italica*, 32.3 (1955), 143-65.
Steinberg, Justin, *Accounting for Dante: Urban Readers and Writers in Late Medieval Italy* (Notre Dame, IN: Notre Dame University Press, 2007).
Steinberg, Justin, *Dante and the Limits of the Law* (Chicago: University of Chicago Press, 2013).
Stoppelli, Pasquale, 'La talpa dei bestiari e la "mala luce" dei dannati', in *Studi di letteratura italiana: In memoria di Achille Tartaro*, ed. Giulia Natali and Pasquale Stoppelli (Rome: Bulzoni, 2009), pp. 51-65.
Storey, H. Wayne, 'Early Editorial Forms of Dante's Lyrics', in *Dante for the New Millennium*, ed. Teodolinda Barolini and H. Wayne Storey (New York: Fordham, 2003), pp. 16-44.
Sturm-Maddox, Sara, 'The *Rime Petrose* and the Purgatorial Palinode', *Studies in Philology*, 84 (1987), 119-33.
Szpiech, Ryan, *Conversion and Narrative: Reading and Religious Authority in Medieval Polemic* (Philadelphia, PA: University of Pennsylvania Press, 2013).
Tateo, Francesco, 'Il tema dell'ineffabile', in *Questioni di poetica dantesca* (Bari: Adriatica, 1972), pp. 173-200.
Tavoni, Mirko, 'Il titolo della *Commedia* di Dante', *Nuova rivista di letteratura italiana*, 1.1 (1998), 9-34.
Tavoni, Mirko, 'La visione di Dio nell'ultimo canto del *Paradiso*', in *Dire l'indicibile: Esperienza religiosa e poesia dalla Bibbia al Novecento*, ed. Cesare Letta (Pisa: Edizioni ETS, 2009), pp. 65-112.

Tavoni, Mirko, 'Guido da Montefeltro dal *Convivio* all'*Inferno*', *Nuova Rivista di Letteratura Italiana*, 13 (2010), 167-98.

The Dante Encyclopedia, ed. Richard Lansing (New York: Routledge, 2000).

The Princeton Encyclopedia of Poetry and Poetics, ed. Roland Greene et al., 4th edn (Princeton, NJ: Princeton University Press, 2012).

Tonelli, Luigi, *Dante e la poesia dell'ineffabile* (Florence: Barbera, 1934).

Vickers, Brian, *In Defence of Rhetoric* (Oxford: Clarendon Press, 1989).

Wakelin, Daniel, *Scribal Correction and Literary Craft: English Manuscripts 1375-1510* (Cambridge: Cambridge University Press, 2014).

Walker Bynum, Caroline, 'Why paradox? The Contradictions of my Life as a Scholar', *Catholic Historical Review*, 98 (2012), 433-55.

Walsh, Richard, 'The Pragmatics of Narrative Fictionality', in *A Companion to Narrative Theory*, ed. James Phelan and Peter J. Rabinowitz (Malden, MA: Blackwell, 2005), pp. 150-64.

Webb, Heather, 'Deceit, Desire, and Conversion in Girard and Dante', *Religion & Literature*, 43.3 (2011), 200-8.

Webb, Heather, 'Power Differentials, Unreliable Models, and Homoerotic Desire in the *Comedy*', *Italian Studies*, 68.1 (2013), 17-35.

Webb, Heather, *Dante's Persons: An Ethics of the Transhuman* (Oxford: Oxford University Press, 2016).

Wetherbee, Winthrop, *The Ancient Flame: Dante and the Poets* (Notre Dame, IN: University of Notre Dame Press, 2008).

Wilkins, Ernest H., 'Reminiscence and Anticipation in the *Divine Comedy*', *Dante Studies*, 118 (2000), 95-107.

Wilson, Robert, *Prophecy and Prophecies in Dante's 'Commedia'* (Florence: Olschki, 2008).

Wlassics, Tibor, *Dante narratore: saggi sullo stile della 'Commedia'* (Florence: Olschki, 1975).

Zakai, Avihu, and David Weinstein, 'Erich Auerbach and His "Figura": An Apology for the Old Testament in the Age of Aryan Philology', *Religions*, 3 (2012), 320-8.

Index of Passages

Commedia
 Inferno I 6, 21, 39–40, 55, 74, 117–119, 128, 143
 Inferno II 8, 22, 124, 128, 143
 Inferno III 64 n.64, 123 n.14
 Inferno V 7, 128
 Inferno VI 150 n.79
 Inferno VII 5 n.8
 Inferno VIII 6, 123 n.14
 Inferno IX 143–144
 Inferno X 149–152
 Inferno XIII 105, 114
 Inferno XIV 54–55, 123 n.14
 Inferno XV 86, 88–90, 105–106
 Inferno XVI 22–25, 31 n.81, 39, 60, 123 n.14
 Inferno XVII 7
 Inferno XIX 8
 Inferno XX 62–63, 65–66, 127, 148–149
 Inferno XXII 123 n.14
 Inferno XXIV 72, 123 n.14
 Inferno XXVI 86–87, 120–123, 160–161, 163
 Inferno XXVII 101–102
 Inferno XXIX 8
 Inferno XXX 56
 Inferno XXXII 123, 154
 Inferno XXXIII 128, 152–156
 Inferno XXXIV 6, 23
 Purgatorio I 6, 39, 125, 128, 167
 Purgatorio II 13 n.33, 20 n.57, 123 n.14
 Purgatorio III 6, 80 n.95, 156 n.87
 Purgatorio V 128
 Purgatorio VI 7
 Purgatorio IX 7
 Purgatorio XI 106–107
 Purgatorio XIII 164 n.101
 Purgatorio XV 60
 Purgatorio XVI 5, 60
 Purgatorio XVII 7
 Purgatorio XIX 8
 Purgatorio XX 162
 Purgatorio XXI 95
 Purgatorio XXII 114, 133
 Purgatorio XXIII 56, 56 n.33, 107, 162
 Purgatorio XXV 6 n.9, 7
 Purgatorio XXVI 60 n.48, 72, 107
 Purgatorio XXVII 22, 123
 Purgatorio XXVIII 21
 Purgatorio XXIX 159–160
 Purgatorio XXX 6, 29, 83–84
 Purgatorio XXXI 85, 85 n.3
 Purgatorio XXXII 5
 Purgatorio XXXIII 6 n.11, 58–59
 Paradiso I 5, 52, 74–75, 125–126, 128
 Paradiso III 52 n.21
 Paradiso IV 64 n.65
 Paradiso V 8 n.16, 128, 139–141
 Paradiso VI 91 n.8, 105
 Paradiso VIII 89–94, 123
 Paradiso X 46, 52 n.21, 81, 111
 Paradiso XI 8, 46 n.9
 Paradiso XII 46 n.9
 Paradiso XIII 46–47, 80 n.95, 111–113, 141
 Paradiso XIV 80 n.95
 Paradiso XV 80 n.95
 Paradiso XVI 60, 123
 Paradiso XVII 6, 8, 64 n.62, 160–163
 Paradiso XX 64 n.66, 65–66, 113
 Paradiso XXI 60 n.48
 Paradiso XXII 5 n.8, 22, 87
 Paradiso XXIV 72 n.76
 Paradiso XXV 163–165
 Paradiso XXVI 5 n.8
 Paradiso XXVII 8, 22
 Paradiso XXVIII 6 n.12, 8 n.16, 60
 Paradiso XXX 142
 Paradiso XXXI 39, 56, 80 n.95
 Paradiso XXXIII 21–22, 50 n.19, 67–71, 75–76 n.82, 76, 78, 80 n.95
Convivio
 Book I 12, 15 n.35, 28, 135
 Book II 29, 31 n.83, 74 n.79
 Book IV 12–14, 15 n.35, 16 n.40, 99–101
Epistole
 VI 164 n.101
 XIII 31 n.83, 37–38

Monarchia
  Book II 135–136
  Book III 46 n.9
Vita nova
  Chapter III 8
  Chapter XXVI 52 n.21
  Chapter XXVII 136
  Chapter XXXIV 136
  Chapter XXXV 29
  Chapter XLII 29, 136–138

Index of Names

Abbott, H. Porter 27–28, 30–32
Adam 45, 47
Adrian V, Pope 8
Aeneas 24–25, 130
Alberigo dei Manfredi, Frate 153–155, 157–158
Albert I, Emperor of Habsburg 7
Alighieri, Pietro 24, 146, 156
Anfiarao (Amphiaraus) 148
Antichrist 5
Aquinas, Thomas 45–47, 111, 141–142
Ariosto, Ludovico 22
Aristotle 5, 10, 12, 46, 49, 51, 62, 79
Ascoli, Albert Russell 9, 18, 32, 37, 171
Auden, W. H. 132, 144
Auerbach, Erich 9, 34–37, 59, 65–66, 98, 103, 108
Augustine of Hippo 27–29
Augustus, Caesar 91
Azzetta, Luca 39

Balzac, Honoré de 33
Bambagioli, Graziolo 156
Barański, Zygmunt G. 22, 34, 127–128
Barolini, Teodolinda 9, 13, 18, 43, 56–57, 60, 61, 66, 77, 132, 140, 171
Barthes, Roland 33, 35
Beatrice 4, 17, 26–27, 29, 35, 47, 64, 83–88, 95, 123, 140–142, 150, 162
Benvenuto da Imola 149, 156
Bernard of Clairvaux 57–59, 67
Bocca degli Abati 154
Boccaccio, Giovanni 133, 144–147, 155
Boethius, Anicius Manlius Severinus 22, 29
Boitani, Piero 161
Bonaventure 4, 48–50
Bonvesin de la Riva 48–49
Booker, Christopher 30
Brilli, Elisa 168, 171
Brooks, Cleanth 53
Brooks, Peter 10–11, 15, 20, 24
Buonconte da Montefeltro 102–104, 110–111, 113–114, 128

Cacciaguida degli Elisei 150, 160–161
Casini, Tommaso 156
Cato of Utica 35, 104
Cavalcanti, Cavalcante 150–152
Cavalcanti, Guido 106, 151–152, 157
Charles Martel of Anjoy 89–94
Chiavacci Leonardi, Anna Maria 28, 58
Chimenz, Siro A. 58
Christ 45, 47, 50, 66, 73
Cicero, Marcus Tullius 22
Cimabue 106
Constantine, Emperor 8
Conte, Gian Biagio 25
Contini, Gianfranco 9, 37, 118, 152, 160
Croce, Benedetto 48
Croesus, King of Lydia 16
Cunizza da Romano 104

Domenico di Michelino 165
Dominic of Caleruega 104
Donati, Forese 103
Donati, Piccarda 103
Doria, Branca 153

Eckhart, Meister 48
Eliot, Thomas Stearns 97–98

Farinata degli Uberti 149–150, 157
Fetonte (Phaëton) 7
Francesca da Rimini 7, 9, 104, 114, 128
Francesco d'Assisi (Francis of Assisi) 8, 104
Franco Bolognese 106
Freccero, John 4–5, 19–20, 85
Freud, Sigmund 10–13
Frost, Robert 97, 103

Ganymede 7
Giacomino da Verona 48–49
Giotto 106
Gragnolati, Manuele 15, 18, 41, 158, 171
Guido da Montefeltro 99, 101–104, 110–111, 113–115
Guido da Pisa 156

INDEX OF NAMES

Heidegger, Martin 160
Hollander, Robert 62, 120–121, 167
Holmes, Olivia 11
Homer 130
Honess, Claire E. 165
Horace (Quintus Horatius Flaccus) 129–130
Hugh of Pisa 38

Iacopone da Todi 48–49
Iannucci, Amilcare A. 102–104, 107–108, 110–111
Inglese, Giorgio 169

Jacopo della Lana 148, 156
Janz, Denis 45, 47
John of Garland 38

Keen, Catherine 166–167
Kermode, Frank 16
Kierkegaard, Søren 116, 134

Latini, Brunetto 86, 88–89, 103–106, 114
Leigh, Matthew 129, 133
Lerner, Ben 98
Lombardi, Elena 41, 171
Lucan, Marcus Annaeus 129, 133

Malaspina, Moroello 145
Manfred of Hohenstaufen 154
Marcellus, Marcus Claudius 91–92
Mary of Nazareth 9, 57–58, 60, 68
Mattalia, Daniele 59
Miller, James 77
Minos 115
Moevs, Christian 4–6
Montaigne, Michel de 16
Myers, K. Sara 134

Oderisi da Gubbio 103–104, 106–107
Ovid (Publius Ovidius Naso) 129–130

Parodi, Ernesto 64–65
Paul of Tarsus 47, 75
Parry, Adam 25

Pertile, Lino 4–6, 120–121, 130, 159
Petrarch, Francis 56–57
Petrocchi, Giorgio 92
Philosophy, Lady 29
Picone, Michelangelo 18
Pier de le Vigne 103–104, 114
Porter, James I. 98
Prince, Gerald 30, 96
Proust, Marcel 109–110

Riccobono, Maria Grazia 117
Romeo di Villanova 103–105, 114
Rushworth, Jennifer 137

Sasso, Gennaro 41, 171
Seung, T. K. 10
Shaw, Prue 34, 135–136
Singleton, Charles S. 21, 109, 158
Sinon 56
Solomon 45, 47
Solon 16
Statius 95, 104, 114, 129–134
Steinberg, Justin 31–32, 144
Swann, Charles 109–110

Tasso, Torquato 22
Tobias, Ronald B. 30

Ugolino della Gherardesca 114–115, 128, 152–153
Uguccione da Lodi 48–49
Ulysses 22, 103–104, 114, 119–120, 123, 130

Virgil 4, 6–7, 24–25, 35–36, 62–63, 65, 91–92, 95, 104, 113–114, 128, 130, 132–133, 143–144, 149–151

Walker Bynum, Caroline 44, 52
Weinstein, David 36
Wilkins, Ernest H. 103–104
Wilson, Robert 122, 152

Zakai, Avihu 36
Zeus 7

Index of Concepts

affectivity 7 n.4, 8, 26, 30, 31 n.83, 65, 89–95, 99, 101–102, 105 n.45, 110, 114–115, 123 n.14, 130, 144, 148, 155, 157
ageing 99–100, 121–122, 158–165, 167
antanaclasis 72–73, 77, 79, 93
authoritarianism 33, 37
authority 18–20, 29–33, 37–38, 41, 43, 75, 88, 126, 133–134, 167, 170–171
autobiography 1, 18–19, 27–28, 30 n.77, 41, 85, 165 n.102, 168–169

body 5–6, 7 n.7, 27, 47, 149, 154–156, 158–159, 161–163, *see also* embodiment

character *see* Dante-*personaggio*
coherence 3, 32, 64, 146, 169–170
comedy 5, 28, 37–39, 162
commentary 18–19, 48, 51, 103, 108
conversion 1, 5, 8, 17, 27–30, 84–85, 99, 102, 107, 113–114
counterfactual 14, 15 n.35, 25, 86, 88, 90–94, 96, 106–107, 121–122, 135, 137, 141, 164–165
creativity 86, 103, 114–115, 124

Dante-*personaggio* 4, 13, 18, 20, 22, 24, 32, 35, 38–39, 88, 117–120, 122–125, 139–140, 142, 147, 149, 152, 157–159, 162
Dante-*poeta* 6, 13, 14, 18, 19, 20, 23–24, 35, 39, 43, 74, 88, 97, 117–126, 128–130, 133–134, 137, 139–142, 147–149, 157–160, 163–164, 171
desire 4, 10, 12–13, 17, 37, 39, 67, 89, 92–95, 100, 106–107, 120, 130, 139 n.57, 139–140, 157, 170
for narrative 11, 23–24, 34, 40, 47, 68, 70, 80, 142, 157
disnarrated 96–98, 102

embodiment 6, 7 n.7, 22, 67, 130, 134, 144, 147, 152–153, 158–159, 171 n.12, *see also* body
errancy 12, 83, 86, 90, 109

eschatology 6, 17, 20, 98, 118–119, 149–150
eternity 39, 43, 51, 58, 60, 61 n.53, 69, 81, 95, 100, 106 n.45, 112, 115, 118
exile 8, 20, 31–32, 37, 41, 88, 95, 105, 114, 139, 145–146, 149, 155, 160–162, 165

failure 25, 41, 71, 73–74, 76–78, 80, 84, 86–89, 103, 107, 110, 121, 135, 143, 158, 164, 165 n.101, 171
freedom 93, 94–96, 98–99, 107, 115, 134, 157, 170
future tense 24, 91, 119, 122–125, 128–136, 138–139, 142–144, 148–150, 152–153, 158, 163, 166–167

gender 10, 41, 141 n.60, 171, 171 n.12
genre 5, 48–49, 109, 128–130

hermeneutic *see* interpretation
hypothetical *see* counterfactual

ineffability 49–50, 52, 74–79, 81
interpretation 1, 7, 9–10, 15, 17, 19–21, 22 n.64, 29, 31–37, 40–44, 47–48, 51, 61–65, 70 n.73, 74 n.78, 75–78, 80, 92, 102–103, 107–108, 111, 117–121, 127, 134, 136 n.49, 141, 148 n.74, 149–150, 157–158, 165 n.103, 168, 170–171
interruption 91, 133, 136 n.50, 139–145, *see also* unfinished

judgement 3, 16, 29, 40, 63, 100–101, 111–113, 115, 134, 150, 152, 161

knowledge 7, 47 n.13, 49, 51, 70, 94, 114, 136, 150, 152, 157, 164

language 6–9, 12, 14, 32, 43, 47, 49–51, 53, 55–57, 59–61, 68, 73–74, 76–77, 95, 100, 108, 111, 125, 162
lyric 2 n.1, 4, 9, 17–18, 27, 48, 57, 129–130, 133, 136 n.50

194 INDEX OF CONCEPTS

manuscript 91 n.7, 126, 127 n.18, 140, 165
materiality 126–127, 138, 140, 146–147, 155
mysticism 5, 45, 48–51, 76, 79

narrative pluralism 25 n.69, 26, 33, 40–42, 66, 88, 93, 95, 98, 164, 172
narrator *see* Dante-*poeta*
negation 14, 96, 107, 131, 141
non-linearity 26, 159 n.93, 169
normativity 7, 32, 85–86, 95–96, 100–101, 122, 148 n.74
novel 10, 30, 43, 96, 98, 109–110, 169

openness 21, 26, 33, 41, 66, 79, 86, 88–89, 92, 94–98, 102, 108, 113, 115–116, 119, 121–122, 128, 130, 132, 134–136, 138, 142 n.61, 147, 151, 154, 166, 169, 171
otherness 26, 37–42, 44, 51, 53, 170
oxymoron 49, 53–62, 68, 72–73, 79, 170

palinode 1, 2 n.2, 6, 9, 17, 67, 120 n.8, 168
passion 62–63, 65–66
past tense 13–14, 18, 20, 23–25, 101, 117, 119–120, 123, 125–126, 135–137, 151, 164
performance 15, 18, 44, 50–51, 73, 79, 82, 136, 153, 158, 167, 170
pilgrim *see* Dante-*personaggio*
pleasure 10–11, 13, 55, 56 n.33, 57, 101, 136–137, 145
plurilingualism 26, 172
pluristylism 26, 172
possibility 8, 12, 14, 25–26, 86, 88, 91–99, 104, 106–107, 113, 131–132, 135, 139–143, 154, 156, 164 n.101, 169
present tense 14, 18, 20, 75, 91, 117–118, 120–121, 123–126, 128–129, 136–138, 163–164

promise 20, 29, 47, 88, 91, 119, 135–138, 141, 152–154, 158, 162
prophecy 20, 87–89, 91, 93, 121–122, 127, 132, 136, 139, 144, 149–150, 152, 156–157, 160–162, 164–165, 170

reader 3, 10–11, 21–23, 26–27, 30, 32–34, 39–41, 44, 47, 50–51, 54–55, 57, 61–62, 67–68, 70–74, 77, 80–82, 84, 88–89, 94, 96–98, 100, 107, 110–111, 115, 121, 126–127, 136–141, 144, 148–152, 155–157, 163–164, 169–172
reading *see* reader
realism 30–31, 35–36, 59–61, 72, 79–80, 82, 115, 126, 165 n.102
resistance 41, 51, 57, 61, 66, 68, 72, 79

Scholasticism 45–54, 69, 94
secret 113–115

textual space 86, 89, 92, 96, 110, 114–115
theology 3, 34, 45–48, 51–52, 65–66, 68, 77, 89, 94–96, 99, 102, 111, 113, 115, 154, 156–158, 170

unfinished 17, 127, 135–136, 136 n.50, 139, 140, 142, 142 n.61, 145–147, 158

vulnerability 26, 32, 41, 139–140, 145–146, 155, 158, 163, 165, 167, 170–171

what might have been 14, 26, 84, 88, 92, 95–97, 136 n.50
writing 10, 18, 21, 23–24, 29–31, 43, 52, 62, 74, 79, 88, 117, 119, 121, 124–128, 130, 132, 134–138, 145–147, 150, 153 n.83, 166–167